SAGE was founded in 1965 by Sara Miller McCune to support the dissemination of usable knowledge by publishing innovative and high-quality research and teaching content. Today, we publish over 900 journals, including those of more than 400 learned societies, more than 800 new books per year, and a growing range of library products including archives, data, case studies, reports, and video. SAGE remains majority-owned by our founder, and after Sara's lifetime will become owned by a charitable trust that secures our continued independence.

Los Angeles | London | New Delhi | Singapore | Washington DC | Melbourne

Myth and Reality

Myth and Reality

Studies in the Formation of Indian Culture

Damodar Dharmanand Kosambi

Popular Prakashan | SAGE | TEXTS

Los Angeles | London | New Delhi
Singapore | Washington DC | Melbourne

First published in 1962 by Popular Prakashan Pvt Ltd

This edition published in 2016 by

SAGE Publications India Pvt Ltd
B1/I-1 Mohan Cooperative Industrial Area
Mathura Road, New Delhi 110 044, India
www.sagepub.in

Popular Prakashan Pvt Ltd
301, Mahalaxmi Chambers
22, Bhulabhai Desai Road
Mumbai 400026
www.popularprakashan.com

SAGE Publications Inc
2455 Teller Road
Thousand Oaks, California 91320, USA

SAGE Publications Ltd
1 Oliver's Yard, 55 City Road
London EC1Y 1SP, United Kingdom

SAGE Publications Asia-Pacific Pte Ltd
3 Church Street
#10-04 Samsung Hub
Singapore 049483

Published by Vivek Mehra for SAGE Publications India Pvt Ltd, typeset in Times New Roman 10.5/12.5 pts by Zaza Eunice, Hosur, Tamil Nadu, India and printed at Sai Print-o-Pack, New Delhi.

Library of Congress Cataloging-in-Publication Data Available

ISBN: 978-93-860-4226-2 (PB)

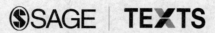

Contents

List of Illustrations

INTRODUCTION

1. SOCIAL AND ECONOMIC ASPECTS OF THE BHAGAVAD-GĪTA

2. URVAŚĪ AND PURŪRAVAS

3. AT THE CROSSROAD: A STUDY OF MOTHER-GODDESS CULT SITES

4. PILGRIM'S PROGRESS: A CONTRIBUTION TO THE PREHISTORY OF THE WESTERN DECCAN PLATEAU

All illustrations in this chapter, not otherwise acknowledged, are from photographs taken by the author.

5. THE VILLAGE COMMUNITY IN THE "OLD CONQUESTS" OF GOA: HISTORY VERSUS THE SKANDA PURĀṆA

Abbreviations

HOS = Harvard Oriental Series, Cambridge, Mass;
NSP = Nirṇay Sāgar Press, Bombay;
PTS = Pāli Text Society, London;
SBE = Sacred Books of The East, Oxford;
TSS = Trivandrum Sanskrit Series, Trivandrum.

A	*Arthaśāstra* of Kauṭalya; ed. T. Ganapati Śāstri, TSS 79, 80, 82; *Kauṭalīyārthaśāstram* of Śrī Viṣṇugupta ed. N. S. Venkaṭanāthācārya, Mysore 1960.
ABORI	*Annals* of the Bhāṇḍārkar Oriental Institute, Poona.
BhG	*Bhagavad-gītā.*
Bṛ	*Bṛhat-saṃhitā* of Varāhamihira; text and English trans. V. Subrahmaṇya Śāstri & M. Rāmakṛṣṇa Bhaṭ, Bangalore 1947.
BṛUp	*Bṛhadāraṇyaka Upaniṣad,* NSP Bombay 1932.
DN	*Dīgha-nikāya* PTS 2 vol. London 1890, 1893; Marāṭhī trans. C. V. Rājvāde I Baroḍā 1918, II Bombay 1932; Hindi trans. Rāhula Sāṅkṛtyāyana & Jagadīśa Kaśyapa, Sārnāth (Banāras) 1936.
El	*Epigraphia Indica.*
Ep Carn	*Epigraphia Carnatica ed. and trans. Lewis Rice.*
G	*BhG*
Gazetteer	*Gazetteer of the Bombay Presidency* 25 vol. Bombay 1880–1901.
GC	J. Gerson da Cunha: *The Koṅkaṇī Language & Literature*, Bombay 1881.
IA	*Indian Antiquary*.
J	In chapter I, this refers to the *Jñāneśvarī*, official Bombay State ed. 1960. The same code letter in chapter III denotes reference to The Pāli *Jātakas* by number.
JAOS	*Journal* of the American Oriental Society.
Jāt.	The *Jātaka* with commentary, ed. V. Fausböll, 6 vol., vol. 7 index (with D. Andersen) London 1877–1897.
JBBRAS	Journal of the Asiatic Society Bombay; formerly the Bombay Branch of the Royal Asiatic Society.
JRAS	*Journal* of the Royal Asiatic Society, London.
KSS	*Kathā-sarit-sāgara* of Somadeva, ed. Durgā Prasād and K. P. Parab, 4th ed. NSP 1930; the 10-volume English translation by G. H. Tawney, annotated by N. M. Penzer (London 1924–) is useful as an index, cited as Tawney-Penzer.
M	G. M. Moraes: M_1 = *The Kadamba Kula,* Bombay 1931; M_2 = Notes on the pre-Kadamba history of Goa (*Trans*. V-th Ind. Hist. Congress, 1941, pp. 164–174); M_3 = A forgotten chapter in the history of the *Koṅkaṇ* (*Bhārata Kaumudī*, Festschrift Radha Kamal Mukherji, Allahabad 1945, pp. 471–475).
Mbh	*Mahābhārata* ed. V. L. Sukṭhaṇkar & others, Poona 1933–.

MN	*Majjhima-nikāya* PTS 3 vol. London 1888–1902; trans. Chalmers 2 vol. London 1926–7; Hindi trans. Rāhula Sāṅkṛtyāyana, Sārnāth (Banāras) 1933.
Mṛc	*Mṛcchakaṭikam* of Śūdraka ed. K. P. Parab, revised (8th ed.) N. R. Acārya NSP 1950. The HOS 9 trans. by A. W. Ryder is attractive.
Ms	*Manusmṛti* 9th ed. with commentary of Kullūka NSP 1933; with commentary of Medhātithi ed. Gangānātha Jhā 3 vol. Calcutta 1932–1939. Trans. G. Bühler SBE 25, 1886.
Pāṇini	*Aṣṭādhyāyī* of Pāṇini and word index by S. Pāṭhak and S. Chitrao, Poona 1935.
Periplus	W. H. Schoff trans. *Periplus of the Erythraean Sea*, travel and trade in the Indian Ocean by a merchant of the first century (New York, 1912).
Rāj	Kalhaṇa's *Rājatarangiṇī*, a chronicle of the kings of Kāśmīr, trans. M. A. Stein 2 vol. London 1900.
RV	*Ṛgveda* ed. with commentary of Sāyaṇa 4 vol. Poona 1933–46.
ŚB	*Śatapatha Brāhmana* trans. J. Eggeling SBE 12, 26, 41, 43, 44; 1882–1900.
SK	*Sahyādrī Khaṇḍa* of the Skanda-Purāṇa, ed. J. Gerson da Cunha, Bombay 1877.
SN	*Sutta-nipāta* ed. V. Fausböll London 1885, revised D. Andersen & H. Smith London 1913.
X	Filippe Nery Xavier, *Bosquejo historico das communidades das aldeas dos concelhos Ilhas, Salcete e Bardez* 2nd ed. 3 vol. Bastora 1903–1907.

Introduction

These essays have one feature in common, namely that they are based upon the collation of field-work with literary evidence. Indian critics whose patriotism outstrips their grasp of reality are sure to express annoyance or derision at the misplaced emphasis. Why should anyone ignore the beautiful lily of Indian philosophy in order to concentrate upon the dismal swamp of popular superstition? That is precisely the point. Anyone with aesthetic sense can enjoy the beauty of the lily; it takes a considerable scientific effort to discover the physiological process whereby the lily grew out of the mud and filth.

This process of development cannot be understood by mere study of the philosophic systems formerly current in India. The great Śaṃkara, the Buddhists who preceded him, and the Vaiṣṇavas who followed, managed to separate a higher from a lower plane of belief. The higher level was purely ideal and theological, the region where the human spirit could soar to ineffable heights of fancied perfection. The common herd might wallow in their day-to-day ritual malpractices upon the lower level. The idealist philosopher was himself excused for joining them in the ritual observances as long as his theory was undefiled by any contact with reality. Only ideas and ideals existed from eternity, whereas the mundane life really did not exist at all on the plane that mattered.

1. Primitive elements survive in all religious beliefs shared by any considerable number of people. The prayer "Give us this day our daily bread" is substantial enough to the greater part of the world's population. It could not have originated before the late stone age, for nothing like bread was known earlier. The idea of prayer to God the Father could also not have been conceived earlier than the pastoral age, in the food-gathering period when the Mother Goddess was predominant. The late stone-age origin of the daily prayer does no fundamental damage to Christian pride. It is as easy to move in the opposite direction with Rousseau and the romanticists as it is to sneer at primitive superstition. They believed that man in the state of nature had been free from the various misguided beliefs and ignoble actions of literate society. This does not need a Frazer or a Malinowski to disprove it. Our present task is to trace the primitive roots of some Indian myths and ritual that survived the beginning of civilization and indeed survive to this day. This is not too difficult in a country where contemporary society is composed of elements that preserve the indelible marks of almost every historical stage. The neglect of such analysis leads to a ridiculous distortion of Indian history and to a misunderstanding of Indian culture, not compensated by subtle theology or the boasts of having risen above crass materialism.

The religious observances of the various human groups in India, particularly those that are lowest in the social, cultural and economic scale, show roughly the order in which the particular groups were enrolled into a greater, productive society. In a general way, this is true of many higher strata as well. The fossilized and stratified remnants of primitive observances, combined with caste and religion, hold a particular group together. The observances also located the coherent group relatively to others within a highly composite society. Change of economic status is reflected in, and acted till recently through some corresponding transformation in caste; sometimes by change in cult as well. One of the main problems for consideration is: Why is a fusion of cults sometimes possible and why do cults stubbornly refuse to merge on other occasions? Naturally, this question cannot be answered on the "highest plane" of Śaṃkara and Rāmānuja, for it simply does not exist on that level. Cults do not clash by themselves. It is the people who observe the cults that find it impossible to come to terms. The followers of Śaṃkara and Rāmānuja, quarrelled bitterly on the worldly plane. It is very doubtful that they could have justified physical violence by the subtle theological differences between their two systems. The theological subtleties which distinguish the two schools are difficult enough to cause any number of headaches; but there seems to be nothing in either system as expounded by its great *ācārya* which should have led to the breaking of heads.

Fig. 1. Three-faced god on Indus seal.

Śiva grew out of rather primitive and aniconic cult-stones along several parallel tracks, into a sublimated highest god—for some people. At one stage his equivalent came into more or less violent conflict with the various mother-goddesses who had previously been the senior deities. We find a naked three-faced god on Mohenjo-dāro seals (fig. 1) who might easily be a prototype of the modern Śiva; but that deity wears buffalo horns on his head-dress. It cannot be a mere accident that the pastoral buffalo-god Mhasobā is also identified with the Mahiṣāsura whom the goddess Pārvatī crushes to gain her title Mahiṣāsura-mardinī (fig. 2). We shall see in one of the present essays that Pārvatī as Yogeśvarī is at times married to an equivalent of Mhasobā who begins to resemble a diluted form of Śiva-Bhairava. This will cast some light upon the Kālīghāṭ painting and other icons where Pārvatī as Kālī tramples (fig. 3) upon Śiva's prostrate body, presumably his corpse; that he comes to life again under her vivifying tread is obviously a mitigating addition to the undeniable conflict. Śiva managed to remain united to Pārvati in marriage, though she is supposed later to have stripped him of everything at a game of dice. His entourage (fig. 4) has the sacred bull Nandi, the cobra, goblins of various sorts, an elephant-headed son Gaṇeśa, another (Skanda) with six heads. It might be noted that the son of Pārvatī's body was not of Śiva's, and he cut off the child's head, later replaced by that of an elephant in the myth. On the other hand, Skanda was born of Śiva's seed, but not of Pārvatī's womb. This complex iconography and ridiculously complicated myth cannot be explained by Śiva's elevation to the highest abstract principle. If, however, we note that Śiva is a cosmic dancer (fig. 5), that a dance by the tribal medicine-man or witch-doctor is essential in most primitive fertility rites, the way to an explanation seems clear. We have only to compare the Ice-age Chamois-masked dancer of Les Trois Frères (fig. 6), or the French stone-age 'diablotins,' with

Fig. 2. Mahiṣāsura-mardini.

Fig. 3. Pārvati trampling upon the dead Śiva, who is thereby vivified as a youth.

Fig. 4. Śiva and his household (Śiva-pañcāyatana). From an 18th century painting (Peshwa period) at Wāï. The main figures are Śiva, Gaṇeśa, Pārvatī, Skanda. The attendants, originally goblins, have become courtiers and flunkeys. On the steps are Śiva's bull (Nandi) and Gaṇeśa's rat; Skanda's *vāhana*, the peacock, is not represented.

Fig. 5. Śiva as *naṭa-rāja*.

Fig. 6. French Ice-age cave painting (Les Trois Frères) of masked dancer.

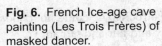

Fig. 7. Dancing Gaṇeśa.

the medieval dancing Śiva-Naṭarāja and the buffalo-horned Indus Śiva. The elephant-headed Gaṇeśa also appears as a dancer, *nṛtta-gaṇeśa* (fig. 7) at times; has he no connection whatever with the European ice-age dancer (fig. 8) who wears a mammoth mask as head-dress, and imitates the mammoth's tusks with his arms? Would not such dancers explain the fact that Gaṇeśa is supposed to have just one tusk; the Indian tribal dancer's two arms would not have sufficed to imitate the trunk and both tusks simultaneously. The monkey-faced Hanumān, depicted carrying a mountain in one hand, leaps about (fig. 9) like any vigorous dancing savage. The meaning of *Hanūmat* is "with a chin"—one human anatomical feature not possessed by any monkey; *Hanumān* dancers who leap high under divine inspiration are still a feature of South Koṅkan *holī* spring festivals. Those who feel ennobled by thinking of Śiva as the fundamental cosmic principle, and his dance as the activating essence of the whole universe of matter, movement, thought and action have no reason to feel offended. They have tried to rise above the primitive man's circumscribed ideology without discarding his imagery.

2. Many other parts of the world passed through parallel stages. This includes Europe and pre-conquest America; contemporary Africa preserves many beliefs that enable us to restore the Indian past. Western history shows far greater stress upon systematic violence in making the change. As Robert Graves put it in his *White Goddess*:

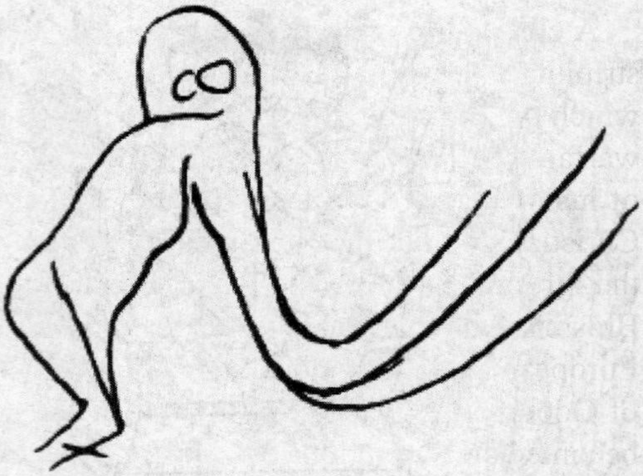

Fig. 8. Mammoth-dancer of Ice-age France.

> Swordsman of the narrow lips,
> Narrow hips and murderous mind
> Fenced with chariots and ships,
> By your joculators hailed
> The mailed wonder of mankind,
> Far to westward have you sailed.
>
> You who, capped with lunar gold
> Like an old and savage dunce,
> Let the central hearth go cold,
> Grinned, and left us here your sword
> Warden of sick fields that once
> Sprouted of their own accord.

Fig. 9. Hanumān.

This is entirely in the European cultural and literary tradition based upon prowess and—later—love, or to put it crudely: violence and sex. In contrast, Indian tradition combines religion with love (or sex with superstition). The *Iliad*, like the *Mahābhārata*, is primarily an epic of warfare. In the extant *Mahābhārata*, the main thread of the narrative is lost in minor narratives (*upākhyāna*) which drown the war story in priestly cant or philosophic lore. The work as it now exists is a formless, illogical mass. It is not that the Greek heroes expressed no philosophy. Achilles says to Priam's defenceless son, caught loitering in a vineyard:

> Far better than thou was Patroclus; he could not choose but die!
> Seest not thou how goodly and fair and tall am I?
> A princely father begat me, a goddess mother bore;
> Yet my death and the o'ermastering doom are hard by the door.
> It shall hap in the dawn or the eventide or at the noon of the day
> That someone shall take my life, even mine, in the midst of the fray.

A clear philosophy, without pity, fear or hesitation, which enabled Achilles to cut the innocent stripling's throat calmly. But it does not seem to fit into the Indian tradition, nor be the way in which the Indian warrior class saw itself, whatever evil practices were actually the usage of Indian warfare. The way was clear in Europe to *Beowulf*, the hero who smote ever too hard for the metal of his own sword. The *Chanson de Roland* loses its military history in legend, but it is hardly to Christianity what the *Mbh* with its *Bhagavad-gītā* is to Hinduism. Horatius at the bridge, Grettir the Strong, Hereward the Wake, Bussy d'Amboise are matched by Indian epic figures like Karṇa, Bhīṣma, Abhimanyu; but the treatment differs beyond comparison. The physical bravery of the European characters stands out as for its own sake, without identification with the immense forces of Good and Evil whereby the Indian war-heroes mitigate the fundamental brutality of warfare to become purely symbolic. To the Carolingian cycle, a new element of romance was added, at the end of the feudal period. Correspondingly, the famous *Rāso* sagas of Rājasthān combine love-making with prowess. But how great the difference! The *Mahābhārata* imposed its form and its formlessness even upon the *Pṛthvī-rāja-rāso*. For the rest, those who deplore the brutal western tradition might briefly consider the undeniable fact that Hellenic *satī* vanished at the dawn of Greek history, whereas the practice of burning widows alive really gained its gruesome force in India in medieval and feudal times. Everything regarded as the best in India's philosophy was then available, but the applications left something to be desired.

Achilles was a real person of the bronze age in Greece, whether or not he performed any of the Homeric feats. His saga is not good history, though history might occasionally peep through isolated battle episodes of the chronicles. Two examples suffice. Earl Simon de Montfort, cornered on a raw English day in August 1265, saw the troops of prince Edward advance in compact order and knew that his time had run out. "How well the churls come on", said he in unwilling admiration; and then, bitterly, "It was from me they learnt it." This is a personal tragedy, which discloses nothing of underlying history. The speaker had founded Parliament, and his death was to show that the same parliament would not serve to make the King of England a puppet in the hands of his barons; but we have to find this out for ourselves from other sources. The last words of Epameinondas serve us better. Struck down in the heat of the battle of Mantineia at the very moment of a signal victory, he tried to entrust the conduct of the remaining operations to another. "Call Deiophantus" was the order, answered by "He has fallen in the battle". "Call Iolaidas"; "He too has fallen in the battle". The general said with his dying breath, "Then you must make your peace with the enemy", pulled the fatal barb out of his chest and expired while friend and foe stood paralysed on the battlefield. There was no third person in the entire Boiotian army who could direct the fairly simple tactical operation of mopping up. These last words are perhaps the most pathetic in the whole of Greek history, for they sum up the basic tragedy of the tiny city-states that could neither co-exist in peace nor combine into sufficiently large groups to resist external aggression. The days when a Macedonian phalanx would annihilate the Theban army in one battle, the reduced legions of Sylla rage through Hellas like a tornado, and Mummius stamp Corinth out almost as a contemptuous gesture, are all reflected in the dying words.

3. Parallels between European Ice-Age drawings and modern Indian representations of certain deities need not imply a direct line of descent. Without discussing any of the numerous diffusionist theses, I merely say that people who live by similar methods and techniques often produce similar cults, just as they produce similar artifacts of stone. For example, we have more than one

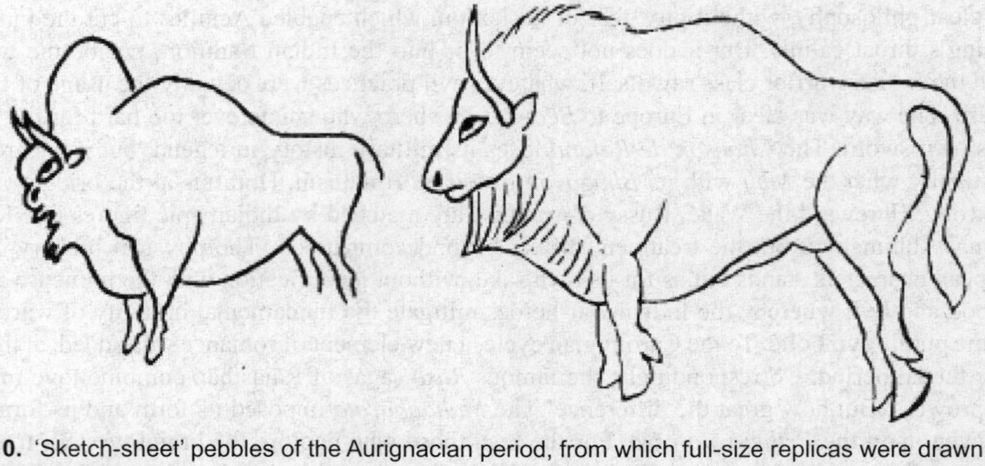

Fig. 10. 'Sketch-sheet' pebbles of the Aurignacian period, from which full-size replicas were drawn; the size here is about 3½″.

'sketch-sheet' which served in Auringnacian France (fig. 10) as model from which cave artists drew full-sized animals faithfully. The exact duplication was undoubtedly an act of faith to promote fertility or success in hunting. The ritual value of duplication continues to later times when a stamp seal about the size of the 'sketch-sheet,' generally with an animal as its main figure, was used in the Indus valley. Stamping the seal upon clay had originally some religious significance. Cultic cylinder seals have been discovered in Mesopotamia while many Indus sealings show no impression upon the underside which might have indicated contact with any package of merchandise. Sealing could protect a parcel at the earliest stages only by imposing a generally understood religious tabu. It took a considerable development of society before the seal became just a signature and its intact condition a sign that the package had not been tampered with.

Some of these sketch-sheets economize by placing many sketches on a single pebble (fig. 11). The obvious development here would be to merge these figures into various fanciful hybrids and chimaeras. An added incentive must have been supplied by the merger of human groups with different totems. This would account for the man-tiger on an Indus seal (fig. 12), the logical ancestor of the man-lion (*Narasiṃha*) incarnation of Viṣṇu (fig. 1. 8). There are many such hybrids in Harappan and Mohenjo-daro seals, so that the idea of iconic fusion was quite familiar. The southern elephant-lion (*Yāḷī*) combination goes back to such ancient pictorial hybridization. Its religious significance is hidden under the modern explanation in Tamil-Nad that the Narasiṃha incarnation got out of hand, so that Viṣṇu had to incarnate himself as a Yāḷī to subdue his own rebellious monster form! The *gaja-vṛṣabha*, or at least a bull-elephant chimaera was noted on a Jamdet Nasr seal by H. Frankfort.* It provides important evidence of intimate contact at a very early

---

* Henri Frankfort: *Cylinder Seals* (New York, 1939, plate VI. c).

The fourth chapter of this book has not been published elsewhere. The new discoveries of pierced microliths, the Karhā-Bhīma track, megaliths of the Poona district, and radiocarbon dating of Buddhist caves are announced here for the first time. The necessary fieldwork was made possible by the cooperation of many. In particular, D. S. Chavda and V. N. Sisodia brought badly needed transport within my means; we were joined in the field by P. Franklin, G. Sontheimer, S. Takahara, and T. Yamazaki. Nothing could have been accomplished without the information

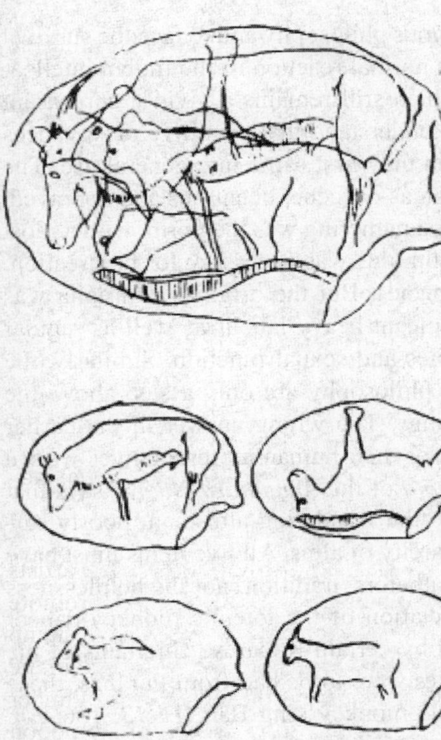

Fig. 11. Multiple Ice-age sketch-sheet from Europe.

Fig. 12. Man-tiger on Indus seal.

Fig. 13. *Ardha-nārīśvara hermaphrodite* Śiva-Pārvati icon.

date between Mesopotamian and Indus cultures, perhaps even a common stratum of people. To my mind, the *ardha-nārīśvara* (fig. 13) utilizes this technique of hybridization to merge two deities, so that simultaneous reverence could be and had to be offered to both. The marriage of Śiva to Pārvatī was unquestionably a later event, when human marriage had become a high ceremonial in the particular society and the pairing marriage was generally recognized. This type of explanation avoids Euhemeristic rationalization as well as the mystic's or theologian's contempt for reality.

---

willingly supplied by innumerable villagers who must remain anonymous. If, some day, an expedition with motor caravans, photographic gadgets, tape recorders, mobile laboratories, sendage apparatus and helicopter-guided surveying equipment takes the field—and the Indian peasant still exists—much more information could be extracted from the same region.

The rest of the book consists of essays slightly modified for re-publication. Chapter I appeared in *Enquiry 2* (1959); in revised form, *JESHO* vol. iv, 1960. Chap. II: *Journal* of the Asiatic Society of Bombay, vol. 27, 1951, pp. 1–30; with additions and illustrations in *Indian Studies: Past & Present*, vol. I, no. 1, Oct. 1959, pp. 141–175. Chapter III. *JRAS*. 1960. pp. 17–31 and 135–144. Chap. V: the *Journal* of the University of Bombay, 1947, vol. xv. pt. 4, pp. 63–78. My thanks are due to the editors of these journals. The illustrations were mostly prepared by my daughter Meera Kosambi. Readers will recognize my debt to B. Malinowski, H. Obermaier, H. Breuil and H. Frankfort, among other giants; but more than any other, to K.Marx.

The reluctance to admit the primitive roots of Indian religious philosophy and to face the survival of primitive belief in the country may stem in part from the normal reaction of the Indian intellectual to the long humiliation of a repressed colonial life which still remains a vividly unpleasant memory. The real difficulty, however, lies in the failure to understand that primitive observances served a totally different purpose under the conditions when they first came into general use. The Hoḷī spring festival, now regarded by law and public opinion as obscene, licentious and depraved, can be traced to remotest savagery. Yet, at the time when food gathering was the norm, with a most uncertain supply of food and meagre diet, a considerable stimulus was necessary for procreation. Obscenity was then essential in order to perpetuate the species. But the original saturnalia was never depraved, as it became inevitably when agriculture meant heavy labour as well as regular nourishment, with a corresponding change in man's appetites and sexual function. Similarly, the Upaniṣadic riddles which display so much mysticism and philosophy are only a step above the deadly riddles asked by *yakṣas* of strangers at sacred springs. The wrong answer in the earlier days meant ritual sacrifice of the intruder. That such *yakṣas* or their human representatives were a real menace is attested by the Pāli canon. The *Pañcaka-nipāta* of the *Aṃguttara-Nikāya* says that contemporary Madhurā (Mathurā) presented five ordeals to the wandering almsman: poorly surfaced roads, excessive dust, fierce dogs, cruel *yakṣas* and scarcity of alms. All five items must have been painfully real to almsmen who represented the food gatherers' tradition, not the helplessness of modern beggars. Finally, those who dislike my interpretation of the totemic monkey-dancer Hanumān might ponder upon the curious ancestry claimed by certain Kanarese chieftains of the 10–12th centuries. Though any number of higher genealogies were to be had from Purāṇas, these worthies insisted upon claiming descent from the *Rāmāyaṇa* monkey-king Bāli (*EI 13*. 186; *Ep. Carn. 4*. Yl. 25; *IA* 1901. 110,260). Surely, primitive superstition was not so very much worse than the economic philosophy of a modern affluent society which destroys surplus grain and potatoes in a hungry world, or the political philosophy which glorifies the ultimate thermonuclear deterrent.

It is not the purpose of these essays to judge but to analyse in so far as the essayist's knowledge suffices for the purpose. It seems to me that a great deal more in the way of fieldwork is needed in every part of the country before we can begin to theorize. However imperfect, the beginning is made here.

1 Social and Economic Aspects of the Bhagavad-Gītā

The *Bhagavad-Gītā*, "Song of the Blessed One", forms part of the great Indian epic *Mahābhārata*.[1] Its 18 *adhyāya* chapters contain the report by Sañjaya of a dialogue between the Pāṇḍava hero Arjuna and his Yadu Charioteer Kṛṣṇa, the eighth incarnation of Viṣṇu. The actual fighting is about to begin when Arjuna feels revulsion at the leading part which he must play in the impending slaughter of cousins and kinsmen. The exhortations of Lord Kṛṣṇa answer every doubt through a complete philosophical cycle, till Arjuna is ready to bend his whole mind, no longer divided against itself, to the great killing. The Gītā has attracted minds of bents entirely different from each other and from that of Arjuna. Each has interpreted the supposedly divine words so differently from all the others that the original seems far more suited to raise doubts and to split a personality than to heal an inner division. Any moral philosophy which managed to receive so many variant interpretations from minds developed in widely different types of society must be highly equivocal. No question remains of its basic validity if the meaning be so flexible. Yet the book has had its uses.

If a *Mahābhārata* war had actually been fought on the scale reported, nearly five million fighting men killed each other in an 18-day battle between Delhi and Thānesar; about 130,000 chariots (with their horses), an equal number of elephants and thrice that many riding horses were deployed. This means at least as many camp-followers and attendants as fighters. A host of this size could not be supplied without a total population of 200 millions, which India did not attain till the British period, and could not have reached without plentiful and cheap iron and steel for ploughshares and farmers' tools. Iron was certainly not available in any quantity to Indian peasants before the 6th century BC. The greatest army camp credibly reported was of 400,000 men under Çandragupta Maurya, who commanded the surplus of the newly developed Gangetic basin. The terms *patti, gulma* etc., given as tactical units in the *Mbh* did not acquire that meaning till after the Mauryans. The heroes fought with bows and arrows from their chariots, as if the numerous cavalry did not exist; but cavalry—which appeared comparatively late in ancient Indian warfare—made the fighting chariots obsolete as was proved by Alexander in the Punjab.

The epic began, like the early Homeric chants, as a series of lays sung at the court of the conquerors. The lament was thinly veiled, presumably by irony; the defeated Kurus survived in legend (*e.g.* the *Kuru-dhamma-jātaka*) as unsurpassable in rectitude and nobility of character. Kṛṣṇa-Nārāyana had no rôle to play even in the first connected epic narrative. Should the reader doubt all this, let him read the final cantos of the extant *Mbh*. The Pāndavas come in the end to disgraceful old age, and unattended death in the wilderness. Their opponents are admitted to heaven as of right, but the heroes are only transferred there from the tortures of hell, after a long and stubborn effort by the eldest brother Yudhisthira. It strikes even the most casual eye that this is still the older heaven of Indra and Yama; Kṛṣṇa-Nārāyana is not its dominant figure, but a palpable and trifling insertion in a corner.

Those legendary Utopians, the pure and unconquerable Uttara-Kurus of the *Dīgha-Nikāya* (*DN* 32) and the *Aitareya Brāhmaṇa* (*AB* 8.14; 8.23) are not to be confused with the Kurus who survived in historical times near Delhi-Meerut. The Buddha preached several of his sermons at the settlement Kammāsa-damma in Kuru-land (*Majjhima Nikāya* 10; 75; 106) while their capital seems to have been at Thullakoṭṭhita (*MN* 82), the seat of the nameless petty tribal Kuru chief, presumably descended from the Pāṇḍava conquerors whom the epic was to inflate beyond all limits. This negligible 'kingdom' either faded away or was among the tribal groups systematically destroyed by the Magadhan emperor Mahāpadma Nanda, a few years before Alexander's raid into the Punjab. The memory, however, remains—as of a tribe, but not a full-fledged kingdom with a class structure—in the eleventh book of the *Arthaśāstra*, along with similar oligarchies like the Licchavis and the Mallas known to have been destroyed about 475 BC. As for Nārāyaṇa, it might be noted here that the famous benedictory initial stanza *Nārāyaṇaṃ namaskṛtya*, which would make the whole of the extant *Mbh* into a Vaiṣṇava document, was stripped off by V. S. Sukṭhaṇkar's text-criticism in 1933 as a late forgery.

1.1. FOR WHAT CLASS?

We know that the *Gītā* exercised a profound influence upon Mahātma Gāndhī, B. G. Ṭiḷak, the 13th century Mahārāṣṭrian reformer Jñāneśvar, the earlier Vaiṣṇava *ācārya* Rāmānuja, and the still earlier Śaṃkara. Though both fought hard in the cause of India's liberation from British rule, Ṭiḷak and the Mahātmā certainly did not draw concordant guidance for action from the *Gītā*. Aurobindo Ghose renounced the struggle for India's freedom to concentrate upon study of the *Gītā*. Lokamānya Ṭiḷak knew the *Jñāneśvarī* comment, but his *Gītā-rahasya* is far from being based upon the earlier work. Jñāneśvar himself did not paraphrase Śaṃkara on the *Gītā*, nor does his very free interpretation follow Rāmānuja; tradition ascribes to him membership of the rather fantastic *nātha* sect. Rāmānuja's Vaiṣṇavism laid a secure foundation for the acrid controversy with the earlier followers of Śiva who came into prominence with the great Śaṃkara. But then, why did Śaṃkara also turn to the *Bhagavad-gītā?*

What common need did these outstanding thinkers have that was at the same time not feit by ordinary people, even of their own class? They all belonged to the leisure-class of what, for lack of a better term, may be called Hindus. The consequent bias must not be ignored, for the great comparable poet-teachers from the common people did very well without the *Gītā*. Kabīr, the Banāras weaver, had both Muslim and Hindu followers for his plain yet profound teaching. Tukārām knew the *Gītā* through the *Jñāneśvarī*, but worshipped Viṣṇu in his own way by meditation upon God and contemporary society in the ancient caves (Buddhist and natural) near the junction of the Indrāyaṇī and Paünā rivers. Neither Jayadeva's *Gītā-govinda*, so musical and supremely beautiful a literary effort, (charged with the love and mystery of Kṛṣṇa's cult) nor the Viṣṇuite reforms of Caitanya that swept the peasantry of Bengal off its feet were founded on the rock of the *Gītā*. I have yet to hear that the heterogeneous collection which forms the Sikh canon owes anything substantial directly to the *Gītā*, though it preserves verses due to Jayadeva, and the Mahārāṣṭrian Nāmdev. Jñāneśvar ran foul of current brahmin belief at Āḷandī, and had to take refuge about 1290 AD on the south bank of the Godāvarī, in the domains of Rāmacandra Yādava, to compose his famous gloss in the common people's language.

We know as little of the historic action taken or instigated by Śaṃkara and Rāmānuja as we should have known of Ṭiḷak's had only his *Gītā-rahasya* survived. Yet, about the year 800, Śaṃkara was active in some manner that resulted—according to tradition—in the abolition of many Buddhist monasteries. That this was achieved by his penetrating logic and sheer ability in disputation is now, the general Hindu belief. The mass of writing left in his name, and what is given therein as the Buddhist doctrine which he refutes, make only one thing clear: that he had not the remotest idea of Gotama Buddha's original teaching. Buddhism as practised in the monasteries had in any case degenerated into Lamaism with opulent *vihāra* foundations which were a serious drain upon the economy of the country. That Śaṃkara's activity provided a stimulus to their abolition, and Rāmānuja's some handle against the wealthier barons whose worship of Śiva was associated in the popular mind with their oppressive land-rent, seems a reasonable conclusion on the evidence before us. Otherwise, it would be difficult to explain why the richer, aristocratic landholders opted for Śiva, the poorer, and relatively plebeian overwhelmingly for Viṣṇu, in the bitter *smārta-vaiṣṇava* feuds, it is difficult to believe that they could come to blows because of differing religious philosophy. Śāṃkara managed to discover a higher and lower knowledge in the Upaniṣads which allowed him "to conform to the whole apparatus of Hindu belief"—whatever that may mean—"on the lower plane, while on the higher he finds no true reality in anything; his logic, it has been well said, starts by denying the truth of the proposition 'A is either B or not B' . . . At death the soul when released is merged in the absolute and does not continue to be distinct from it". According to Rāmānuja, "if in a sense there is an absolute whence all is derived, the individual souls and matter still have a reality of their own, and the end of life is not merger in the absolute but continued blissful existence. This state is to be won by *bhakti*, faith in and devotion to God." It is not possible to imagine that subtle arguments on these tenuous ideas gripped the masses, that people could be whipped up to a frenzy merely by the concept of restricted dualism (*viśiṣṭādvaita*) or thoroughgoing dualism (*dvaita*). Yet frenzied conflict there was, for centuries. Neither side objected to rendering faithful service at the same time to beef-eating Muslim overlords, who knocked brahmins off without compunction or retribution, and desecrated temples without divine punishment.

The main conclusion is surely the following: Practically anything can be read into the *Gītā* by a determined person, without denying the validity of a class system. THE GĪTĀ FURNISHED THE ONE SCRIPTURAL SOURCE WHICH COULD BE USED WITHOUT VIOLENCE TO ACCEPTED BRAHMIN METHODOLOGY, TO DRAW INSPIRATION AND JUSTIFICATION FOR SOCIAL ACTIONS IN SOME WAY DISAGREEABLE TO A BRANCH OF THE RULING CLASS upon whose mercy the brahmins depended at the moment. That the action was not mere personal opportunism is obvious in each of the cases cited above. It remains to show how the document achieved this unique position.

1.2. A REMARKABLE INTERPOLATION

That the song divine is sung for the upper classes by the brahmins, and only through them for others, is clear. We hear from the mouth of Kṛṣṇa himself (*G.*9.32): "For those who take refuge in Me, be they even of the sinful breeds such as women, vaiśyas, and śūdras..." That is, all women and all men of the working and producing classes are defiled by their very birth, though they may in after-life be freed by their faith in the god who degrades them so casually in this one. Not only that, the god himself had created such differences (*G*.4.13): "The four-caste (-class) division has been created by Me"; this is proclaimed in the list of great achievements.

The doctrines are certainly not timeless[2]. Ethics come into being only as they serve some social need. Food-producing society (as distinct from conflicting aggregates of food-gathering tribal groups) originated in the fairly recent and definite historical past, so that the principles upon which it may work at some given stage could not have been expressed from eternity. The *Gītā* sets out each preceding doctrine in a masterly and sympathetic way without naming or dissecting it, and with consummate skill passes smoothly on to another when Arjuna asks "why then do you ask me to do something so repulsive and clearly against this?" Thus, we have a brilliant (if plagiarist) review-synthesis of many schools of thought which were in many respects mutually incompatible. The incompatibility is never brought out; all views are simply facets of the one divine mind. The best in each system is derived, naturally, as from the high God. There is none of the polemic so characteristic of disputatious Indian philosophy; only the Vedic ritual beloved of the Mīmāṃsakas is condemned outright. The Upaniṣads are well—if anonymously—represented, though the *Śvetāśvatara Upaniṣad* alone contains the germ of *bhakti*, and none the theory of per fection through a large succession of rebirths. This function of *karma* is characteristically Buddhist. Without Buddhism, *G*.2.55–72 (recited daily as prayers at Mahātmā Gāndhi's āśrama) would be impossible. The *brahma-nirvāṇa of G*. 2.72, and 5.25 is the Buddhist ideal state of escape from the effect of *karma*. We may similarly trace other—unlabelled—schools of thought such as Sāṃkhya and Mīmāṃsā down to early Vedānta (*G*. 15.15 supported by the reference to the *Brahma-sūtra* in *G*. 13.4). This helps date the work as somewhere between 150–350 AD, nearer the later than the earlier date. The ideas are older, not original, except perhaps the novel use of *bhakti*. The language is high classical Sanskrit such as could not have been written much before the Guptas, though the metre still shows the occasional irregularity (*G*. 8. 10^d, 8. 11^b, 15. 3^a, &c) in *triṣṭubhs*, characteristic of the *Mbh* as a whole. The Sanskrit of the high Gupta period, shortly after the time of the *Gītā*, would have been more careful in versification.

It is known in any case that the *Mbh* and the Purāṇas suffered a major revision[3] in the period given above. The *Mbh* in particular was in the hands of Brahmins belonging to the Bhṛgu clan, who inflated it to about its present bulk (though the process of inflation continued afterwards) before the Gupta age came to flower. The Purāṇas also continued to be written or rewritten to assimilate some particular cult to Brahminism. The last discernible redaction of the main Purāṇa group refers to the Guptas still as local princes between Fyzābād and Prayāg.[4] This context fits the *Gītā* quite well. The earliest dated mention of anything that could possibly represent the *Gītā* is by Hsiuen Chuäng,[5] early in the seventh century, who refers to a Brahmin having forged at his king's order such a text, (supposedly of antiquity) which was then 'discovered', in order to foment war. The fact does remain that the *Mbh* existed in two versions at the time of the *Āśvalāyana Gṛhya Sūtra*, which refers both to the *Bhārata* and the *Mahābhārata*.[6] The prologue of the present *Mbh* repeats much the same information in such a way as to make it evident that the older 24,000-*śloka Bhārata* was still current at the time the longer version was promulgated. Every attempt was made to ascribe both to the great 'expander', Vyāsa, to whom almost every Purāṇa is also ascribed. A common factor is the number *18*, which had some particular sanctity for the whole complex, and for the Brahmins connected therewith. There are *18* main *gotra* clan-groups of brahmins[7] though the main *ṛṣī* sages are only seven in number; many of the *18* (e.g. the *kevala* Bhārgavas and *kevala* Āṅgirasas) are difficult to fit into a rational scheme. Correspondingly, there are *18* main Purāṇas, and *18 parvan* sections of the *Mbh*, though the previous division was into *100*, as we learn from the prologue. The very action of the Bhāratan war was fought over *18* days between *18* legions. The *Gītā* has also *18 adhyāyas*, which is surely not without significance. That the older *Bhārata* epic had a shorter but similar *Gītā* is most unlikely. One could expect some sort of an exhortation to war, as is actually contained in *G*. 2.37: "If slain, you gain heaven; if victorious, the earth; so up, son of Kunti, and concentrate on fighting". These lines fit the occasion very well. Such pre-battle urging was customary in all lands at all times (advocated even by the supremely practical *Arthaśāstra*, 10.3) through invocations and incantations, songs of bards, proclamations by heralds, and speech of captain or king. What is highly improbable—except to the brahmin bent upon getting his *nīti* revisions into a popular lay of war—is this most intricate three-hour discourse, on moral philosophy, after the battle-conches had blared out in mutual defiance and two vast armies had begun their inexorable movement towards collision.

To put it bluntly, the utility of the *Gītā* derives from its peculiar fundamental defect, namely dexterity in seeming to reconcile the irreconcilable. The high god repeatedly emphasizes the great virtue of non-killing (*ahiṃsā*), yet the entire discourse is an incentive to war. So. *G*. 2.19 ff. says that it is impossible to kill or be killed. The soul merely puts off an old body as a man his old clothes, in exchange for new; it cannot be cut by weapons, nor suffer from fire, water or the storm. In *G*. 11, the terrified Arjuna sees all the warriors of both sides rush into a gigantic Viṣṇu-Kṛṣṇa's innumerable voracious mouths, to be swallowed up or crushed. The moral is pointed by the demoniac god himself (*G*. 11.33): that all the warriors on the field had really been destroyed by him; Arjuna's killing them would be a purely formal affair whereby he could win the opulent kingdom. Again, though the *yajña* sacrifice is played down or derided, it is admitted in *G*. 3.14 to be the generator of rain, without which food and life would be impossible. This slippery opportunism characterizes the whole book. Naturally, it is not surprising to find so many *Gītā* lovers imbued therewith. Once it is admitted that material reality is gross illusion, the rest follows quite simply; the world of "doublethink" is the only one that matters.

The *Gītā* was obviously a new composition, not the expansion of some proportionately shorter religious instruction in the old version. I next propose to show that the effort did not take hold for some centuries after the composition.

1.3. NOT SUFFICIENT UNTO THE PURPOSE

The lower classes were necessary as an audience, and the heroic lays of ancient war drew, them to the recitation. This made the epic a most convenient vehicle for any doctrine which the brahmins wanted to insert; even better than rewriting the Purāṇas, or faking new Purāṇas for age-old cults. The Sanskrit language was convenient, if kept simple, because the Prakrits were breaking apart into far too many regional languages; Sanskrit was also the language which the upper classes had begun to utilize more and more. Kuṣāṇa and Sātavāhana inscriptions are in the popular *lingua franca* used by monk and trader. But from 150 AD, there appears a new type of chief (oftener than not of foreign origin like Rudradāman) who brags[8] in ornate Sanskrit of his achievements, including knowledge of Sanskrit. The Buddhists had begun to ignore the Teacher's injunction to use the common people's languages; they too adopted Sanskrit. The high period of classical Sanskrit literature really begins with their religious passion-plays and poems, such as those written by Aśvaghoṣa.[9] A patrician class favouring Sanskrit as well as the Sanskrit-knowing priestly class was in existence.

No one could object to the interpolation[10] of a story (*ākhyāna*) or episode. After all, the *Mbh* purports to be the recitation in the Naimiṣa forest to the assembled sages and ascetics by a bard Ugraśravas, who repeated what Vyāsa had sung to Janamejaya as having been reported by Sañjaya to Dhṛtarāṣṭra! The brahmins were dissatisfied with the profit derived from the *Gītā*, not with its authenticity. So, we have the *Anu-gītā*[11] as a prominent sequel in the 14th Canto (*Aśvamedha-parvan*). Arjuna confesses that he has forgotten all the fine things told before the battle, and prays for another lesson. Kṛṣṇa replies that it would be impossible even for him to dredge it out of his memory once again; the great effort was not to be duplicated. However, an incredibly shoddy second *Gītā* is offered instead which simply extols brahminism and the brahmin. Clearly, that was felt necessary at the time by the inflators though no one reads it now, and it cannot be compared to the first *Gītā* even for a moment.

Secondly, the *Gītā* as it stands could not possibly help any kṣatriya in an imminent struggle, if indeed he could take his mind off the battle long enough to understand even a fraction thereof. The ostensible moral is: "Kill your brother, if duty calls, without passion; as long as you have faith in Me, all sins are forgiven." Now the history of India always shows not only brothers but even father and son fighting to the death over the throne, without the slightest hesitation or need for divine guidance. Indra took his own father by the foot and smashed him (*RV* 4. 18. 12), a feat which the brahmin Vāmadeva applauds. Ajātaśatru, king of Magadha, imprisoned his father Bimbisāra to usurp the throne, and then had the old man killed in prison. Yet, even the Buddhists[12] and Jains as well as *Bṛhadāraṇyaka Upaniṣad* (2.1) praise the son (who was the founder of India's first great empire) as a wise and able king. The *Arthaśāstra* (*A*. 1. 17–18) devotes a chapter to precautions against such ambitious heirs-apparent; and shows in the next how the heir-apparent could circumvent them if he were in a hurry to wear the crown. Krsna himself at Kuruksetra had simply to point to the Yādava contingent, his own people, who were fighting in the opposite ranks. The legend tells us that all the Yādavas ultimately perished fighting among themselves. Earlier, Kṛṣṇa had killed his maternal uncle Kaṃsa. The tale gains a new and peculiar force if it be remembered that under mother-right, the new chief must always be the sister's son of the old.

Thirdly, Kṛṣṇa as he appears in the *Mbh* is singularly ill-suited to propound any really moral doctrine. The most venerable character of the epic, Bhīṣma, takes up the greatest of *Mbh* parvans (*Śānti*) with preaching morality on three important questions: King-craft (*rāja-dharma*), conduct in distress (*āpad-dharma*), and emancipation (*mokṣa-dharma*). As regent, he had administered the kingdom to which he had freely surrendered his own right. He had shown irresistible prowess and incomparable knightly honour throughout a long life of unquestioned integrity The sole reproach anyone can make is that he uses far too many words for a man shot full of arrows, dying like a hedgehog on a support of its own quills. Still, Bhīṣma seems eminently fitted to teach rectitude. But Kṛṣṇa? At every single crisis of the war, his advice wins the day by the crookedest of means which could never have occurred to the others. To kill Bhīṣma, Śikhaṇḍin was used as a living shield against whom that perfect knight would not raise a weapon, because of doubtful sex. Droṇa was polished off while stunned by the deliberate false report of his son's death. Karṇa was shot down against all rules of chivalry when dismounted and unarmed; Duryodhana was bludgeoned to death after a foul mace blow that shattered his thigh. This is by no means the complete list of iniquities. When taxed with these transgressions, Kṛṣṇa replies bluntly at the end of the *Śalya-parvan* that the man could not have been killed in any other way, that victory could never have been won otherwise. The calculated treachery of the *Arthaśāstra* saturates the actions of this divine exponent of the

Bhagavad-gītā. It is perhaps in the same spirit that leading modern exponents of the *Gītā* and of *ahiṃsā* like Rājāji have declared openly that non-violence is all very well as a method of gaining power, but to be scrapped when power has been captured: "When in the driver's seat, one must use the whip."[13]

Fig. 1.1. Nārayaṇa asleep on the waters.

1.4 WHY KṚṢṆA?

Just as the *Mbh* could be used as a basis only because people came to hear the war-story recited, Kṛṣṇa could have been of importance only if his cult were rising in popularity, yet sufficiently unformed for such barefaced remoulding. The cult, however, is clearly synthetic. The identification with Nārāyaṇa is a syncretism, taking originally distinct cults as one. In the same direction is the assimilation of many sagas to a single Kṛṣṇa legend, whether or not the original hero bore the epithet of Kṛṣṇa. There would, however, be no question of creating a new cult out of whole cloth; some worship or set of similar worships must already have been in existence among the common people before any brahmins could be attracted thereto. The best such recent example is that of Satya-narayaṇa, 'the true Nārāyaṇa', so popular all over the country, but which has no foundation whatever in scripture, and which is not even mentioned 200 years ago. Indeed, the origin seems to be in the popular legends of one Satya Pīr,[14] in Bengal; the Pīr himself became Satyanārāyaṇa.

Fig. 1.2. Ea-Enki in his water-surrounded chamber; detail of Mesopotamian seal.

The vedas have a Viṣṇu, but no Nārāyaṇa. The etymology seems to be 'he who sleeps upon the flowing waters (*nārā*)' and this is taken as the steady state (fig. 1.1) of Nārāyaṇa.[15] It precisely describes the Mesopotamian Ea or Enki, who sleeps in his chamber in the midst of the waters, as Sumerian myth and many a Sumerian seal, (fig. 1.2) tell us. The word *nārā* (plural) for 'the waters' is not Indo-Aryan. Both the word and the god might conceivably go back to the Indus Valley. The later appearance in Sanskrit only means that the peaceful assimilation of the people who transmitted the legend was late. At any rate, the flood-and-creation myth (so natural in a Monsoon country) connects the first three *avatāras*, (figs. 1.3, 1.5, 1.6, 1.7) Fish, Tortoise and Boar—surely related to primitive totemic worships. The Fish has its Mesopotamian counterparts (fig. 1.4). One performance of this Nārāyaṇa is shared by Kṛṣṇa in the *Gītā*: the *viśva-rūpa-darśana* showing that the god contains the whole universe; he individually represents the best specimen of each species in it. Though familiar

Fig. 1.3. The Fish incarnation of Viṣṇu.

to most of us as in *Gitā* 10–11, there is a prototype version without Kṛṣṇa in *Mbh* 3.186.39–112, which shows that an all-pervading Nārāyaṇa had been invented much earlier.

The speech-goddess *Vāg-ambhṛṇī*, in a famous but late hymn of the Ṛgveda (*RV*. 10. 125), declares that she draws Rudra's bow, and is herself Soma and the substance of all that is best. The original god whose misdeeds are never sin is surely the upaniṣadic Indra who says to Pratardana Daivodāsi: "Know thou Me alone; this indeed do I deem man's supreme good—that he should know Me. I slew the three-headed Tvāṣtra, threw the Arurmagha ascetics to the wolves, and transgressing many a treaty, I pierced through and through the Prahlādīyans in the heavens, the Paulomas in the upper air, and the Kālakāñjas on this earth. Yet such was I then that I never turned a hair. So, he who understands Me, his world is not injured by any deed whatever of his: not by his killing his own mother, by killing his own father, by robbery, killing an embryo, or the commission of any sin whatever does his complexion fade" (*Kauṣ .Brāh. Up*. 3.2). The 'breaking many a treaty' is again the *Arthaśāstra* king's normal practice, though that book mentions that in olden days even a treaty concluded by simple word of mouth was sacred (*A*. 7. 17). Indra performed all these dismal feats in vedic tradition, but that tradition nowhere makes him proclaim himself as the supreme object for *bhakti; pāpa* and *bhakti* are not vedic concepts. No vedic god can bestow plenary absolution as in *G*.18.66: "Having cast off all (other) beliefs, rites and observances, yield to Me alone; I shall deliver you from all sins, never fear". The reason Kṛṣṇa could do this and not Indra was that the older god was clearly circumscribed by immutable vedic *sūktas* and tied to the vedic *yajña* fine-ritual. He was the model of the barbarous Aryan war-leader who could get drunk with his followers and lead them to victory in the fight. His lustre had been sadly tarnished by intervening Buddhism, which had flatly denied *yajña* and brought in a whole new conception of morality and social justice. The pastoral form of bronze-age society with which Indra was indissolubly connected had gone out of productive existence.

Fig. 1.4. Merman and Mermaid on Mesopotamian button-seal.

Fig. 1.5. The Tortoise incarnation.

Kṛṣṇa or rather one of the many Kṛṣṇas also represented this antagonism. The legend of his enmity to Indra reflects in the Ṛgveda[16] the historical struggle of the dark pre-Aryans against the marauding Aryans. The black skin-colour was not an insurmountable obstacle, for we find a Kṛṣṇa Āṅgirasa as a vedic seer. The Yadus are a vedic tribe too, but no Kṛṣṇa seems associated with them though the 'bound Yadu' prisoner of war is mentioned. There was a 'Kṛṣṇa the son of Devakī' to whom Ghora Āṅgirasa imparted some moral discipline, according to *Chāndogya Up*. 3.17.1–7. The Mahānubhāvas take Sāṃdīpani as Kṛṣṇa's *guru*, and a few include the irascible Durvāsa in the list of his teachers. Kṛṣṇa the athletic Kaṃsa-killer could beat anyone in the arena, whether or not he was the same Kṛṣṇa who trampled down Kāliya (fig.1.15), the many-headed *Nāga* snake-demon that infested the Yamunā river at Mathurā. Naturally the Greeks who saw his cult in India at the time of Alexander's invasion identified Kṛṣṇa with their own Herakles.

One feature of the Kṛṣṇa myth, which still puzzles Indians, would have been quite familiar to the Greeks. The incarnate god was killed—unique in all Indian tradition—by an arrow shot into his heel, as were Achilles and other Bronze-age heroes. Moreover, the archer Jaras is given in most accounts as Kṛṣṇa's half-brother, obviously the tanist of the sacred king who had to kill the senior twin. Kṛṣṇa himself consoles the repentant killer, and absolves him by saying that his own time had come; the sacred king's appointed term had ended. One might venture the guess that the original unpardonable sin committed by Indra and perhaps by Kṛṣṇa as well was the violation of matriarchal custom, unthinkable in the older society, but which they managed to survive triumphantly, and in comparison to which all other sins paled into insignificance. Certainly, the *gokula* in which Kṛṣṇa was brought up would be patriarchal, as a cattle-herders' commune. But the *Vṛndāvana* where he played his pranks was sacred to a mother-goddess, the goddess of a group (*vṛnda*) symbolized by the Tulasī (Basil) plant. Kṛṣṇa had to marry that goddess, and is still married to her every year, though she does not appear in the normal list of his wives; originally, this meant a *hieros gamos* with the priestess who represented the goddess, and the annual sacrifice of the male consort. Inasmuch as there is no myth of Kṛṣṇa's annual sacrifice, but only of his having substituted for the husband, he seems to have broken the primitive usage, as did Herakles and Theseus.

The taming of the *Nāga* has perhaps a deeper significance than Herakles decapitating the Hydra, a feat still earlier portrayed (fig. 1.16) in the Mesopotamian glyptic. The *Nāga* was the patron deity, perhaps aboriginal cult-object of the place. The trampling down of Kāliya instead of killing indicates the obvious survival of *Nāga* worship, and parallels the action of *Mahiṣāsura-mardinī*. Such cults survive to this day, as for example that of Maṇi-nāga, which has come down through the centuries near Orissa. Nīlamata-nāga, for whom the brahmins wrote a special purana,[17] was the primitive deity of Kaśmīr. The Nāga Śrikaṇṭha had to be faced in a duel by Puṣyabhūti, king of Thānesar. Such

Fig. 1.6. The Boar incarnation.

Fig. 1.7. The Boar incarnation.

Fig. 1.8. The Man-lion (*Narasiṃha*).

local guardian nāgas are current down to the 10th century work *Navasāhasāṅka-carita*. So, our hero had a considerable following among the Indian people, even in the 4th century BC. By the later Śuṅga period, he was called Bhagavat, originally the Buddha's title. A Greek ambassador Heliodoros[18] proclaims himself convert to the cult, on the pillar near Bhilsā. That Kṛṣṇa had risen from the pre-Aryan people is clean from a Pāṇinian reference (Pāṇ.4.3.98, explained away by the commentator Patañjali) to the effect that neither Kṛṣṇa nor Arjuna counted as kṣatriyas. But his antiquity is considerable, for he is the one god who uses the sharp wheel, the missile discus, as his peculiar weapon. This particular weapon is not known to the Vedas and went out of fashion well before the time of the Buddha. Its historicity is attested only by cave paintings (fig. 1.17) in Mirzāpūr which show raiding horse-charioteers (clearly enemies of the aboriginal stone-age artists) one of whom is about to hurl such a wheel. The event and the painting may fairly be put at about 800 BC[19] by which date the dark god was on the side of the angels, no longer an aborigine himself.

A historical tribe of Vṛṣṇis is actually known about the 2nd century AD by a single coin (fig. 1.18) in the British Museum found near Hoshiarpur in the Punjab. When Kṛṣṇa's people were driven out of Mathurā by fear of Jarāsaṃdha (*Mbh.* 2.13.47–49 and 2.13.65), they retreated WESTWARDS to found a new mountain-locked city of Dvārakā, which is, therefore, more likely to have been near modern Darwāz in Afghanistan rather than the Kathiawad seaport. When the Buddhist *Mahāmāyūrī mantra* (circa 3rd century AD) speaks of

Fig. 1.9. The Dwarf (*Vāmana*).

Fig. 1.10. Paraśurāma.

Fig. 1.11. Rāma.

Viṣṇu as the guardian *yakṣa* of Dvārakā however (Sylvain Lévi, *Journal Asiatique* 1915.19–138; line 13 of Sanskrit text), presumably the latter city was meant; it is notable that Viṣṇu and not Kṛṣṇa is named. As for the Deccan Yādavas, the brahmins who found a genealogy which connected them to the dark god had no deeper aim in the forgery than to raise the chiefs of a local clan above the surrounding population.

Finally, there was also the useful messianic aspect as in *G.* 4.7.[20] The many proto-historic Kṛṣṇas and current belief in transmigration made the *avatāra* syncretism possible. It could also lead the devotee in his misery to hope for a new *avatāra* to deliver him from oppression in this world, as he hoped for salvation in the next.

Fig. 1.12. Kṛṣṇa.

Fig. 1.13. Buddha.

1.5. WHEN DOES A SYNTHESIS WORK?

Like the *avatāras* of Viṣṇu-Nārāyaṇa, the various Kṛṣṇas gathered many different worships into one without doing violence to any, without smashing or antagonizing any. Kṛṣṇa the mischievous and beloved shepherd lad is not incompatible with Kṛṣṇa the extraordinarily virile husband of many women. His 'wives' were originally local mother-goddesses, each in her own right. The 'husband' eased the transition from mother-right to patriarchal life, and allowed the original cults to be practised on a subordinate level. This is even better seen in the marriage of Śiva and Pārvatī which was supplemented by the *Ardha-nārīśvara* hermaphrodite [half Śiva, half Pārvatī, (fig. 13) just to prevent any separation]. Mahiṣāsura (Mhasobā), the demon "killed" by that once independent goddess, is still occasionally worshipped near her temple (as at the foot of Parvati hill[21] in Poona). Sometimes, (as at Vīr) he is found married to a goddess (Jogubāī) now equated to Durgā while another goddess (Tukāī) similarly identified is shown crushing the buffalo demon on the adjacent hillock. The widespread Nāga cult was absorbed by putting the cobra about Śiva's neck, using him as the canopied bed on which Nārāyaṇa floats in perpetual sleep upon the waters, and putting him also in the hand of Gaṇeśa. The bull Nandi was worshipped by stone-age people long before Śiva had been invented to ride on his back. The list can be extended by reference to our complex iconography, and study of the divine households. Gaṇeśa's animal

Fig. 1.14. Kalki, the future incarnation.

head and human body equate him to the 'sorcerers' and diablotins[22] painted by ice-age men (fig. 1.19) in European caves.

This is "in the Indian character", and we have remarked that a similar attitude is reflected in the philosophy of the *Gītā*. No violence is done to any preceding doctrine except vedic *yajña*. The essential is taken from each by a remarkably keen mind capable of deep and sympathetic study; all are fitted together with consummate skill and literary ability, and cemented by *bhakti* without developing their contradictions. The thing to mark is that the Indian character was not always so tolerant. There are periods when people came to blows over doctrine, ritual, and worship. Emperor Harṣa Śilāditya (circa 600–640 AD) of Kanauj found no difficulty in worshipping Gaurī, Maheśvara-Śiva, and the Sun, while at the same time he gave the fullest devotion to Buddhism.[23] His enemy Narendragupta-Śaśāṅka, raided Magadha from Bengal, cut down the Bodhi tree at Gayā, and wrecked Buddhist foundations wherever he could. What was the difference? Why was a synthesis of the two religions, actually practised by others besides Harṣa (as literary references can show) not successful?

Let me put it that the underlying difficulties were economic. Images locked up too much useful metal; monasteries and temples after the Gupta age withdrew far too much from circulation without replacement or compensation by adding to or stimulating production in any way. Thus, the most thoroughgoing iconoclast in Indian history was another king Hansa (1089–1101 AD) who broke up all images[24] in Kaśmīr, except four that were spared. This was done systematically under a special minister *devotpāṭana-nāyaka*, without adducing the least theological excuse, though one could easily have been found. The Kaśmīrian king remained a man of culture, a patron of Sanskrit literature and the arts; he presumably read the *Gītā* too. But he needed funds for his desperate fight against the Ḍāmara group of local barons. The particular campaign was won, at the cost of making feudalism stronger than ever.

The conclusion to bẹ drawn is that a dovetailing of the superstructure will be possible only when the underlying differences are not too great. Thus, the *Gītā* was a logical performance for the early Gupta period, when expanding village settlement brought in new wealth to a powerful central government. Trade was again on the increase, and many sects could obtain economic support in plenty. The situation had changed entirely by the time of Harṣa Śīlāditya, though many generous donations to monasteries were still made. The villages had to be more or less self-contained and self-supporting. Tax-collection by a highly centralized but non-trading state was no longer a paying proposition, because commodity production per head and cash trade were low:[25] this is fully attested by the miserable coinage. The valuable, concentrated luxury trade of the Kuṣaṇa-Sātavāhana era had suffered relative decline in spite of feudal and monastic accumulation of gold, silver, jewels, etc. Once magnificent cities like Patna, no longer necessary for production, had dwindled to villages containing ruins which people could regard only as the work of superhuman beings. There was no longer enough for all; one or the other group had to be driven to the wall. One such instance is the combined Hari-Hara cult [with an image half Śiva, half Viṣṇu (fig. 1.20)] which had its brief day but could not remain in fashion much beyond the 11th century. The followers of Hari and Hara found their interests too widely separated, and we have the *smārta-vaiṣṇava* struggle instead. With Mughal prosperity at its height, Akbar could dream of a synthetic *Din-e-ilāhī;* Aurangzeb could only try to augment his falling revenue by increased religious persecution and the *Jizyā* tax on unbelievers.

To sum up, writing the *Gītā* was possible only in a period when it was not absolutely necessary. Śaṃkara could not do without the intense polemic of theological controversy. To treat all views tolerantly and to merge them into one implies that the crisis in the means of production is not too acute. FUSION AND TOLERANCE BECOME IMPOSSIBLE WHEN THE CRISIS DEEPENS, WHEN THERE IS NOT ENOUGH OF THE SURPLUS PRODUCT TO GO AROUND, AND THE SYNTHETIC METHOD DOES NOT LEAD TO INCREASED PRODUCTION. Marrying the gods to goddesses had worked earlier because the conjoint society produced much more after differences between matriarchal and patriarchal forms of property were thus reconciled. The primitive deities adopted into Śiva's or Viṣṇu's household helped enlist food-gathering aboriginals into a much greater food-producing society. The alternative would have been extermination or enslavement, each of which entailed violence with excessive strain upon contemporary production. The vedic Aryans who tried naked force had ultimately to recombine with the autochthonous people. The *Gītā* might help reconcile certain factions of the ruling class. Its inner contradictions could stimulate some exceptional reformer to make the upper classes admit a new reality by recruiting new members. But it could not possibly bring about any fundamental change in the means of production, nor could its fundamental lack of contact with reality and disdain for logical consistency promote a rational approach to the basic problems of Indian society.

Fig. 1.15. Kāliyā trampled by the boy Kṛṣṇa.

1.6. THE SOCIAL FUNCTIONS OF BHAKTI

Fig. 1.16. Killing of the seven-headed Hydra; detail of Mesopotamian seal.

However, the *Gītā* did contain one innovation which precisely fitted the needs of a later period: *bhakti*, personal devotion. To whoever composed that document, *bhakti* was the justification, the one way of deriving all views from a single divine source. As we have seen from the demand for the quite insipid *Anu-Gītā* sequel, this did not suffice in its own day. But with the end of the great centralized personal empires in sight Harṣa's being the last—the new state had to be feudal from top to bottom. The essence of fully developed feudalism is the chain of personal loyalty which binds retainer to chief, tenant to lord, and baron to king or emperor. Not loyalty in the abstract but with a secure foundation in the means and relations of production: land ownership, military service, tax-collection and the conversion of local produce into commodities through the magnates. This system was certainly not possible before the end of the 6th century AD. The key word[26] is *sāmanta* which till 532 at last meant 'neighbouring ruler' and by 592 AD had come to mean feudal baron. The new barons were personally responsible to the king, and part of a tax-gathering mechanism. The *Manusmṛti* king, for example, had no *ṣāmantas*; he had to administer everything himself, directly or through agents without independent status. The further development of feudalism 'from below' meant a class of people at the village level who had special rights over the land (whether of cultivation, occupation, or hereditary ownership) and performed special armed service as well as service in tax-collection. To hold this type of society and its state together, the best religion is one which emphasizes the role of *bhakti*, personal faith, even though the object of devotion may have clearly visible flaws.

Innumerable medieval rustic 'hero' stones[27] commemorate the death in battle—usually a local cattle-raid—of an individual whose status was above that of the ordinary villager. In older days, the duty of protecting the disarmed villages would have been performed by the *gulma* garrisoning the locality. The right to bear arms (with the concomitant obligation to answer a call to arms) was now distributed among a select class of persons scattered through the villages. Many inscriptions vaunt the Gāṅga barons' sacrifice of their own heads in front of some idol, to confer benefit upon their king. More than one epigraph declares the local warrior's firm intention not to survive his chief.[28] Marco Polo[29] reported of the 13th century Pāṇḍyas that the seigneurs actually cast themselves upon the king's funeral pyre, to be consumed with the royal corpse. This suits the *bhakti* temperament very well. Though barbarous, it is not the type of loyalty that a savage tribal chief could expect or receive from his followers, unless his tribe were in some abnormal situation.

Though *bhakti* was the basic need in feudal ideology, its fruits were not enjoyed equally by all. By the 12th century, feudal taxation had begun to weigh heavily upon the peasantry, who paid not only for the luxurious palace but also its counterpart the equally rich and even more ornate temple. Brahminism had definitely come to the top, as may be seen from two monumental collections of the period, namely the *Kṛtyakalpataru* of Bhaṭṭa Lakṣmīdhara (minister of Govindacandra Gahaḍavala of Kanauj, circa 1150 AD); and a century later, Hemadri's quite similar *Caturvargacintamani*. The latter was chancellor of the exchequer (*mahā-karaṇādhipa*) under the last Yādavas of Devagiri (Daulatābād). He is described as the outstanding computer

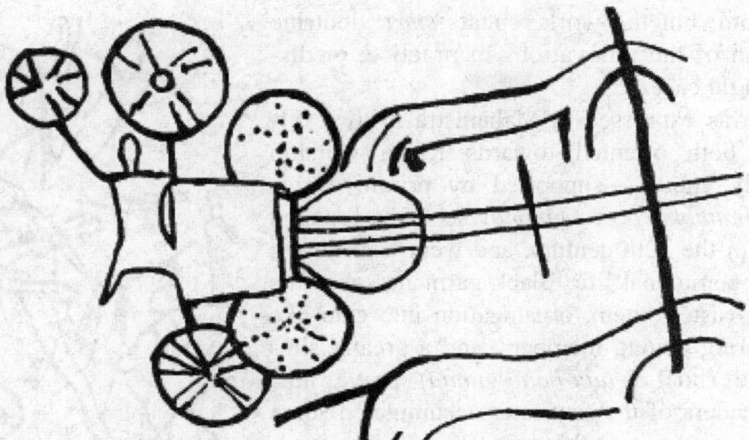

Fig. 1.17. Discus-throwing charioteer in a Mirzapur cave.

Fig. 1.18a 1.18b. Vṛṣṇi tribal coin (enlarged).

(*gaṇakāgraṇi*). A few tables for quick assessment survive in Hemādri's name; the name is also (wrongly) coupled in Marāṭhī tradition with the general use of *bājrī* as cultivated food-grain, the cursive *Moḍī* alphabet, and the numerous close-jointed mortarless Yādava temples that had been built centuries earlier, to develop from little shrines of matchless proportion and balance into rank clumsy, richly endowed structures by the 12th century. Yet his *magnum opus*, far from being another *Arthaśāstra*, or an *'Ain-i-Akbarī*, or an Indian *Corpus Juris Civilīs*, is concerned almost entirely with brahminical rites and ritual codified from Puraṇas and other accepted religious books. The published seven volumes contain perhaps three fifths of the original. Any person who performed even a tenth of the special rites prescribed for any given deity, lunar date, transgression, celebration, worship, festival or occasion would have no time for anything else; as a document of a superstitious leisure class, none other known today will bear comparison with it. A section on jurisprudence preserved in Lakṣmīdhara's compendium shows that common law was practised and decisions for each caste, tribe, and locality based upon their particular custom; but the work repeats *smṛti* doctrine without mention of the innovations in practice, or discussion of a single case.

The protest was expressed in Mahārāṣṭra by two different groups, both oriented towards Kṛṣṇa worship and—remarkably enough—supported by primitive survivals. The *Mahānubhāva* or *Mānbhāv* sect was founded by Cakradhara in the 12th century, and went back to the ideals of tribal, communal life. Black garments, absolute rejection of the caste system, organization into clan-like sub-groups, sharing among members, and a greatly simplified marriage ritual (*gaḍa-baḍa-guṇḍā*) prove this, though a few leaders of the sect later accumulated some property, with a concomitant thirst for Hindu respectability. The other movement, crystallized by Jñāneśvar was particularly strong among the seasonal *vārkarī* pilgrims to Paṇḍharpür, who followed a custom which seems to date back to the mesolithic age. Jñāneśvar was under brahmin interdict, as begotten by an apostate monk; his aged parents drowned themselves in the Ganges while he himself committed ritual suicide at Āḷandī, after a short but exceptionally bitter life. The Marāthā saints who followed him all wrote like him in the vernacular, had personally experienced the hardships of the common people, and came from all castes. Nāmdev, though a tailor, carried the new doctrine to the far north, with success. I am told that some of his work was absorbed directly into the Sikh Canon (*Granth Saheb*), or provided stimulus and inspiration even at so great a distance to what became a great religious movement among the common people of the Punjab. Gorā was a potter by caste and craft. The untouchable Cokhā Meḷā was killed by collapse of Mangaḷveḍhe town wall for the construction of which he had been pressed by corvée, old as he was. The Paiṭhaṇ brahmin Eknāth (fig 1.22), to whom we owe the present text of the *Jñāneśvarī* (in 1590 AD) as well as many fine Marāṭhī poems, went out of his way to break the crudest restrictions of untouchability. The greatest of them all, the 16th century *kuṇabī* peasant and petty grain-dealer Tukārām survived grim famine, the unremitting jealousy of contemporary folk-poets, and the contemptuous hatred of brahmins, ultimately to drown himself in the river. These men represent a general movement by no mean confined to their province and language. The generally painful tenor of their lives shows that they were in the opposition, and did not care to exercise the meretricious art of pleasing those in power—quite unlike the brahmins, who did not scorn to develop the cult of these saints whenever it paid, but always pandered to the rich.

Fig. 1.19. Diablotin at Les Trois Frères cave.

The real military strength of the Marāṭhās, as later of the Sikhs, derived obviously from the simpler, less caste-ridden, and less unequal life. The later Marāṭhā generals like the Śinde and Gāekwād rose from relatively obscure families, unlike the earlier and more distinguished Candrarao More, Bhonsle, and Jādhav, the last of whom might claim kinship with the Yādava emperors of Devagiri and through them perhaps with Kṛṣṇa himself. Malhārrāo Hoḷkar was of the Dhangar shepherd caste, and would normally not have been allowed to rise to the status of a general, duke, and eventually king. It seems to me that some of this goes back, like the *bhagvā jheṇḍā* flag of Marāṭhā

Fig. 1.20. Hari-Hara.

armies, to Vārkarī custom. In spite of the brahmin *Baḍave* priests, and the rampant brahminism of the Peshwā days, the Vārkarī pilgrims minimized caste observances and distinctions on the journey. However, the reform and its struggle was never consciously directed against feudalism, so that its very success meant feudal patronage—and ultimately feudal decay by diversion of a democratic movement into the dismal channels of conquest and rapine.

The conglomerate *Gītā* philosophy might provide a loophole for innovation, but never the analytical tools necessary to make a way out of the social impasse. Jñāneśvar's life and tragic career illustrate this in full measure. He does not give a literal translation of the divine message, but its meaning and essence in his own terms, and in words that any Marāṭhā peasant could understand. Jñāneśvar's longest comment on the original comes in the 13th *adhyāya* of the *Gītā*, the chapter on 'the field and field-knower', particularly on *G*. 13. 7 (where he himself apologizes in *J*. 13. 314–338 for having been carried away far from the original) and on *G*. 13. 11. In the former, (*J*. 13.218–224), he flays the rainmaking *yājñika* fire-sacrificers; yet in *J*. 3. 134–5, these very sacrifices were taken as normal and necessary by him as by his divine exemplar; and once again (*G*. 18.5; *J*. 18. 149–152) both warn us that the *yajña* must not be abandoned any more than charity (*dāna*) or ascetic practices (*tapas*). The suffocating contradictions of mixed superstition are neatly brought out in *J.* 13. 812–822: "The peasant farmer sets up cult after cult, according to convenience. He follows the preacher who seems most impressive at the moment, learns his mystic formula. Harsh to the living, he relies heavily on stones and images; but even then never lives true to any one of them. He will have My (= Kṛṣṇa's) image made, established in a corner of the house, and then go off on pilgrimages to some god or other. He will pray to Me daily, but also worship the family's tutelary deity at need, and other gods as well, each at the particular auspicious moment. He founds My cult, but makes vows to others; on anniversary days, he is devoted to the ancestral Manes. The worship he gives Us on the eleventh (lunar date) is no more than that he renders to the sacred cobras on the fifth. He is devotee solely of Gaṇésa on the (annual) fourth; on the fourteenth, says he, 'Mother Durgā, I am yours alone' . . . At the Nine Nights (of the Mother-goddesses) he will recite the set praise of Caṇḍī, serve meals outdoors on the Sunday, and rush off on Monday with a *bel* fruit offering to Śiva's phallic symbol. Thus he prays unemittingly, never still for a moment, like a prostitute at the town gate". In Jñāneśvar's society, however, such eclectic worship was the universal practice at all levels, to the very highest people for whom Lakṣmīdhara and Hemādri indited their monstrous compendia. To that extent, though indirectly, the commentator voices a protest against the growth of an oppressive upper class. The *Gītā* doctrine is given a remarkably attractive turn by Jñāneśvar's quite original interpretation (*J.* 9. 460–470): "Kṣatriya, vaiśya, woman, śūdra and untouchable retain their separate existence only so long as they have not attained Me. . .Just as rivers have their individual names, whether coming from east or west, only till they merge into the ocean. Whatever be the reason for which one's mind enters into Me, he then becomes Me, even as the iron that strikes to break the philosopher's stone turns into gold at the contact. So, by carnal love like the milkmaids, Kaṃsa in fear, Śiśupāla by undying hatred, Vasudeva and the Yādavas by kinship, or Nārada, Dhruva, Akrūra, Śuka and Sanatkumāra through devotion—they all attained Me. I am the final resting place, whether they come to Me by the right or the wrong path, *bhakti*, lust or the purest love, or in enmity". Neither the callous *G.* 9.32 on which this charming comment is made, nor the fundamentally brutal Kṛṣṇa saga manifest such a calm elevation above jealous, exclusive *bhakti*. Yet,

Fig. 1.21. Jñāneśvar.

Fig. 1.22. Eknāth.

on the very next stanza, the scholiast extols brahmins as veritable gods on earth! His rejection by contemporary brahmins, which must surely have been a main reason for the decision to render the *Gītā* into Marāṭhī, never prevented him from striving after the brahmin vedic lore officially denied to all but initiates. That is, he embodied the inner contradictions which he discerned in contemporary society but failed to discover in the *Gītā*. Therefore, he could launch no movement towards their solution. Though an adept in *yoga* as a path towards physical immortality and mystical perfection (*cf. J.* on *G.* 6. 13–15), there was nothing left for him except suicide. That the gods remained silent at the unexpected Muslim blow which devastated their many richly endowed temples and no incarnation of *Kṛṣṇa* turned up to save the Yādava kingdom, might have been another cause for despair.

Fig. 1.23. Tukārām.

1.7. THE GĪTĀ TODAY

The main social problem was violently placed upon a new footing by Alāuddin Khilji and the Muslim conquest which imposed payment of heavy tribute. This intensified the need for more effective tax collection; that in turn encouraged a new, powerful but more efficient feudalism. Some optimists have maintained that the poorer classes benefited because Alauddin squeezed only the rich, who were rendered powerless. This disingenuous view carefully neglects to mention that even in the Doabs (which were directly administered) none of the former burdens of the peasantry were lifted. Their dues were collected by a different agency, though it remains true that the *Hindu* upper classes were prevented for a while from imposing fresh exactions. The provinces had not even this consolation, for the throne of Delhi exacted harsh tribute from conquered areas, without troubling itself about how provincial magnates gathered it—and how much more besides. Local military power was reduced only to a stage where it constituted little danger to the imperial forces, but the mechanism of violence more than sufficed for its main purpose, revenue collection. Whether the tribute was actually paid or not, and even over regions not subject to tribute, the imposts and exactions grew steadily. The class that collected the surplus retained an increasing portion, so that the needs of the state could be satisfied only in the earlier period, when feudalism stimulated trade and fresh agrarian production. Then the crisis was aggravated, to be resolved by another foreign conquest that introduced a totally different form of production, the bourgeois-capitalist. The modern independence movement did not challenge the productive form; it only asked that the newly developed Indian bourgeoisie be in power.

Modern life is founded upon science and freedom. That is, modern production rests in the final analysis upon accurate cognition of material reality (science), and recognition of necessity (freedom). A myth may grip us by its imagery, and may indeed have portrayed some natural phenomenon or process at a time when mankind had not learned to probe nature's secrets or to discover the endless properties of matter. Religion clothes some myth in dogma. "Science needs religion" is a poor way of saying that the scientists and those who utilize his discoveries must not dispense with social ethics. There is no need to dig into the *Gītā* or the Bible for an ethical system sandwiched with pure superstition. Such books can still be enjoyed for their aesthetic value. Those who claim more usually try to shackle the minds of other people, and to impede man's progress, under the most specious claims.

Individual human perfection on the spiritual plane becomes much easier when every individual's material needs are first satisfied on a scale agreed upon as reasonable[30] by the society of his day. That is, the main root of evil is social. The fundamental causes of social evil are no longer concealed from human sight. Their cure does not lie in theology but in socialism; the application of modern science, based upon logical deduction from planned experiment, to the structure of society itself. Science is at the basis of modern production; and no other tools of production are in sight for the satisfaction of man's needs. Moreover, the material needs could certainly be satisfied for all, if the relations of production did not hinder it.

NOTES TO CHAPTER 1

The following abbreviations have been used: *G* = the *Bhagavad-gītā; J* = the *Jñāneśvarī; Mbh* = the *Mahābhārata; Up* = *Upaniṣad; RV* = the *Ṛg-veda; JBBRAS* = *Journal* of the Asiatic Society, Bombay (formerly Bombay Branch of the Royal Asiatic Society); *ABORI* = *Annals* of the Bhandarkar Oriental Research Institute, Poona; *A* = the *Arthaśāstra of Kauṭalya; JRAS* = Journal of the Royal Asiatic Society, London. For the historical background, my own *Introduction to the Study of Indian History* has been used without detailed reference.

1. *Mbh.* 6.23–40 of the Poona edition, begun under the editorship of the late V. S. Sukṭhaṇkar, with the *Ādi, Sabhā, Āraṇyaka, Udyoga* and *Virāṭa parvans* completed under his direction. Succeeding volumes have been less satisfactory, and the edition is not yet complete. For the *Gītā* in particular, the readings generally assumed to be Śaṃkara's have been retained against the norm accepted for the rest of the edition. Among the many useful translations of the *Gītā* are those of F. Edgerton (Harvard Oriental Series), K. T. Telang (Sacred Books of the East), and S. Radhakrishnan (London 1948).
2. R. G. Bhāṇḍārkar's *Vaiṣṇavism, Śaivism, and Minor Religious Systems* (originally published in 1913 in the *Grundriss d. Indo-Arischen Philologie u. Altertumskunde*; re-issued. Poona 1929, in vol. IV of his collected works) gives a good summary of the influence of the doctrine in the classical and medieval period, but without reference to the historical context, which was indeed not known at the time. Its influence upon Bhāṇḍārkar himself led to a petty reformist movement, the Prārthanā Samāj (an offshoot of the Brāhmo Samāj) in which RGB was the dominant figure; and support of widow remarriage, then unheard of for brahmins, though practised by some 85% at least of the population. That he spoke for a very narrow class in the attempt to speak for the whole of India never struck him, nor for that matter other contemporary 'reformers'. Still, the silent change of emphasis from caste to class was a necessary advance.
3. In particular, the translation of *dharma* as religion, or even a universal Law for all society was a new concept with Buddhism, not accepted even after the time of the *G*. For example: *Manusmṛti* 8.41 reads "The (king) must inquire into the laws (*dharma*) of each caste (*jāti*), district (*janapada*), guild (*śreṇī*), and household (*kula*), and only then give his own legal decision (*svadharma*)". A great deal of the confusion over the *Gītā* derives from ignorance of reality, of the actual practices of large social groups; and from taking brahmin documents as representative of all Indian society.
4. The standard reference work is F. E. Pargiter's *The purāṇa text of the dynasties of the Kali age* (Oxford, 1913). Some of the theories have been contested e.g. A. B. Keith's review in the *JRAS*, but the work has survived and gained a well-deserved reputation for its synoptic edition of the historical kernel in the major puranas.
5. Translated in S. Beal: *Buddhist Records of the Western World* (London 1884, vol. I, pp. 184–186). The equivalent of *G*. 2.37 does occur on p. 185, and the association with a great battle at *Dharmakṣetra*, where bones still whitened the earth, is explicit, in an otherwise garbled account.

6. V. S. Sukṭhaṇkar: *The Nala episode and the Rāmāyaṇa* in *Festschrift* F. W. Thomas, pp. 294–303, especially p. 302, where he concludes that the two versions bracket the extant *Rāmāyaṇa*. The paper is reprinted in his Memorial edition (Poona 1944), pp. 406–415. For the mechanism of inflation, see his *Epic Studies VI*; and my notes on the *Parvasaṃgraha*, in the *JAOS*. 69.110–117; for the *Bhīṣmaparvan* and the 745 stanzas of the *Gītā*, ibid, 71.21–25.
7. J. Brough: *The early Brahmanical system of gotra and pravara* (Cambridge, 1953) p. 27, notes that the *kevala* Āṅgirasas are completely omitted by Hiraṇyakeśi-Satyāṣāḍha, but takes this to be a casual lacuna. So great an omission is highly improbable. My review in *JAOS* 73.202–208 was mistaken for a polemic, when the point being made was that theoretical works on *gotra* need to be checked by independent observation. For example, the *segrava* (= śaigrava) gotra found in Brāhmī inscriptions at Mathurā is not known to the books. Even more striking are the innumerable local brahmin groups whose conforming to theory has never been tested. City people in Mahārāṣṭra take brahmins to be primarily of the Sārasvat, Citpāvan, Deśastha and Karhāḍā groups. The 1941 *Census* caste tables for Bombay province as published show that such categories are together outnumbered by the 'Other Brahmans', and that local brahmin groups are the rule, though the books and theory are in the hands of the major groups named. The Bhṛgus are specially connected with the *Mbh* inflation, as was shown by V. S. Sukṭhaṇkar in his magnificent *Epic Studies VI* (ABORI 18.1–76; *Mem. Ed.* 1.278–337). It is important to note that the Bhārgava inflation was independent of though not hostile to the Nārāyaṇīya inflation, which continued after the first had tapered off. So much so, that the famous benedictory stanza *Nārāyaṇam namaskṛtya* of the popular editions drops out of the critical text, but most of the properly Bhārgava inflations (e.g. needless emphasis upon Paraśurāma) all remain. In *G.* 10.25, the Lord reveals himself as Bhṛgu among the great sages (*maharśīṇām Bhṛgur aham*), though that sage occupies no position in vedic tradition, and a trifling one even later.
8. *Epigraphia Indica* 8.36 ff.
9. Aśvaghoṣa's *Buddhacarita* and *Saundarananda* still exist, not to speak of *subhāṣita* verses scattered through anthologies in his name. The fragments of a play *Śāriputra-prakaraṇa* were arranged in order by H. Lüders, from Central Asian (Turfan) finds. This or another play of the same name was acted by hired actors in Fa Hsien's time in the Gupta heartland, as were also similar plays on the conversion of Moggallāna and Kassapa; note that all three disciples and Aśvaghoṣa himself were brahmins.
10. The *Mbh* diaskeuasts proclaim their desire to include everything. In *Mbh* 1.1–2, the work is successively an *itihāsa*, a *purāṇa*, an *upaniṣad*, a veda, and outweighs all four vedas together. It is the storehouse for poets. *Mbh*. 1.56.33 boasts: *yad ihāsti tad anyatra, yan nehāsti na tat kva-cit*: whatever is here might be elsewhere, but what was not here could hardly ever be found!
11. Translated by K. T. Telang, see Note 1. There is an *Uttaragītā*, a quite modern apocryphal work.
12. This is the second *sutta* of the *Dīgha-nikāya*, and has served as the model, in many ways, for the later *Milindpañho*, questions of king Menander.
13. This was clearly stated by Mr. C. Rajagopalachari in a press interview.
14. The only published source I have been able to locate for the original cult is the *Satya Pirer Kathā* in Bengali by Rāmeśvara Bhaṭṭācāryya (*ed.* by Śrī-Nagendranāth Gupta. Calcutta University 1930).
15. This paragraph and the next are treated in greater detail in a paper of mine on the *avatāra* syncretism and possible sources of the *Bhagavad-gītā, JBBRAS*. vol. 24–25 (1948–9), pp. 121–134.
16. *RV*. 8.96.13–14, but sometimes interpreted mystically as part of the Soma legend. The traditional explanation is that this Kṛṣṇa was an 'Asura', i.e. non-Aryan, and the fighting against Indra on the banks of the Aṃśumatī river was real, not symbolic of something else.
17. Ed. K. de Vreese, Leiden 1936. This particular *nāga* cult had been virtually killed by the Buddhist monks (*Rājataraṅgiṇī* 1.177–8), while the brahmins had also been reduced to helplessness at the time of the Buddhist teacher Nāgārjuna. They made a come-back by writing the *Nīlamatapurāṇa* (*Rāj*. 1. 182–6), Kalhaṇa informs us in passing.
18. *ABORI* 1.59–66; *JRAS* 1909.1055–6, 1087–92; 1910.813–5, 815–7.
19. See *JRAS* 1960; 17–31, 135–144, or chapter IV of this book; for the cave painting (originally discovered by Carlleyle) Mrs. B. Allchin in *Man*, 58.1958, article 207 + plate *M* (pp. 153–5).
20. The assurance is unmistakable: "Whenever true belief (*dharma*) pales and unrighteousness flourishes, then do I throw out another offshoot of myself". The next stanza proclaims that the god comes into being from age to

age, to protect the good people, destroy the wicked, and to establish *dharma*. It need not be further emphasized that the superfluous incarnation in *Mbh.* times wasted a perfectly good *avatāra*, badly needed elsewhere.

21. The cult is coeval with the foundation of Parvatī village, hence older than the Peshwā temple to the goddess who killed that demon. Cf. Bombay Gazetteer vol. 18, pt. 3 (Poona District), p. 388.
22. *Art In The Ice Age* by J. Maringer and H. G. Bandi, after Hugo Obermaier (London 1953); especially figures 30, 31, 70 (with mask, and arms imitating mammoth tusks), 142, 143. and perhaps 166.
23. This shows in Harṣa's inscriptions (e.g. *Epigraphia Indica* 7.155–60); benedictory verses at the beginning of his Buddhist drama *Nāgānanda*, addressed to Gaurī; Bāṇa's description in the *Harṣacarita* and Hsiuen Chuāng's account (*Beal* 1.223; the stūpa, vihāra, fine Maheśvara temple and the Sun-temple were all close together near Kanauj, and all constantly thronged with worshippers).
24. For the iconoclasm of Harṣa of Kaśmīr, *Rājataraṅgiṇī* 7.1080–1098. He had predecessors of similar bent, though less systematic: Jayāpīḍa in the 8th century (*Rāj.* 631–3: 638.9) and Śaṃkaravarman (5.168–70) in 883–902 AD.
25. The Gupta gold coinage is impressive, but hardly useful for normal transactions. Their silver coinage is notoriously inferior to, say, pre-Mauryan punch-marked coins, and rather rare in hoards; of Harṣa, only one coinage is known, and even that rather doubtful, in silver. The Chinese travellers Fa Hsien and Hsiuen Chuāng are emphatic in the assertion that most of the transactions were barter, and that cowry shells were also used, but very little currency. The accumulation by temples, monasteries and barons did nothing for the circulation of wealth or of commodities.
26. This is discussed in a paper of mine to appear in the *Journal* for the Economic and Social History of the Orient (Leiden), on feudal trade charters. Yaśodharman of Mālwā uses *sāmanta* as neighbouring ruler, whereas Viṣṇuṣeṇa (a Maitraka king) issued a charter in 592 AD where *sāmanta* can only have the feudal meaning.
27. The hero-stones carved in bas-relief are to be found in almost any village not recently settled, throughout Mahārāṣṭra and the south. A good collection is in the National Defence Academy's Museum at Khaḍakwāslā, near Poona. The death in fending off cattle raiders seems to be symbolized in many cases by a pair of ox-heads in the lowest panels. The story progresses upwards, to the funeral, perhaps with a *satī*, and going to heaven. The top of the relief slab is generally carved in the semblance of a funerary urn, familiar since Buddhist days. For inscriptions, even a single volume (*Epigraphia Carnatica X*, for example): Kolār 79, feudal grant for family of baron killed in battle (about 890 AD); Kolār 226 (*circa* 950 AD), grant of a field, on account of the death of a warrior fighting against cattle raiders; Kolār 232 (750 AD), Kolar 233 (815 AD), Muḷbāgal 92, 780 AD: Muḷbāgal 93, 970 AD, etc., with the hero-relief in every case.
28. Less well known than Gāṅga inscriptions are the minor ones showing how widely the custom was spread: *e.g.* from the *Ep. Carnatica*, Goribindnur 73 (*circa* 900 AD), the village watchman sacrifices his own head.; Cintāmaṇi 31 1050 AD), when the Oḍeya of the village went to heaven, his servant had his own head cut off—and a field was dedicated to his memory; oaths of not surviving the lord are taken in Kolar 129 (*circa* 1220 AD), Muḷbāgal 77 (1250 AD), Muḷbāgal 78 etc. Occasionally, a memorial was erected to a particularly able hound, as in Muḷbāgal 85 (975 AD), and Muḷbāgal 162, though the dog's prowess rather than *bhakti* is praised.
29. Penguin Classics L 57, *Travels of Marco Polo* (trans. R. E. Latham), pp. 236–8, for the cremation, and ritual suicide in front of some idol, by royal consent.
30. By 'society' is meant not only the rulers but the ruled. If the śūdra should agree that he ought to starve for imaginary sins committed in some supposed previous birth, either his group will die out, or at best be unable as well as unwilling to fight against invaders. Indian feudal history, however, is full of raids and counter-raids, not only by Muslims. It follows that the expropriated class will not show by its actions that they regard the expropriation as reasonable on religious grounds, particularly when they see the very same religion unable to defend its proponents against armed heretics. My point is simply that the fulfilment of certain material needs is as essential to health of the mind as it is to that of the body. It seems to me that the *Gītā* philosophy, like so much else in India's 'spiritual' heritage, is based in the final analysis upon the inability to satisfy more than the barest material needs of a large number.

2 | Urvaśī and Purūravas

2.1. INTRODUCTION

One of Kālīdāsa's finest plays, *Vikramorvaśīyam,* has for its theme the love, separations, and final reunion of King Purūravas of the lunar race and the nymph Urvaśī. The *apsaras*, on her way to heaven, is abducted by the demon Keśī, from whose clutches the mortal king rescues her. This led to their falling in love. She finds the divine city of Amaravati no longer attractive, and proves her lover's reciprocal sentiment by a masked visit to his park. From the joy of this discovery, she is recalled to heaven, to act the part of Lakṣmī in a play staged before Indra. But the divine stage-director Bharata sentences her to assume human form for mispronouncing Viṣṇu's name Puruṣottama as Purūravas. The curse is no great burden, as it enables her to mate with Purūravas, but the course of their true love is interrupted again and again. The heroine is turned into a vine, because of an unwitting transgression: she stepped into a grove sacred to the six-headed god Skanda-Kārttikeya, where no woman was allowed to tread without suffering metamorphosis because of the taboo. But she is changed back and restored to her husband by a charmed jewel. The jewel is stolen by a bird of prey; the bird is found shot dead by an arrow bearing a legend which tells the king that Urvaśī has borne him a son. This means another reunion, which would be terminated by Urvaśī's restoration to heaven; but Indra, having a war on his hands, allows her to remain on earth till her husband's death.

This crude analysis of a beautiful play by one of the world's great poets and India's great dramatist does no justice to the consummate skill with which the theme is handled and embellished. What interests me here is the theme itself. It can be traced right back to our oldest extant records, namely the Śatapatha Brāhmaṇa and the Ṛgveda. The oldest report still contains some features of the play, for it is a dialogue between the two principal characters, totally foreign in appearance to anything else in the Ṛgveda. The action takes place at a crucial moment when the hero pleads with the heroine and she refuses his request. Thus the happy ending is a much later invention. As we shall see, there is a greater change than this in the structure of the story. This change reflects precisely the difference between Vedic society and the Gupta period, being in fact a transition from ritual to drama.

2.2. KĀLIDĀSA'S TREATMENT

The theme attracted Kālidāsa sufficiently to be treated more than once, being for him simply the reunion of lovers separated by circumstances or by disfavour with the gods. On the purely human level, we have his play the *Mālavikāgnimitram*, which contains some of the most brilliant passages composed by the poet. There, however, the heroine is a princess forced to serve as a handmaid. On the other hand, the *Śākuntala* finds the hero unwilling to recognize either his wife or their son after a period of separation, some petty miracles being needed to bring him back to his senses. However, the lovers are always royal; the entire level is that of the court, but for an occasional scene in the forest or a hermitage. The king is always noble in character with his full complement of courtiers. In each of the three plays, there is at least one other queen between the two lovers, a variety of the eternal triangle that caused no difficulty in polygamous society, for the extra queen could yield gracefully while still remaining a queen. The characters are certainly oriented towards the contemporary reigning family, presumably the Guptas, as is seen from the language, and the title Vikrama. Also by the fact that Purūravas is the founder of the lunar line of kings while the son of Śakuntalā is Bharata (the eponymous ancestor of the greatest Ṛgvedic tribe) who is again enrolled into the Soma line of descent. The women and servants speak Prākrit, a practice which reflects a situation prevalent to this day in many parts of the country where formal school education has not yet made its way or is still confined to the males of a small upper class. For example, the men of the land-holder class in Goa believe their language to be Marāṭhī or Portuguese, according to their religion, but the women speak Koṅkaṇī. Similarly in many parts of the Gangetic basin, where the Hindi spoken by the men of the upper class differs very much from that spoken by the womenfolk, and of course from that of the peasants. But the aristocrats also generally speak the supposedly cruder language or dialect, particularly when addressing women or servants, which never happens with Kālidāsa or any of the other Sanskrit dramatists with the solitary exception of the Sūtradhāra in the *Mṛcchakaṭikaṃ prologue*. We have here one of the concomitants of a peculiarly Brahmanic renaissance, which did its best to create a class language, refusing to acknowledge the failure that was absolutely inevitable. Their only success was in preserving a dead language for religion, as with Sumerian for the priesthood in Mesopotamia. The Sanskrit renaissance was due in fact to concessions made to the popular idiom such as Mahārāṣṭrī or its prototypes. Language is a means of communication for the whole of society. It develops, just as does money and the concept of value, from social intercourse.[1] At most, a class can MARK its unity by means of a specialized vocabulary, or a particular accent, but both must belong to the whole of their society for comprehension. In much the same way, no class can have a special currency for itself, nor can it monopolize all the means of barter-exchange (money) in the realm. Kālidāsa, therefore, has not even depicted his own times very carefully, beyond the brahminized concept of a royal court. But in the earliest times the story could not be meant to delineate a royal court, which had not come into existence. Though the scriptures in which it seems to originate became a monopoly of the Brahmin class, their purpose was liturgical. So, we have to look much deeper into the details of the story, and into their historical development, before coming to any understanding of its origin.

2.3. MODERN INTERPRETATIONS

Before trying our own analysis, let us consider what has been done by scholars of repute. Keith[2] admits that the explanation does not suffice for the earliest stage; the Ṛgvedic hymn is 'of considerable interest and obscurity'. He finds the sun-dawn myth of Weber and Max Müller 'quite unnecessary.' The whole story has no deep significance according to him: "The hymn clearly refers to one of those alliances of nymphs and men, which are common in all literature as in the stories of Thetis and of the German swan maidens, who often for as long as seven years are allowed to stay with mortal men......the taboo of seeing the hero naked is of interest and primitive in nature......Purūravas is simply a hero, not necessarily ever a real man, but conceived as one: later tradition derives the lunar race of kings from him." The trouble with this is that it explains nothing. If the legend is common, and primitive, it has to have some fairly deep significance, particularly in view of its later survival and repetition in different ways.

Max Müller[3] had a very simple formula for these primitive myths, which he succeeded in translating into purely almanac language: Thus—'Urvaśī loves Purūravas' meant 'the sun rises'; 'Urvaśī sees Purūravas naked' meant 'the dawn is gone'; 'Urvaśī finds Purūravas again' meant 'the sun is setting'. Against this sort of fatuous equivalence, as in the Nirukta and Kumārila, there is no argument. Müller, however, gives an abstract of Kālidāsa's play, yet only explains the *Śatapatha* legend; for there is no mention in Kālidāsa of the tabu against Urvaśī seeing her lover naked. Just why the simple sun-dawn myth had to undergo all these changes doesn't transpire from a reading of Müller's critique.

This is not to deny either Müller's substantial contributions to Indic philology or the legend's similarity to a sun-myth. To Müller, India owes the first complete edition of the Ṛgveda, the circumstances being explained in detail in the very book cited: the Veda was generally misquoted by learned Brahmins who used this method at will to refute any inconvenient legal decision supported by the Manusmṛti or similar works, and even to justify the practice of widow-burning (*satī*). The East India Company's officers forbade the latter practice, but wanted as far as possible to yield to Brahminism, as it was always a convenient tool for subjection of the 'natives'. So came into existence Müller's edition of the *Ṛksaṃhitā*, giving the Brahmins themselves a complete text which hardly any of them possessed in Bengal and none could have edited there at that time. One may note that it was the Germans who took and maintained the lead in Indic studies, though one should have expected British scholars to occupy that position. The British attitude is shown by Colebrooke's sneer against the Vedas, 'They are too voluminous for a complete translation of the whole; and what they contain, would hardly reward the labour of the reader; much less, that of the translator." The contrast is surely to be explained by the satiety of a nation which had completed its industrial revolution and wanted only to exploit its colonies, as against a nation that had begun to catch up with and surpass its older rival by means of superior technique, which necessarily implied the profound scientific method and outlook that characterized Germany of the last century.

Now, if the difference in the means of production explains so much even in the attitude of modern European scholars, is it not necessary to ask just what differences in social structure prevailed at the various stages of the Purūravas-Urvaśī legend? But this is precisely what has not been done. As we saw, Keith never gave the matter a thought. Geldner, whose account represents the heaviest labour of mature German scholarship,[4] saw nothing essential in the earliest version that did not survive in its developments. To him, the whole episode was just one more of many such *Itihāsapurāṇas*. The same attitude led Geldner to see a far greater continuity between the Veda and later Sanskrit literature, just as Sāyaṇa did, than the facts (as now exemplified by archaeology) justify. When he said (p. 244) of Urvaśī "Sie vermag die Natur der Hetäre nicht zu verleugnen," did he realize that the hetaerism (strictly speaking, hierodule-prostitution, but I shall continue to use "hetaera" loosely) originates in, and in many parts of India still remains connected with, temple cults; at the earliest stages, with the cult of the mother-goddess? For our purpose, Geldner's main service was a painstaking report on the principal versions of the story; to these we may proceed forthwith, with the remark that Geldner's essay well repays close study in spite of its insufficient explanation of the original legend.

2.4. VERSIONS OF THE STORY

Geldner reported upon eight different sources, in his order: 1) the Śatapatha Brāhmaṇa 11.5 1 ff. 2) The Kāṭhakam. 8. 10. 3) Ṣaḍguruśiṣya's commentary to the Sarvānukramaṇī. 4) Harivaṃśa (noting virtual identity with the Vāyu-purāṇa 2.29). 5) Viṣṇu-purāṇa 4. 6. 19 ff. 6) The Bṛhaddevatā. 7) Kathāsaritsāgara 17.4. (Trans. Tawney-Penzer Vol. II. pp. 34–6; and note II. 245, 5). 8) The Mahābhārata (Crit. ed. 1.70. 16–22).

Of these, the first is given at the end of this section for comparison with RV. x. 95, from which it shows some important differences, even at so early a stage. Geldner noted that accounts 1,4,5 follow much the same lines, 2 is a dry excerpt; 3 adds the story of Ila, a son of Manu metamorphosed into a woman by stepping into a grove sacred to the mother-goddess Pārvatī, and in that state bearing Purūravas as a son to Budha; 3 also gives a motif to the curse upon Urvaśī by adding the legend of Vaśiṣṭha's birth from the combined semen of Mitra and Varuṇa poured into a *kumbha*.

The most important admission made by Geldner is that there are essentially two versions of the latter half of the legend, of which the older was tragic. The lovers never were united, at least in this world. Of course, this can be seen by any translation of the Ṛgvedic hymn, but it is essential to know that it survived in Indian tradition though Kālidāsa could not accept it for his romance. What the German scholar failed to inquire was what was supposed to have happened, in the original version, to the pair after they parted. On this point, the Ṛgveda gives no direct information while the Śatapatha Brāhmaṇa ends by saying that Purūravas himself became a Gandharva after performing the correct sacrifice; the Gandharvas are the superhuman beings assigned as natural consorts to the Apsaras, but some doubt is added as to exactly what happened by the further statement that anyone who sacrifices in the manner of Purūravas becomes himself a Gandharva. However, Geldner should have followed the Mahābhārata version further in the Purāṇas. The relationship is rather confused, in the absence of any extensive analysis; but specimen legends have shown that the Mahābhārata in its critically edited form contains the source of many important puranic stories, though both may be derived from some older common source. The epic says briefly (Mbh. 1.70. 16–22) that "the learned Purūravas was born of Ilā, WHO WAS BOTH HIS FATHER AND HIS MOTHER, or so have we heard. Ruling over (*aśnan*) thirteen islands of the sea, the victorious one was always surrounded by superhuman powers, though himself human. Intoxicated by (his own) prowess, he crossed the Brahmins, tore their treasures from the Brahmins in spite of their outcries. O king, Sanatkumāra, having come from the Brahmā-world, gave him advice which he did not take. Then cursed by the angered sages he was at once destroyed, he, the king, who had been overcome by greed and lost his reason by force of pride. The same hero brought from the Gandharva-world, along with Urvaśī, the fires arranged into three for sacrificial purposes. Six sons were begotten of Aila (Purūravas): Āyu, Dhīmān, Amāvasu, Dṛḍhāyu, Vanāyu, and Śrutāyu, the sons of Urvaśī."

Of these six sons, only Āyu is known at the earliest stage; seeing that the last three have *āyu* as termination of a compound name, it may be admitted that an Āyu tribe derived their descent, from Urvaśī and Purūravas. At least two of the Purāṇas allow this story to be traced, the direct influence being proved by the fact that there the Nahuṣa story follows immediately after, as in the above Mahābhārata section. The moral of both epic and purāṇic narrative is that it is dangerous for any king to rob Brahmins, to tax them, or press them into forced labour. The *Arthaśāstra* 1.6, on the other hand, says that Aila (Purūravas) came to a sad end by squeezing (taxes, mercilessly out of) all four caste-classes. The Purāṇic specialization to brahmins is a late modification. But the Vāyu Purāṇa 1.2.13–21, which is copied with only trifling variants by Brahmāṇḍa 1.2.14–23, gives the exact manner in which Purūravas came to die. His greed for treasure was never satisfied. Once, while hunting, he stumbled upon a golden altar made by Viśvakarman at which the seers of the Naimiṣa forest were sacrificing, and tried to loot that. The angry sacrificers struck him with the sacrificial grass which had become as Indra's *vajra*; so crushed, the king yielded up the ghost.

Clearly, PURŪRAVAS WAS KILLED AT A SACRIFICE, according to this Brahmin tradition; that his extortionate greed was the cause is merely a warning to later kings. I submit that the cause may have been invented, but the killing cannot have been wholly divorced from current inherited legend. At this stage, let us repeat the Śatapatha Brāhmaṇa (xi. 5.1) version, in Eggeling's translation:

"The nymph Urvaśī loved Purūravas, the son of Iḍā. When she wedded with him, she said, 'Thrice a day shalt thou embrace me; but do not lie with me against my will, and let me not see thee naked, for such is the way to behave to us women', (2) She then dwelt with him a long time, and was even with child of him, so long did she dwell with him. Then the Gandharvas said to one another, 'For a long time, indeed, has this Urvaśī dwelt among men: devise ye some means how she may come back to us.' Now, a ewe with two lambs was tied to her couch: the Gandharvas then carried off one of the lambs. (3) 'Alas', she cried, 'they are taking away my darling, as if I were where there is no hero and no man!' They carried off the second and she spoke in the selfsame manner. (4) He then thought within himself, 'How can that be (a place) without a hero and without a man where I am? And naked, as he was, he sprang up after them: too long he deemed it that he should put on his garment. Then the Gandharvas produced a flash of lightning, and she beheld him naked even as by daylight. Then, indeed, she vanished: 'Here am I back', he said, and lo! she had vanished. Wailing with sorrow, he wandered all over Kurukṣetra. Now there is a lotus lake there called Anyataḥplakṣā: He walked along its bank; and there nymphs were swimming about in the shape of swans. (5) And she (Urvaśī) recognising him, said, 'This is the man with whom I have dwelt.' They then said, 'Let us appear to him.'—'So be it!' she replied; and they appeared to him. (6) He then recognised her and implored her (RV. x. 95.1) 'Oh my wife, stay though, cruel in mind: let us now exchange words! Untold, these secrets of ours will not bring us joy in days to come';—'Stop, pray, let us speak together!' this is what he meant to say to her. (7) She replied (x. 95.2). 'What concern have I with speaking to thee? I have passed away like the first of the dawns. Purūravas, go home again: I am like the wind, difficult to catch';—'Thou didst not do what I told thee; hard to catch am I for thee, go to thy home again!' this is what she meant to say. (8) He then said sorrowing (x. 95. 14), 'Then will thy friend rush away this day never to come back, to go to the farthest distance: then will he lie in Nirṛti's lap, or the fierce wolves will devour him'; 'Thy friend will either hang himself, or start forth; or the wolves, or dogs will devour him'! this is what he meant to say. (9) She replied (x. 95. 15), 'Purūravas, do not die! do not rush away! let not the cruel wolves devour thee! Truly, there is no friendship with women, and theirs are the hearts of hyenas;—'Do not take this to heart! there is no friendship with women: return home!' this is what she meant to say. (10) (RV. x. 95. 16) 'When changed in form, I walked among mortals, and passed the nights there during four autumns. I ate a little ghee, once a day, and even now I feel satisfied therewith.'—This discourse in fifteen verses had been handed down by the Bahvṛcas. Then her heart took pity on him."

Thus the Śatapatha Brāhmaṇa account is a commentary on the Ṛgvedic hymn, though not explaining its most obscure features. The Brāhmaṇa then goes on (by itself) to say how Urvaśī gave him a night of her company, and gave him his son. The Gandharvas granted him a boon, which he chose as being one of themselves. Thereto, he received directions for the proper sacrifices. The account ends: (17) "He then made himself an upper *araṇī* of Aśvattha wood, and a lower *araṇī* of Aśvattha

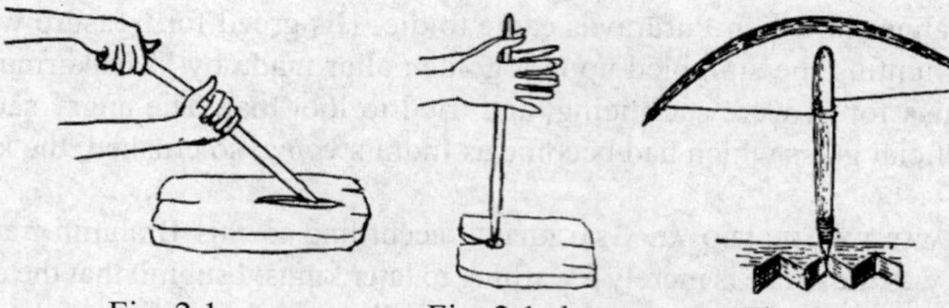

Fig. 2.1. *a*. Fig. 2.1. *b*. Fig. 2.1. *c*.

Fig. 2.1. *a*, fire-plough; 2. 1. ***b*, *c*** fire-drills.

wood; and the fine which resulted therefrom was that very fire: by offering therewith he became one of the Gandharvas. Let him therefore make himself an upper and a lower *araṇī* of Aśvattha wood, and the fire which results therefrom will be that very fire: by offering therewith he becomes one of the Gandharvas." Kālidāsa retained the heroine on earth till the hero's death, rather than translate him to heaven forthwith. That the *ŚB* account was not authenticated by any strong textual basis in antiquity follows from the other Brāhmaṇa accounts which do their poor best to explain the same hymn (cf. W. Caland in *Album Kern*, Leiden 1003, pp. 57–60).

The last sentence of the Śatapatha quotation is meant for any later sacrificer. The similarity of Urvaśī-Purūravas (or for that matter any human coupling) with the two portions of the fire-plough[5] (Fig. 2.1) has been noted, the more so because the son's name *āyu* is also used as an adjective for *agni*. This is one more natural interpretation of the whole myth. But let us remark for the time being that a definite locality was recognized for the dialogue, and that the 'happy ending' was not part of the Vedic discourse, being clearly a later addition. The Ṛgvedic hymn is in eighteen instead of fifteen verses, which has been taken by some to denote a difference of version. Finally, what is the original meaning of 'became a Gandharva'? This could not have happened while Purūravas was alive, for the Gandharva at the time of the Brāhmaṇas is recognized as a spirit who could possess women, say the spirit that caused their hysteria: Bhujyu Lāhyāyani in the Bṛhadāraṇyaka Upaniṣad 3. 4. 1 says to Yājñavalkya… "We were travelling around as wanderers among the Madras. As such we came to the house of Patañcala Kāpya. He had a daughter who was possessed by a Gandharva". We asked him, 'who are you'? He said: 'I am Sudhanvan, a descendant of Aṅgiras'". Patañcala Kāpya could not have had a very happy family life, for Uddālaka Āruṇi reports a little further: (Br. Up. 3. 7. 1) "He had a wife possessed by a *gandharva*. We asked him, 'Who are you?' He said 'I am Kabandha Ātharvaṇa'". The Aṅgirasas left human descendants, and the Atharvan is clearly at one time a human fire-priest. Hence, though the Gandharvas possess a separate minor heaven of their own, a human being can attain it only as a spirit. For a Buddhist the Gandharva is a condition of existence between death and rebirth.

If we combine the Brāhmaṇa with the purāṇa account, the common feature is that Purūravas became a spirit, i.e., lost his life, in some way connected with a sacrifice.

2.5. ṚGVEDA X. 95

At this stage, let me introduce the original hymn which forms our ultimate source at present, and which will have to be accounted for if some new interpretation of the legend is to be proposed.

haye jāye manasā tiṣṭha ghore vacāṃsi miśrā kṛṇavāvahai nu
na nau mantrā anuditāsa ete mayaskaran paratare ca nāhan (1)

(Purūravas) "Alas, O wife, desist from your intentions, O dreadful one, let us discourse together. If our chants remain un-uttered, they will bear no fruit for distant days."

kimetā vācā kṛṇavā tavāhaṃ prākramiśam uṣasām agriyeva
purūravaḥ punar astaṃ parehi durāpanā vāta-ivāham asmi (2)

(Urvaśī) "What shall I do with these discourses of yours? I have gone over like the first of the Uṣas. O Purūravas, go back to your destiny; I am as hard to get as the wind."

iṣur na sriya iṣudher, asanā goṣāḥ śatasā na raṃhiḥ
avīre kratau vi davidyutan norā na māyuṃ citayanta dhunayaḥ. (3)

(Pur.) "Like an arrow to the target that wins cattle a hundred hold. Without heroic determination there is no shining; the chorus sets up a keening like (bleating) lambs."

sā vasu dadhatī śvaśurāya vaya uṣo yadi vaṣṭy antigṛhāt
astaṃ nanakṣe yasmiñ cākan divā naktaṃ śnathitā vaitasena (4)

(Extra.) That Usas giving wealth and nourishment to the father-in-law, as long as wished, reached her destiny (*astaṃ nanakṣe*) from the inner house, which pleased her; rammed night and day by the (lover's) member.

triḥ sma māhnaḥ śnathayo vaitasen ota sma me'vyatyai pṛṇāsi
purūravo'nu te ketam āyaṃ rājā me vīra tanvas tad āsīḥ (5)

(Urv.) "Thrice a day didst thou ram me with the member, and impregnated me unwilling (as I was). Purūravas, I yielded to thy desires; O hero, then wert thou king of my body".

yā sujūrṇiḥ śreṇiḥ sumnaāpi hradecakṣur na granthinī caraṇyuḥ
ta añjayo'ruṇayo na sasruḥ śriye gāvo na dhenavo'navanta (6)

(?) This excited……line, knotted together, moving, reflected in the pool; these drawn-red ointments flowed; they lowed like cows, the cattle decorated (?).

sam asmiñ jāyamāna āsata gnā ut em avardhan nadyaḥ svagūrtāḥ
mahe yat tvā purūravo raṇāyāvardhayan dasyuhatyāya devāḥ (7)

(?Urv.) "As he was born, there sat the gods' wives; the self-made rivers made him grow. Thee, O Purūravas, the gods have raised for the great battle, for victory over the Dasyus."

sacā yad āsu jahatīṣv atkam amānuṣīṣu mānuṣo niṣeve
apa sma mat tarasantī na bhujyus tā atrasan rathaspṛśo nāśvāḥ (8)

(Pur.) "When I, though human, embraced the superhuman (females) who cast off their clothing, they started away from me like does (? *bhujyus*) or like horses touching the chariot".

yad āsu marto amṛtāsu nispṛk saṃ kṣoṇībhiḥ kratubhir na pṛṅkte
tā ātayo na tanvaḥ śumbhata svā aśvāso na krīḷayo dandaśānāḥ (9)

(Urv.) "If the mortal lusting after (us) goddesses mingles with the water-nymphs according to their will, then do they display their bodies like swans, nipping each other like stallions at play".

vidyun na yā patantī davidyod bharanitī me apyā kāmyāni
janiṣṭo apo naryaḥ sujātaḥ prorvaśī tirata dīrgham āyuḥ (10)

(Pur.) "She flashed like falling lightning, bringing me the craved waters—from, the water was bom a noble lad. May Urvaśī grant (me) long-life".

jajñisa ithā gopīthyāya hi dadkātha tat purūravo ma ojaḥ
aśāsaṃ tvā vtduṣī sasminn ahan na māśṛṇoḥ kim abhug vadāsi (11)

(Urv.) "Thou wert surely born for protection; this power didst thou hand over to me. I, the initiate, warned you on that very day. Thou didst not listen to me, why dost thou (now) speak like an innocent?"

kadā sūnuḥ pitaraṃ jāta icchāc cakran nāśru vartayad vijānan
ko dampatī samanasā vi yūyod adha yad agniḥ śvaśureṣu dīdayat (12)

(Pur.) "When will the son that is born yearn after his father? He will have shed flooding tears, knowing (what happened). Who dares separate the wedded pair in accord as long as the (ancestral) fire burns at the hours of the fathers-in-law?"

prati bravāṇi vartayate aśru cakran na krandad ādhye śivāyai
pra tat te hinavā yat te asme parehy astaṃ nahi mūra māpaḥ (13)

(Urv.) "I answer you, let him shed ample tears, he will not cry, heedful of (my) sacred office; I shall send you that or thine that thou hast with us. Go to thy destiny; thou fool thou canst not reach me".

sudevo adya prapated anāvṛt parāvataṃ paramāṃ ganatvā u
adhā śayīta nirṛter upasthe' dhainaṃ vṛkā rabhasāso adyuḥ (14)

(Pur.) "Let (your) lover (*sudevaḥ*) today drop (dead) uncovered, let him go to the very farthest distance, never to return; let him lie down in the lap of Nirṛti (the death-goddess), let him be eaten by raging wolves".

purūravo mā mṛthā mā pra papto mā tvā vṛkāso aśivāsa u kṣan
na vai strāiṇani sakhyāni santi sālāvṛkāṇāṃ hṛdayāny etā (15)

(Urv.) "O, Purūravas, thou art not to die, not to drop (dead), the unholy wolves are not to eat thee."
(Pur.) "There is no friendship with womenfolk, their hearts are the hearts of hyenas".

yad virūpācaraṃ martyeśvavasaṃ rātrīḥ śaradaś catasraḥ
ghṛtasya stokaṃ sakṛdahna āsnām, tād ev edam tatṛpāṇā carāmi (16)

(Urv.) "When I wandered among mortals in another guise and stayed (with them) for the nights of four years, I ate just a drop of clarified butter once a day; sated with that do I wander here now."

āntarikṣaprāṃ rajaso vimānīṃ upa śikṣyāmy urvaśīm vasiṣṭhaḥ
upa tvā rātiḥ sukṛtasya tiṣṭhān ni vartasva hṛdayaṃ tapyate me (17)

(Pur.) "I, the best (of men) submit to the atmosphere-filling, sky-crossing Urvaśī. May the blessings of good deeds be thine; turn back, my heart is heated (with fear)"

iti tvā devā ima āhur aiḷa yathem etad bhavasi mṛtyubandhuḥ
prajā te devān haviṣā yajāti svarga u tvam api mādayāse (18)

(Urv.) 'Thus speak these gods to thee, son of Iḷā: inasmuch as thou art now doomed to death, thy offspring will offer sacrifice to the gods, but thou thyself rejoice in heaven."

Hermann Oldenberg's discussion (*ZDMG* xxix, 1885, 52–90: Ākhyāna-Hymnen im Ṛgveda; our legend, pp. 72–86) postulates a (lost) prose shell for the vedic hymn without attempting to explain its many intrinsic difficulties. The original suggestion was made by Windisch, on the model of Irish myth and legend. The argument is that the Śatapatha Brāhmaṇa version is much more comprehensible than the bare Ṛgveda dialogue, hence some such explanatory padding must originally have existed. Unfortunately for this reasoning, Oldenberg himself shows at the end of his discussion that many details of the Śatapatha story arise from misread or badly understood phrases in the veda. For instance, the nymphs have been turned by the *ŚB* into swans from the ṛgvedic simple *ātayo na*. The ewes tied to Ūrvaśī's bed may derive from reading the vedic *urā na māyum* as *uraṇamāyum*; the lack of a hero (to stop the Gandharvas taking away her darling) bewailed by Urvaśī may come from the ṛgveda's *avīre kratau*, the lightning flash from *vi davidyutan na*. For all that, Oldenberg agrees with Ludwig that "es kaum möglich ist die beiden Darstellungen (des *RV* und des *ŚB*) in Uebereinstimmung zu bringen." The conclusion is that the original dialogue had become incomprehensible by the time of the Brāhmaṇa, and if these very able German scholars understood the *ŚB* account better, it was only because that account was manufactured specially to provide such understanding, in place of that which had already been lost. Whether prose passages were lost therewith or not is immaterial, though the possibility seems to me very remote. There is a great deal in the Śatapatha and other Brāhmaṇas which shows to what extent vedic rites had gained currency and the form in which they were practised. But unconvincing prose stories inserted as explanations—for the whole of the Brāhmaṇic literature is meant as commentary to ritual practice—and, fantastic etymologies show that in many cases the origin of the rite (and consequently the real meaning of a hymn) had been forgotten, or was something entirely different from the modes of contemporary society. To give better-known examples of such development: we know that down into imperial Roman times a hymn was sung whose archaic

Latin was incomprehensible to the singers; that the opening of the Sybilline books meant reversion in times of the utmost civic peril to ancient and virtually forbidden sacrifices; undoubtedly, that is why the praetor Petilius gave his opinion that certain books rediscovered after long burial should be burnt (Plutarch's *Numa Pompilius*). We must try to unearth for ourselves the original ritual whose lapse had led the *ŚB* to account so badly for *ṛks* fixed by the Bahvṛcas' memory.

2.6. COMMENTARY TO RV X. 95

The hymn undoubtedly contains the germs of *all* the later stories that developed about Urvaśī and Purūravas, and from which Kālidāsa drew his material with such unrestricted freedom. But to take *some* of them and then seek to explain the obscurities of the hymn thereby with Geldner leads to nothing except a great exercise of ingenuity in twisting the meaning of Sanskrit words—a pastime to which the language unfortunately lends itself far too well. The meteorological explanation will certainly not do, for then all details vanish completely. The Buddha, Napoleon, and Gladstone (as by Andrew Lang) can all be written off as sun-myths. Nor does it do to say that prose explanations must have been lost or that such myths are found in many other people's folklore. We have to explain what survives, and to explain it on its own merits with reference to a form of society in which no prose additions were needed.

The primary reason for the survival of any vedic hymn is its liturgical function. If an odd hymn like this remains, it can only be because it had some very marked significance or utility which was lost after the composition of the particular verses. Of course, during the period of mere survival, all other parallel aspects[6] are of the utmost help, including the fire-drill, the sun-myth, the romantic tale, the psychological image. The last may be seen in the preface to Grassmann's translation: "The hymn is of late origin … and seems to have been carried from an original religious idea into the region of crude sensuality, and to have been increased by further displacements that move within this latter region with ease. Purūravas, the 'much-calling', the son of Iḷā (the libation) and Urvaśī, the much-desiring or the much-offering, the spirit of ardour, appear here no longer in this ethico-religious relationship. On the contrary, the yearning of the man who calls to the gods and the granting of the goddess that awakens and recompenses ardour are here transformed into material desire and sensuality." This, naturally, raises far too many objections to satisfy anyone. There is still plenty of sensuality in the Ṛgveda, and if the movement of motifs be admitted, it can in general have been only from the sensual to the ideal ethico-religious, not in the opposite direction. Why should that have happened here, and in so mysterious a manner that the very meaning of the actual hymn is lost?

My explanation derives from as literal a reading as possible, with the ambiguities left unresolved till the end, and then determined—as far as possible—by taking the sense of the whole. PURŪRAVAS IS TO BE SACRIFICED AFTER HAVING BEGOTTEN A SON AND SUCCESSOR UPON URVAŚĪ; HE PLEADS IN VAIN AGAINST HER DETERMINATION. This is quite well-known to anthropologists as a sequel to some kinds of primitive sacred marriage.

Most of the Ṛgvedic hymns are meant to be chanted by one or more priests. But there are a few exceptions where *the hymn can only be explained as what remains of a ritual performance.*[7] For example, three (or four) characters, Indra, Indrāṇī, and Vṛṣākapi (and perhaps his wife) take part in x. 86, which is unquestionably sensual with its quite erotic passages; the refrain *'viśvasmād Indra uttara'* is treated as a later addition by all scholars, and so ignored, simply because it comes at the end of every *ṛk* without fitting into the metre. Why was it added at all, and why so systematically, when we have plenty of other examples of refrains fitting into the ṛgvedic verse, and of later additions with smoother join? The only possible explanation is that this refrain is meant to be chanted by others than the principal characters, presumably by all those who attended the performance. The dialogue of Urvaśī and Purūravas is likewise meant to be *part of a ritual act performed by two characters representing the principals and is thus a substitute for an earlier, actual sacrifice of the male*. The extra verses are to be chanted by someone else, to round out the action. That is, Kālidāsa's play is very naturally based upon the oldest of plays. This is not a startling conclusion; even modern European drama develops from the mystery plays of the medieval church, which themselves develop from and supplement church ritual. They offer a substitute for pagan, pre-Christian rites of similar purport. It has also been shown that Aeschylus at least among the Greek dramatists developed his plays from the mysteries related to tribal cults and initiation ceremonies, by adopting the themes to changes in contemporary society.

If anything has been omitted, it could at most have been stage-directions for the mime, and not some prose narrative. The original meaning of *nāṭya* is precisely miming, not acting in the modern sense. Quite apart from foreign parallels and the still-surviving semi-ritual dances and songs in the countryside which come at least to the threshold of drama (M. Winternitz: *Geschichte der Indischen Literatur* 3.162ff.), the Sanskrit texts of the dramas are quite explicit. For example, in the *Mṛcchakaṭikam*, the villain Śakāra dances (*nartayati*) with joy in the 9th act, a simple enough demonstration. But the masseur-monk in act 3 takes the place of an image to escape his pursuers, after miming various sentiments: *bahuvidhaṃ nāṭyaṃ kṛtvā*. Śakāra mimes a sentiment, not an action (in the 9th act) when he manifests temptation: *iti mohaṃ nāṭayati*. In the same act, the hero Cārudatta mimes his shame (*lajjāṃ nāṭayati*) without verbal answer when the shocked judge asks him, "Sir, is a courtezan then your friend?"; fear is mimed by him on his way to execution. I choose this drama deliberately because this hero is led to his death bedecked like a beast to be sacrificed to the gods, with a garland of red flowers and red hand prints all over his body. This will be of interest to us later. Here, I only raise one further question, namely, whether the *nāndī* prologue to any Sanskrit drama was not originally pure mime, with the verbal benediction added later.

It will be seen at once that this explanation serves to remove *all* the major obscurities of the hymn, without doing any violence to the meaning of the words; the explanation fits better than any of the others that have been offered, and shows at the same time why certain divergent accounts with a tragic ending survived in the Purāṇas. Let us look further into the details.

Purūravas addresses his wife as *ghore*, which means the grim or dreaded one, used for gods like Indra; hardly a lover's term, though later this is taken as denoting her hard-heartedness. But he is emphatic that if their *mantras* remain unspoken, there will be no benefit in distant days; that is, the chant (and action) is meant to confer upon the audience the benefits associated with all fertility rites. Urvaśī apparently tells her lover to get back to his home, *punar astam parehi*, and this is supported by similar interpretations of the word *astam* in the fourth *ṛk*, which is admitted to be an extra verse. But look at the funerary hymn x.14.8 where the dead man is sent back to his ancestors and Yama with the words *punar astam ehi*. This has sometimes been taken as a request to be reborn in the original family, but such transmigration is not a Ṛgvedic idea. There is no doubt that Purūravas is to go to his final destiny, pass from the sight of men (*astam adarśane*, Amarakośa 3. 4. 17). He himself says that he is to die, in 14, where going to a far distance, lying down in the lap of Nirṛti and so on are familiar idiomatic circumlocutions for death. This has, again, been taken as a desire to commit suicide for being bereft of his love—a proposition far too romantic for the Ṛgveda, particularly as no word of endearment passes between these two! Urvaśī seems to console him in the next *ṛk* by assuring him that he is not to die. But look closer, and it is clear only that he is not to die a common profane death, not to be eaten by wolves like any untended corpse in the Iranian *dakhma* (predecessor of the tower of silence) or the corresponding open corpse-enclosure, the *śmaśāna* described in so many Buddhist works, and even in the *Kathāsaritsāgara*. No, he is to be sacrificed to or by the gods; that was his destiny. Purūravas was raised for the battle of the gods against the demons so it is not straining the sense to see in this (x. 95.7) the necessity for sacrificing Purūravas. The assurance 'thou dost not die' is given in almost identical terms to the sacrificed, cooked, and eaten horse in *RV*, i. 162. 21 *na vai u etan mriyase*. In fact, the horse is going to the gods, freed from all his earthly troubles and brings victory to the sacrificers. We should not be surprised to find Purūravas assured at the very end that he is going straight to heaven. That is why he is *mṛtyubandhuḥ*, not an ordinary mortal, but one literally bound to death at the sacrifice. This surely explains why Urvaśī has the heart of hyena (15), why Purūravas's son can never know his father, but must console himself with thinking of his mother's sacred office (12, 13). Even when he asks Urvaśī to turn, *ni vartasva* (17) Purūravas does not ask her to turn back to him, but to turn away from him for his heart quails with dread; quite naturally, seeing what she is about to do to him. Earlier, he had begged her for long life (10) (Geldner's translation "die Urvaśī soll noch lange leben" is piffle, seeing that she is immortal anyway) to which her only answer (11) was that he had been amply warned in advance as to what fate awaited him, if he insisted upon mating with her. The light diet admitted by Urvaśī in (16) is perhaps a denial of cannibalism as a motive for killing the hero; the demon wives of the *Kathāsaritsāgara* derive or sustain their supernatural powers by feeding upon human flesh. The Tulasī (holy basil) plant is worshipped throughout the country, being planted in the courtyard or near the entrance of every devout Hindu household, on square *vṛndāvana* pedestals which are really horned altars almost identical in form with those found (Fig. 2.2) at non-Israelite 10th century BC Megiddo, and others still further away from India. The plant goddess is married every year (now, to Kṛṣṇa), the reason buried deep in the mass of her legends (*māhātmya*) being given that she is a widow. This can only mean the annual death (by sacrifice) of the husband, which brings us back to Urvaśī and Purūravas. It is not too fanciful to see the ancient sacrifice and its derivative legend reflected in Keats' *Isabella*, a poem based upon a story in Boccaccio. The heroine buries her murdered lover's head in a flower-pot, and plants a Basil tuft over it, always keeping the Basil-pot by her side.

Fig. 2.2. Pre-Israelite altar.

2.7. URVAŚĪ'S ASSOCIATES

There is some doubt still as to the translation of the first half of x 95.6. Are *sujūrṇiḥ. . .granthinī caraṇyuḥ* to be taken as names, or are they adjectives of *śreṇiḥ?* Taking the latter meaning, we might have a description of the line of dancers at sacrifice. In the first sense, they are other apsarasas, companions of Urvaśī. These particular names are not to be found anywhere else, while the peculiar hiatus in *sumnaāpi* can't be explained in either case. No apsaras are named in the Ṛgveda, except Urvaśī, if we leave out this passage. The Atharva-veda does have several others (AV. iv. 37.3 etc.): Guggulu, Pīlā, Nāladī, Aukṣagandhī, Pramandinī whose names indicate some sort of a smell in each case. The Vājasaneyi Saṃhitā (xv. 15ff. cf. also Taitt. Sam. iv. 4.3) names a different lot, two by two, to accompany several gods: Puñjikasthala, Kratusthalā for Agni; Menakā, Sahajanyā for Vāyu, Pramlocantī, Anulocantī (both prone to strip themselves) for Sūrya; Viśvācī, Ghṛtācī; Urvaśī and Pūrvacitti (for Parjanya). As pairs of female attendants for each male god, they are a normal feature of temple-reliefs, especially in the South, and may be studied also in the Ambarnāth temple (1060 AD). These anticipate the later *śaktis*, or the regular mates of the gods (Lakṣmī for Viṣṇu etc.), and it is remarkable that they should occur so early. There are plenty more, as in *AV*. vi. 118. 1–2, Ugrajit, Ugrampaśyā, Rāṣṭrabhṛt though only two of these might be apsaras. Clearly, the number of these nymphs is legion. Menakā (the name is a pre-Aryan word for 'woman') is known in the Śakuntalā episode for her seduction of Viśvāmitra. Her daughter Śakuntalā is, remarkably enough, herself called an apsaras in the Śatapatha Brāhmaṇa (xiii. 5.4.11). She has some quite extraordinary features, for her name is derived from birds having fed her as an exposed infant; these birds were carrion-eaters, presumably vultures (*Mbh*. 1.67.10–11) and birds of ill-omen, *Śakunta*. But Urvaśī is the most prominent of these, and is unquestionably a water-goddess besides being able to traverse the air as in x. 95.17 above.

The apsarasas as water-goddesses appear in the legend of Vasiṣṭha's birth (RV. vii.33), where the sage is surrounded by these nymphs (vii. 33.9). Vasiṣṭha is apparently clad in the lightning *vidyuto jyotiḥ pari saṃjihānam* (vii. 33.10) which recalls the lightning flash of the later Purūravas legend that disclosed the hero in his nakedness. The actual birth of Vasiṣṭha is obscured by vii. 33.11–13 which report variously: *utāsi maitrāvaruṇo vasiṭho'rvaśyā brahman manaso' dhi jātaḥ*, then *apsarasaḥ pari jajñe vasiṣṭhaḥ*, and then that he was born from the seed of Mitra and Varuṇa poured into a *kumbha*, um, and that the all-gods culled him from the lotuspond: *viśve devāḥ puṣkare tvādadanta*. Being born from or because of the *apsaras* Urvaśī and brought to human beings by the similarly born Agastya was Vasiṣṭha's origin as a Brahmin, obviously un-Aryan as we shall see later.

We may note in passing that several *apsarasas* occupy such prominent place near the beginning of some royal genealogy: Menakā (Śakuntalā), Ghṛtācī, Alambusā, etc. The marriage had to be in some way legal for such a genealogy to be valid in patriarchal society, while it was notorious both by actual matriarchal custom and later tradition that the *apsaras* could not submit to a husband as permanent lord and master. Thus Rāvaṇa said bluntly in violating the sea-born nymph Rambhā: *apsarāṇāṃ patir nāsti*, and was conscious neither of sin nor crime. This obstacle was neatly avoided by the *apsaras* being cursed to human form and mortality for a period. Kālidāsa found this convenient in ascribing a reborn *apsaras* as ancestress to Rāma in the 8th *sarga* of his *Raghuvaṃśa*, though some such tradition must have been current in his day.

There is no doubt that the apsaras is a water-goddess (like the Nereids including Thetis, and most Greek nymphs with names ending in *neira*), though her consort, the Gandharva, is generally in the sky (but again the golden-heelel Gandareva of the deep, in Iranian mythology) In RV. x. 10. 4–5, Yama and his twin sister Yamī the first humans are born of the Gandharva and the water-woman (*apyā yoṣā*), being fashioned by Tvaṣṭṛ, even in the womb, to be husband and wife. In x. 85, the Gandharva seems to have special rights over all women, especially the virgins. This partly accounts for the *apyā kāmyāni* of x. 95.10, and the child born from the waters, *janiṣo apo naryaḥ*.

Of course, there is a clear physiological erotic[8] factor also present, Psychoanalysts have maintained that "drawn from the waters" is an old representation for just ordinary human birth. The treatment by Freud and Otto Rank of this motive propounds that Sargon, Moses, or even Pope Gregory the great (in the *Gesta Romanorum*) being taken from the waters (like Karṇa in the Mbh.) is merely a birth story, the waters being uterine or those within the amnionic sac. Be that as it may, we do have two other points of support.

Iḷā is a prominent goddess in the Ṛgveda, remembering that goddesses in general are far less important there than the male gods. She is associated with Urvaśī and rivers in v. 41.19: *abhi na iḷā yūthasya mātā sman nadībhir urvaśī vā gṛṇātu; urvaśī vā bṛhaddivā gṛṇānā abhyūrṇvānā prabhṛthasya āyoḥ*. The Āyu at the end may be Urvaśī's son. The Mbh. tells us that Iḷā was both father and mother of the hero, and the change of sex in later accounts is clearly meant to link Purūravas to Manu inspite of his having no father nor any known parent except Ilā. Such changes are not unknown when matriarchy is superseded (cf. Tawney-Penzer Vol. 7 p. 231; Frazer *Golden Bough* 2. p. 253ff.); one example īs the Buddhist Avalokiteśvara, who displaced a mother-goddess, and is often equated to one, *e.g.* Kuan-Yin. The implication is that Purūravas is a figure of the transitional period when fatherhood became of prime importance; that is, of the period when the patriarchal form of society was imposing itself upon an earlier one. We shall have to consider whether this happened in India, or represents some extraneous change preserved in Aryan myths brought into India. But it is clear as far as x. 95 goes that Purūravas is pleading the newer type of custom in marriage in the twelfth *ṛk* when he asks, who can separate the married pair as long as the ancestral fire burns in the husband's paternal house? (The plural *śvaśureṣu* is rather intriguing, but not unusual grammatically for the singular). That the Purūravas of x. 95 is actually the son of Iḷā and not some other character is clear from the appellation Aiḷa in the concluding lines of the hymn. He is mentioned in just one other place in the whole of the Ṛgveda: *tvam agne manave dyām avāśayah purūravase sukṛte sukṛttaraḥ* (i. 31. 4), where the word *manave* may imply a separate favour by Agni to Manu, and not necessarily that Purūravas is a son or descendant of Manu (or just 'the human' Purūravas); why thundering from the sky is a sign of special favour is not clear, nor whether that was the favour received by Purūravas rather than Manu. We have, therefore, necessarily to concerntrate upon Urvaśī's side of the story, more being known about her.

To return to the birth from the waters, one may point out an episode whose parallelism has been partially recognised, namely, the story of Bhīṣma (Mbh. 1.91ff.). This great figure dominates the extant Mahābhārata even more than the god Kṛṣṇa. He is born of the river Ganges, who assumes human form to woo Pratīpa, but accepts consortship of his son Śāntanu instead. She kills her first seven sons by drowning them one after the other in the river, which is surely her own natural form; hence the sons are sacrificed to her if one ignores the revision. The eighth is saved by the father's pleading, but then the river-queen leaves her husband. That son is Devavrata or Gāṅgeya (with two names, *dvināmā* as we are specially told in Mbh. 1.93.44), later named Bhīṣma. The change of name is occasioned by his strict vow to remain celibate. This leads him to abduct, or capture, for his step-brother, the three daughters of the king of Kāśī, named curiously enough Ambā, Ambikā, Ambālikā. ALL THREE NAMES MEAN 'MOTHER', and are connected with water by the words *ambu* and *ambhas*. One should guess that they might be river-goddesses, even forms of the Ganges, who has a triune image at Elephanta. Their names are particularly notable because of their joint invocation in the horse-sacrifice (Śat. Brāh. xiii. 2.8.3. etc.). Of the three, the two younger are married off to Bhīṣma's stepbrother Vicitravīrya, who dies without issue. Bhīṣma is asked to beget sons upon them for continuity of the family, but refuses though his vow has no longer served any purpose. The eldest sister finds herself cast off by Śālva, her former chosen one and asks Bhīṣma to take his place, but is also rejected. She vows to kill Bhīṣma, though he has the boon of virtual immortality from his father, being able to live as long as he likes. Ambā commits suicide, is reborn as or is transformed after rebirth into the male Śikhaṇḍin, and ultimately kills the hitherto invincible Bhīṣma in battle because he cannot fight against a woman, not even against a man who had been a woman. I might add here that Śikhaṇḍin, which means "crested", and might be used of a peacock, is given as name or appellation of a Gandharva in AV. iv. 37.7, so that the narrative is again closer to the Urvaśī story than would appear. Bhīṣma is killed by the river-goddess[9] whom he rejected; the explanation that his opponent was a sexual invert will not suffice.

We may compare the story of Bhīṣma with that of the doomed hero of another Aryan battle epic. Achilles is also the son of a water-goddess by a royal but human father. The mother dips him into the Styx to confer invulnerability upon him, not to drown him. The son spends some time dressed as a girl and living among girls as one of them. This is accounted for as an attempt to keep him out of the fatal campaign against Troy. But the matter cannot be so simple, for we have Cretan frescos that show boys in girl's clothing as attendants at a sacrifice or other ritual which is to be performed entirely by women. This must be some ancient story thrust upon the marauding, hronze-age, Aryan chief; the original connection between the sacred immersion, girl's clothing and life, and the hero's death must have been much stronger, if it be admitted that Thetis is also pre-Aryan in Greece.

Other ramifications of river-goddess worshipped are known (J. Przyluski: *IHQ*. 1934 p. 405–430), perhaps the Indian custom of *visarjana*, committing images, and at times ashes of the dead to the waters, hearkens back in some way to this tradition. Ritual marriage to mother-and river-goddesses was definitely known to be dangerous (as with the Danäides) in other lands; it underlies the refusal of Gilgameś to consort with Iśtar, and the Ahqat and An'at story which, as is well-known, was periodically acted out. The gradual fading of the danger is seen in the Manusmṛti injunction (3.19) not to choose a bride with any sort of terrifying name, among them specifically the name of any river. A similar caution is given by the quite practical and generally irreligious *Kāmasūtra* 3.1.13. Therefore, though the naming of Indian girls after rivers is common nowadays, and has no effect upon their prospects of marriage, the fashion was definitely frowned upon in earlier days, undoubtedly for very good reasons. On the other hand, the *apsaras* and water-goddess cult survives, e.g. near Poona, particularly in the Mlāvaḷ region, the *māmāla-hāra* of Sātāvāhana inscriptions at Kārle. These goddesses (Mlāvaḷā-devī: "the mother-goddesses") have given their name to the country, are identified with the 'seven *apsaras*' (*sātī āsarā*), and are worshipped only in the plural, always near the water,—whether well, pond, or river. But they do not seem to demand blood-sacrifices nowadays, such as other rustic goddesses still require at least once a year. Their aniconic stones are still coated with red minium, or the goddesses themselves are symbolised by red streaks on a rock or tree.

2.8. THE DAWN-GODDESS IN THE ṚGVEDA

The most important of Urvaśī's associations has been lost in most translations. This is with Uṣas, the goddess of the dawn and possibly the *bṛhaddivā* of v. 41. 19. In x. 95.2, Urvaśī says that she has passed over like the first of the dawns, and this seems a mere simile. The problem then is to explain away the *uṣo* in 4, and this is done in many different ways, none convincing. The explanation I offer is that Urvaśī has reached the status of an Uṣas, and that this status is that of a mother-goddess[10], not of a mere goddess of the dawn. That was HER destiny, as being sacrificed was her lover's. We proceed to consider this in detail.

Fig. 2.3. Detail of Syro-Hittite seal.

In x. 95. 8.9, we noted that the apsaras and her companions strip off their clothing; that was also the way in which Menakā and others seduced the sages. Quite remarkably, it is the goddess Uṣas who most often bares herself to the sight of men in this way. In i. 123. 11, she reveals her body like a young woman decorated by her mother: *āvis tanvaṃ kṛṇuṣe dṛṣe kam*. In i. 124.7 *uṣā hasreva ni riṇīte apsaḥ*, she reveals her secret charms like a lascivious woman, or like a smiling one, as you take *hasrā*. But in the same *ṛk* she goes towards men like a brotherless woman, mounting the throne, platform, or stage for the sake of wealth: *abhrāteva puṃsa eti pratīcī, gartārug iva sanaya dhanānām*, where the meaning of *gartāruk* is not clear. Obviously the reference is to one who has no brother to make a match for her, hence must display herself upon some high place to collect a dowry. Perhaps v. 80.4–6 contain the oftenest repeated mention of this self-exposure of the dawn goddess, but her revealing her bossom and charms to men is quite common. Remarkably enough, this performance is seen often on Syro-Hittite seals (W. H. Ward: *Seal Cylinders of Western Asia*. chap. L). where the Indian humped bull is shown: at times as her pedestal. (Fig. 2.3) There is no shame attached to this: *nodhā ivāvir akṛta priyāṇt* like a girl with yet immature breasts (*nodhā iva*, after Grassmann's suggestion). We can understand the bewitching apsaras doing this, for it is her function to attract men. But why Uṣas?

In any case, why should this goddess of the dawn be so specially prominent in the Ṛgveda, when she seems to have no important function; her counterpart Eos is negligible in Greece. There are at least twenty one complete hymns dedicated to her, and she is important enough to be invited in the special sacrificial chants known as *āprī*-hymns. In these hymns, with their rigidly fixed structure, Uṣas comes just after the opening of the divine doors, to be mentioned either together with the night (*uṣasā-naktā*) or in the dual, which would again mean the same pair. That is too high an honour for a mere witch, or one who behaves like a hetaera. Clearly, she once had a higher position, for which we must search to explain the survival.

The former high position is not difficult to trace. She is the sun's wife on occasion, as in vii. 75.5 *sūryasya yoṣā*, but perhaps his sister and also his mother iii. 61.4 *svarjanantī*. Yet this is not enough to explain her importance. In i. 113.19, she is the mother of all the gods, a numen of Aditi: *mātā devānām aditer anīkam*. Her real status slips out in a most important reference, which is in a hymn dedicated to Agni (iv. 2. 15).

adhā mātur uṣasā sapta viprāḥ jāyemahi prathmā vedhaso nṛn
divas-putrā aṅgiraso bhavema adriṃ rujema dhaninaṃ śucantaḥ.

"We seven sages shall generate (or be born) from mother Uṣas, the first men sacrificers; we shall become Aṅgirasas, sons of heaven, we shall burst the rich mountain, shining forth." Uṣas was, therefore, a high mother goddess, literally Mater Matuta. How did she come to lose this position?

Vasiṣṭha says *abhūd uṣā indratamā maghonī* (vii. 79.3), where the aorist past tense seems to me to indicate that Uṣas had once been but was no longer superlatively Indra's equal. The support for this is from the tale of conflict between the two deities. The mention is not isolated, for we find it in ii. 15.6, x.138.5, x.73.6, but with greatest detail in iv. 30.8–11:

etad ghed uta vīryam indra cakartha pauṃsyam
striyaṃ yad durhaṇāyuvaṃ vadhīr duhitaraṃ divaḥ (8)
divaś cid ghā duhitaraṃ mahān mahīyamānām; uṣāsam indra saṃ piṇak (9)
apa uṣa anasaḥ sarat saṃpiṣṭād aha bibhyuṣī; ne yat sīṃ śiśnathad vṛṣa (10)
etad asyā anaḥ śaye susaṃpiṣṭaṃ vipāśyā; sasāra sīṃ parāvataḥ (11)

"This heroic and virile deed didst thou also do, O Indra, that thou didst strike down (or kill) the evil-plotting woman, the daughter of heaven. Uṣas, verily the daughter of heaven, the great, to be regarded as great didst thou crush, O Indra. Uṣas fled from the shattered wagon in fright, when the Bull (Indra) had rammed her. Her wagon lay completely smashed to bits on the Vipāś (river), she (herself) fled to the furthest distance".

There is no reason or explanation given for this conflict. Indra is the young god, one whose birth is mentioned several times, and who takes the lead over all other gods because of his prowess in battle. In fact, he reflects the typical Aryan tribal war-chieftain, irresistible in strife after getting drunk on Soma. His displacement of Varuṇa is just barely to be seen in a dialogue (iv. 42). Indra and the older chief god Tvaṣṭṛ (whose position I have traced elsewhere) have no such open conflict as this. To Keith, the wagon (*anas*) signified merely that the image of Uṣas was carried around the fields in such a cart, like the Germanic[11] field deities, or Demeter. But why was it smashed up by the new leader? Her fleeing to the furthest distance is equivalent to her death. She is ascribed only an ordinary horse-chariot (*ratha*) in most later hymns. The ox-cart, like the archaism *sīm*, must represent great antiquity. At the same time, she is an ancient goddess in spite of her virginity and youth, which are preserved by her being born again and again: *punaḥ punar jāyamānā purāṇī* (i.92.10). The only possible explanation lies in a clash of cults, that of the old mother-goddess being crushed on the river Beas by the new war-god of the patriarchal invaders, Indra. That she survives after being 'killed' can only indicate progressive, comparatively peaceful, assimilation of her surviving pre-Aryan worshippers who still regarded her as mother of the sun, wife of the sun, daughter of heaven. Her behaviour is reflected in that of apsarasas like Urvaśī, who degenerate into the witches of the Atharva-veda by natural development of the combined society, which really and finally kills their cult, except for local survivals in villages and the jungle.

The former (probable) role of Uṣas as the mother of creation and certainly of the Aṅgirasas—who claim affinity with the light-deities—can be untangled with some difficulty from the extant Ṛgveda. Later mythology takes creation as resulting from the incest of Prajāpati with his own daughter, the root stanzas being found in the RV. But in i.72.5, it is clear that the father is the sky-god (here a male though often elsewhere a female in the same veda, hence a later fiction coupled to the original mother-goddess), while Uṣas is emphatically the daughter of heaven as both commentators and translators point out here; the progeny are the Aṅgirasas. In iii. 31.1. *seq*. we have much the same theme, as also in x. 61.7, while in i. 164.33, the daughter has become the Earth. This shows heterogenity among Brahmin traditions. Her connection with later hetaerism may be seen from Sāyaṇa's comment upon the word *vrā*, which he takes as a name of Uṣas, as for example in i. 121.2, and iv. 1.16; in the latter hymn, it would make much better sense to take Uṣas as the cow-mother, the goddess whose thrice seven secret names were known only to the initiates.

There is only one more reference to Urvaśī in the Ṛgveda (iv. 2.18; AV. xviii. 3.23), just after the striking mention of Uṣas with the seven seers:

ā yūtkeva kṣumati paśvo akhyad devānām yaj janīm anty
ugra martānām cid urvaśīr akṛpran vṛdhe cid arya uparasyāyoḥ.

The Urvaśīs are here in the plural; *āyu* can again be taken as the legendary son, or some adjective. Graṣsmann makes Urvaśī also into an abstraction 'der Menschen heisse Wünsche', but seeing that the Uṣās do also occur in the plural, and that Urvaśī had become an Uṣas before finishing with Purūravas, there is no reason why we should not take the word as still referring to the nymphs.[12] The proper translation of the second line, therefore, would be something like "The Urvaśīs have taken pity upon mortals, even to helping the later kinsman Āyu". Presumably, the son and successors of Aiḷa Purūravas were not sacrificed, patriarchy had conquered finally.

One further if rather slight bit of evidence points to the great antiquity of such goddesses, in spite of the dominant patriarchal gods in the Ṛgveda. That is that they had wings at one time, a feature lost in our iconography that may be seen in the Hittite glyptic (Fig. 2.4. *c*), the Burney Lillith (Fig. 2.4. *b*) and a unique Mesopotamian representation (Fig. 2.4.*c*) of Ishtar, who is a mother-goddess and a dawn-goddess, being also mother, sister and wife of Tammuz, the sun-god whom she frees periodically from his mountain grave. The apsaras traverses the sky, without being called winged. Just where the Ṛgvedic seers got this notion is difficult to see unless originally the sun itself was the winged goddess; for we have nothing like it in the known Indus valley glyptic, though bird-*headed* figurines (Fig. 4. *d*), ideograms of homo-signs with four arms, and perhaps one (winged?) symbol on a seal are found (M. S. Vats, *Excavations at Harappā*, Delhi 1940, pl. 91.255). On the other hand Suparṇa is used of the sun, which reminds us of the winged sundisc of the Assyrians;

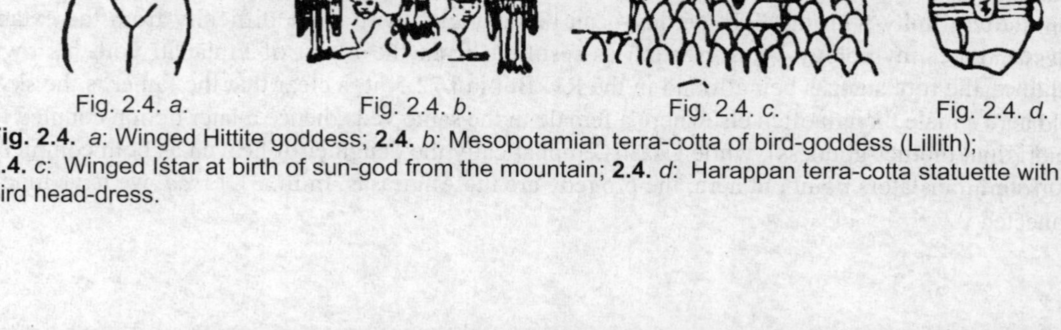

Fig. 2.4. *a*. Fig. 2.4. *b*. Fig. 2.4. *c*. Fig. 2.4. *d*.

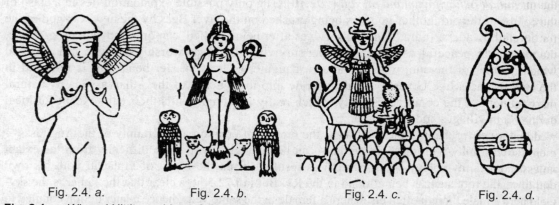

Fig. 2.4. *a*: Winged Hittite goddess; **2.4.** *b*: Mesopotamian terra-cotta of bird-goddess (Lillith); **2.4.** *c*: Winged Iśtar at birth of sun-god from the mountain; **2.4.** *d*: Harappan terra-cotta statuette with bird head-dress.

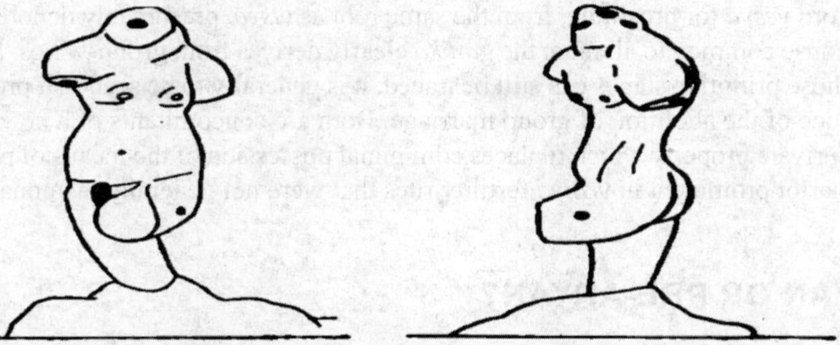

Fig. 2.5. *a, b.* Harappan stone statuette of dancing girl, originally dressed like 2.4 *d*, as shown by peg-holes for head-dress and for girdle bosses.

in i. 105.1, it refers to the moon. The only male god with wings as well as arms is explicitly Viśvakarman in x. 81.3. There is a winged demon *suparṇayātu* against which the Vasiṣṭhas pray for protection in vii. 104.22. But i. 22.11 hopes that the gods' wives would be with unbroken wings, *acchinna-patrāḥ sacantām*. That the dawns, or the dawn-night pair were winged seems quite clear from two prayers in distress: i. 105.11 *suparṇā eta āsate,*[13] and *mā mām ime patatriṇī vi dugdhām* (i. 58.4). These goddesses reduce man's life day by day, and so are death-goddesses themselves as probably were also the terrifying bird-headed Indus terracottas. All the more natural if, as mother-goddess, one of them were to cause the death of her consort in a sacrifice. The tradition survived in the west, in the Sirens that lured mariners to their death and the Harpies. In India, the last contact seems to have been with Śakuntalā, the rejected apsaras.

The Ṛgveda shows fainter traces of a different type of "hetaerism", which seems related to survivals of Aryan group marriage rather than to the cult of the pre-Aryan mother-goddess, though the two need not be independent. The specific reference may be seen in RV. i. 167.4, where the goddess Rodasī is common to all the Maruts, under the title of *sādhāraṇī* (plus the incomprehensible *yavyā* = fertile?). Whether this indicates fraternal polyandry (as I incline to think) or a form of prostitution is not clear; the question is further complicated by Rodasī (with a displaced accent) being elsewhere equated to the combination of earth and sky, hence two goddesses rather than one. The Aśvins are go-betweens for arranging the marriage of Sūryā with Soma (in x. 85.8–9 hence originally of the sun-goddess to the moon-god), which would make them her brothers; but they are clearly her husbands in iv. 43.6, which again is not a contradiction in terms of group-marriage of the older sort. We have already noted the identity of Sūryā with Uṣas and Urvaśī in later tradition, while the later hymn reduces Sūryā's marriage to a still current ritual which can only have arisen by a human couple impersonating the divine bridal pair. The bridegroom in x. 85.36 takes his bride by the hand at the crucial stage of the wedding, yet in the very next *ṛk*, the woman is spoken of as she who receives the seed of (many) men: *yasyāṃ bījaṃ manuṣyā vapanti*, and it would be odd to have this generic mode of designation unless indeed, in some older days at least, she would automatically have become the bride of several brothers, or clansmen.[14] In RV. 1.126.5, the *viśyā iva vrā anasvantaḥ* seems best translated by Geldner's 'die auf Karren wie die Clandirnen fahrend…', for *viśyāḥ* is feminine plural. Dime, prostitute, is rather a strong word to use, and I should prefer to see here the nomadic common clan-wives by group-marriage, riding bullock-carts which might just be a means of transport not necessarily connected with the older vehicle of Uṣas, though we have seen that Sāyaṇa takes *vrā* = Uṣas, twice.

The later word *veśyā* for prostitute, from the same root as *viśyā*, presumably denotes the woman who dwelt in a house common to all men; the *gaṇikā* clearly derives from group-wives. In most developed societies whose primitive stages can still be traced, it is generally to be seen that prostitution arises as a consequence of the abolition of group marriage. Both are concomitants of a new form of property, patriarchal private property which replaces communal possession of the means of production. *AV*. xv. shows the harlot prominent in *vrātya* fertility rites that were not generally fashionable.

2.9. ARYAN OR PRE-ARYAN?

The character of Urvaśī and her higher form Uṣas has been delineated in the foregoing, but we have still to consider whether she was Aryan in the same sense as Indra, Varuṇa, Agni, or inherited from older civilizations. The parallelism with Ishtar-Innanna[15] is unquestioned, but there would seem to be no direct etymological connection, though we must mention the ingenious conjecture that the Indo-European word for star (*star* in the RV) is actually derived from Ishtar and her symbol, the star. There is a lily-goddess in Asia Minor, probably some derivative of Astarte, and prototype of the Hebrew Susannah. It is not enough even so to point out once again the hetaera-hierodule-bayadère character of our heroine and of the mother goddess which she claimed to have become. For, admitting this, and the fact that such attendance upon a mother-goddess has no ancient basis in any Sanskrit text or scripture, we should still have to explain whether the actual temple cults of this sort still extant in India derive from religions outside India, or from the Indus Valley pre-Aryans. However, we find enough in the extant literature for our purpose to complete the analysis without pretending to solve all possible problems that may arise. It might be said in passing that Indian mother-goddess temples are a direct growth from primitive tribal cults, each of local origin, later brahminized.

Of course, the question of some plausible mechanism for the adoption of pre-Aryan cults will be raised; it will also be objected that, after all, the Indus seals portray exclusively male animals, the rare human figures are demonstrably masculine where identifiable. The reasoning is in full agreement with this, for the seals belonged to a different set of people than the female figurines, to the men of the trader class which was destroyed along with the houses behind whose massive, undecorated walls they had piled up their wealth. The women with their cults survived, either as wives or slaves, which would account for all the traces of their cults that we have shown in Aryan documents though at variance with the mode of living (not race) which is denoted by the word Aryan.

The Ṛgvedic references to the dancing-girl are casual, as if the institution were familiar to all; yet temples of any sort could not have been pastoral-Aryan-vedic, there is no direct mother-goddess worship, and we have seen that the Uṣas cult was smashed up by no less a personage than Indra. In i. 92.3 we hear women chanting at their work, presumably ritual: *arcanti nārīr apaso na viṣṭibhiḥ*. In the next *ṛk*, we have Uṣas wearing decorative clothes like a dancing girl: *adhi peśāṃsi vapate nṛtūr iva*. The patterned cloth appears again in ii. 3.6 figuratively, as the woven pattern of the sacrifice: *yajñasya peśas*. This profession of weaving clearly belongs to the women, and is in the process of being usurped by men, as I shall now show.

In *RV*. v.47.6, the Mothers weave clothes for their son, the sun. The night weaves the sun's garment for him in i. 115.4, and is a weaving woman again in Sāyaṇa on ii.38.4: *vastraṃ vayantī nārīva rātriḥ*. Most significant for my main theme, Uṣas is also a weaver with the night: *uṣasā-naktā vayyā iva…tantuṃ tataṃ saṃvayantī* (ii.3.6). Therefore it is again natural to find the apsarasas in vii.33.9 weaving the garment stretched by the all-regulating god of death, Yama: *yamena tataṃ paridhiṃ vayantas*. In vii.33.12, the sage Vasiṣṭha was born of the apsaras, the jar, and the lake to take over the work of these nymphs who are like the Norns in weaving the pattern of fate. Nevertheless, men other than Vasiṣṭha succeeded to less fateful types of weaving. The *yajña* being woven is not only a common figure of speech, but the male seer of ii.28.8 weaves his song, just as the paternal ancestors in x. 130.1 weave the sacrifice.

This change over to patriarchal production must have occurred at the time early Ṛgvedic society was formed from pre-Aryan conquered as well as their Aryan conquerors. Men seem always to have monopolized ploughing (iv. 57) while Brahmaṇaspati, a male priest-god, swedges the world together like a smith (x.72.2).

We are now in a position to understand why in x.95.4 Urvaśī claimed (as an Uṣas) to have given clothing and food to her father-in-law. That is, though she had a dread ritual to perform as *viduṣī* in x.95.11, she was initiated into certain arts as well which had been the prerogative of her sex, and weaving was one of them. Thus the Sāyaṇa gloss *vasu* = *vāsakam*, clothing, is quite correct. The word later comes to mean wealth in general, and the Brahmanical renaissance with its spicing and embalming of the Sanskrit language makes this synonymous with all other forms of wealth. Nevertheless, the original meanings of the three main terms seem to have been separate: *dhana* would indicate precious metals, loot in general; *rayī* must have originally denoted wealth in cattle and horses, seeing that *gomat* is used as its adjective so often; *vasu*, I take it, meant primarily wealth manufactured and worn, like clothing. At the time of the Atharva-veda (*AV* ix. 5. 14), weaving must have been a household industry carried on by women, for home-woven garments are there mentīoned, along with gold, as a sacrificial gift; spinning, and weaving but not needlework appear in the list of a good wife's accomplishments in the *Kāmasūtra* (4. 1. 33).

This raises the next question, in what way did Urvaśī supply food to her father-in-law? For the *vayas* in question might have been merely the result of her cooking. Of course, Uṣas is often *gavāṃ mātā*, mother of the cattle and the older ploughless hoe agriculture may have again been a prerogative of the women, as we find it in most primitive societies, but there is no direct evidence before us. However, we may use archaeology and anthropology to solve another riddle, namely the multiple account of Vasiṣṭha's birth in vii. 33, where he is born of the apsaras, the lotus or lotus-pond, and also from the seed of Mitra-Varuṇa poured into a jar, *kumbha*. The answer is very simple, namely that THE KUMBHA IS ITSELF THE MOTHER GODDESS in spite of the masculine gender of the word. It is known that prehistoric hand-made pottery, before the introduction of the wheel and mass production, is fabricated by women. To this day, pots made by hand or on the potter's disc in India are made by women, and smoothed by men with paddles and a stone anvil-block; but no woman is allowed to work the fast potter's wheel in India, so far as I know. Moreover, the pots generally represent (fig. 2.6. *b*) the mother-goddess, either by their decorations, the oculi or necklaces incised or painted on them as patterns, or by actual additions to complete the image. The latter has left its mark upon the Sanskrit language, for the word for ear *karṇa* means pot-handle as well, like the Scots 'lug'. The Rāmāyaṇa demon Kumbhakarṇa may have had ears like the handles of a pot. However, other ancient names with the termination *karṇa* can only be explained as of totemic origin: Jatūkarṇa, Tūṇakarṇa, Mayūrakarṇa, Masūrakarṇa, Kharjūrakarṇa, (cf. *Kāśīkā* on Pāṇini 4.1.112, and the *gaṇapāṭha*).

Fig. 2.6. *a.* Pot-sherd from Nāvḍā-Tolī (Maheśvar) *circa* 1600 BC with painted group of dancers; girls still dance the *hātagā* dance in a circle, holding hands aṣ shown here.

Fig. 2.6. *b.*: Later sherd in relief *circa* 1000 BC from same site with naked goddess in relief (after Sankalia).

The apsaras in general is a mother-goddess, as would appear from the AV hymns called *mātṛnāmāni*. Later tradition, mixed as usual, is even stronger. Lakṣmī, like Aphrodite, was born of the sea. She has the name Ramā, Mā and 'mother of the people' (*Lokamātā* cf. *Amarakośa*, 1.1 29). This makes her a mother-goddess, as should be all goddesses whose names have a suffix-m*ā*: Umā, Rumā, Ruśamā, etc. But there is some reason to think of her as originally as apsaras, apart from her being born of the waters. Though she is a goddess, wife of Viṣṇu-Nārāyaṇa, she counts as sister to the sea-born demon Jālaṃdhara (*Skanda-P*. 2.4.8, 2.4.14–22), husband of the plant-goddess Tulasī-Vṛndā whose story we have already reviewed above. The reader knows that the original 'grove of Vṛndā' (*vṛndāvana*) was on Kṛṣṇa's home ground, in the *gokula* at Mathura, according to ancient tradition as well as modern pilgrims' belief. Her cult most obviously has been separate from, and older than that of Kṛṣṇa. So Kṛṣṇa-Nārāyaṇa being married to Tulasī-Vṛndā annually is a comparatively late step in the assimilation of a mother-goddess cult to that of a pastoral god. Certainly, Kṛṣṇa's numerous wives, like the countless wives, mistresses and casually violated nymphs of Herakles, must have been mother-goddesses in their own right before the union, the ultimate fusion of cults rounded upon the merger of two entirely different forms of society.

We have already referred to the terra cotta figurines that prove the worship of the mother-goddess to have been prominent in the pre-Aryan Indus valley. I now suggest that the 'Great Bath' at Mohenjo-daro (fig. 2.10) is ceremonial *puṣkara*. This curious building, situated apart from the city on the citadel-zikkurat mound, could not have been utilitarian seeing that so much labour had to be expended to fill the tank with water. There is no imagery or decoration of any sort, but the tank is surrounded by rooms, which may have been used by living representatives, companions, or servants of the goddess, the *apsaras* of the day; the water need not have been so labouriously drawn, unless for water-deities to whom it was essential. The range of seemingly unconnected meanings for the word *puṣkara* is highly suggestive: lake, lotus, art of dancing, the sky; the root *puṣ* from which it is derived, like the very close *puskala*, denotes fertility, nourishment, plenty. The whole nexus of ideas is connected with the apsaras though she appears in the classical Sanskrit literature only as dancer and houri. According to the Dhammapada-aṭṭhakathā iv. 3 and the preamble story to Jātaka 465, the Licchavi oligarchs of Vesāli had a special, heavily guarded, sacred investiture-puṣkara = *abhi-Se-ka-maṅgala-pokkharaṇī*. About 120 AD Nahapāna's son-in-law Usavadāta went far out of his way to have the *abhiṣeka* investiture performed at the "Pokṣara (*sic*) tank" (EI. 7, p. 78, inscription at

Nāsik). The Cambodian apsaras dancers of Angkor Vat are portrayed with the lotus flower in one hand and lotus seed-pod in the other, the first symbolizing the puṣkara while the second is obviously a fertility symbol. How old the tradition really is may be seen from the Indo-Greek coin of Peukelaotis (fig. 2.7) where the lotus-crowned patron-goddess of the city Puṣkaravatī is portrayed in precisely the same way, with the name Ambi = mother-goddess. The Śatapatha Brāhmaṇa vii. 4. 1. 11 tells us that the lotus-leaf (*puṣkaraparṇa*) is the womb (*yoni*), and in 13 that the puṣkara is the lotus-leaf. Thus Vasiṣṭha's birth has a completely consistent account, multiple only in the symbolism used. The *gotra* lists mention a *Pauṣkarasādi* gotra among the Vasiṣṭhas. The gotra is historical as a Brahmin priest of that gens was priest of king Pasenadi (*Dīghanikāya* 4), and a grammarian of that name is also known. The name means descendant of *puṣkara-sad*, he who resides in the *puṣkara*, which clearly indicates Vasiṣṭha. So does Kunḍin, from which the Kauṇḍinya gotra of the Vasiṣṭhas is derived. Neither the lotus-pond nor the apsaras that tarries there could be Aryan in origin. It would be difficult to explain the fundamental and distinctive role of the lotus in all Indian iconography without relating it to pre-Aryan cults, for the Aryan-vedic center about the sacred fire. One may note further that one of the holiest places of pilgrimage is a *tīrtha* named Puṣkara, identified with one of that name in Rajputana, but presumably representing earlier artificial tanks of the sort. The *puṣkara* is a necessary adjunct to every Hindu temple not actually by a river, even in well-watered regions.

Fig. 2.7. Indo-Greek coin of Peukelaotis; Kharoṣṭī legend *pakhalavadi devada ambi*.

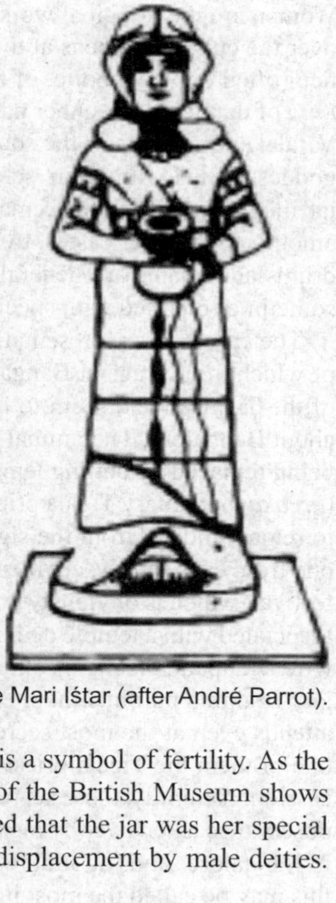

Fig. 2.8. The Mari Iśtar (after André Parrot).

The *Mahābhārata* birth-story of the hundred Kauravas and their sister tells us that they were not born directly of their mother Gāndhārī but from ghee-filled jars into which the undeveloped embryos were placed. Significantly, *kumbhā* is still used for harlot by lexica like the Viśvakoṣa. Mesopotamian glyptic represents two rivers flowing from a jar held by Ea or his attendant. As pointed out by Mr. R. D. Barnett, the flowing jar is a symbol of fertility. As the Mari statue of Iśtar (Fig. 2.8) shows her holding it, and seal 89762 of the British Museum shows the two rivers issuing from her shoulders, the guess would be justified that the jar was her special fertility symbol—hence the representation of an uterus—before her displacement by male deities.

The Vidhūra-paṇḍita-jātaka (Fausböll 545) gives an extraordinary rule for success (*gāthā* 1307), namely that a *kumbha* filled with water must always be reverently saluted with joined hands. The *udakumbha*, urn filled with water, does not appear to be particularly important in the Ṛgveda, but has a very prominent position in the *gṛhyasūtras*, and in current practice. For example, the bridal pair must circumambulate the sacred fire which is accompanied by the water-jar, though the vedic god is *agni* alone, without the jar. The fire is addressed in some Ṛgvedic funerary humns, but again the water-jar plays an important part in modern Hindu cremation rites, symbolising the whole course of the dead man's life.

2.10. THE GODDESSES OF BIRTH AND DEATH

The *Kathā-sarit-sāgara* 70.112 equates the *kumbha* or *ghaṭa* explicitly to the uterus. The equivalence may explain why the *navarātra* 'nine-nights' fertility festival to all mother-goddesses begins on the first of Āśvin by establishing a fertility-jar (*ghaṭa-sthāpanā*). The jar is set in some earth in which seed-grain is carefully planted "to encourage the fields". The cella of the shrine is decorated with food of all sorts. In the villages, this is the special time for blood-sacrifices to the goddesses. Women are the principal worshippers during these nine nights, even when male priests have taken over the cult, as happens at the more profitable cult-spots. The festival ends officially with a sacrifice (often only symbolic, of flour, but still officially called *bali-dāna*) to Sarasvatī, and the *visarjana* of that goddess. Other parts of the country have their own equivalent observances, such as the Varalakṣmī worship in the south. Here, the pot is decorated with a painting, or a silver mask of the goddess, filled with grain, set up with due ceremony, and worshipped. The special function of the jar may, account for the remarkable fact that potters rather than brahmins are in general demand among many lower castes, to officiate at funerals, and some other ceremonies. Their special hand-drums and chants are generally required for prophylactic ritual before a wedding ceremony, and sometimes credited with special power over ghosts.

The *kumbha* as representation of a mother-goddess still survives in many south Indian festivals, of which the Karagā at Bangalore may be taken as a specimen. It is the special annual fertility rite of the Tigaḷas, who seem to have come from North Arcot, and are professional market-gardeners about Bangalore. The animal sacrifices formerly made to the pot are now reduced to one, the rest being replaced by cutting lemons, or by boiled cereals. In the final procession, the main participant (*arcaka*; hereditary Tigaḷa priest) carries the pot on his head, but is dressed as a woman; his wife has to remain hidden from the sight of men all during the festival. The Tigaḷa representatives, at least one from each family, cut themselves with sharp swords, but no blood flows during the ordeal. This festival, which is obviously not Aryan, has been Brahminized only during the last 150 years, is now associated with a temple dedicated to the eldest Pāṇḍava Dharmarāja, and the goddess made into his wife Draupadī, the main content[16] of the sacred pot being a gold fetish known as her *śakti*. An auxiliary Brahmin purohita (at present śri Veṅkaṭarāya Vādyar, from whom I obtained these details) now attends even at the most secret part of the ritual which is performed in a shelter with two Tigaḷas, one of them the Tigaḷa priest mentioned before, the other a Tigaḷa who leads the way for the procession. Naturally, these secret rites are not divulged, but the whole festival is obviously a women's observance taken over by men. It is to be noted that though the Tigaḷas are a low caste, every temple in Bangalore sends an idol representing its god to follow in the final procession, and on the whole, this may be called the most impressive local festival. The untouchables have a similar one a couple of months later, the real Karagā ends on *caitra* (April) full-moon after nine days of observances and celebrations. The triple pot which is itself the Karagā is not made by a Tigaḷa nowadays, but by a professional potter. Nevertheless, it must still be made from the sediment of one particular artificial pond; not turned on the wheel but hand-made, and not burnt but sun-dried; the final procession ends with the Karagā pot being thrown into the pond, though the golden *śakti* representing Draupadī is quietly rescued by the priest for use again next year.

There are two different conceptions of death in the Ṛgveda, which gives several distinct funerary rites in its later book, namely x. 14, x. 18, x. 35. The earlier concept of death in the *RV* is unquestionably going to sleep, the long sleep from which there is no awakening. Many of the demons killed by Indra sink down into this eternal sleep. The Vasiṣṭha hymn vii. 55 seems to have begun as a funeral hymn, then mistaken for and further transformed into a lullaby. Correspondingly, we have the lower level of the cemetery H at Harappā with extended burials. The dead sleep peacefully, furnished with grave goods and supplied with jars that must once have contained the drink of immortality, Soma. This cemetery is undoubtedly Aryan, and the city itself to be identified with the Hariyūpīyā of vi.27.5–6, though the battle mentioned there might refer equally well to conflict between two waves of Aryan invaders as to the first Aryan conquest of the city. When we come to the top layer of cemetery H, however, the character of the burials changes abruptly. The dead adults survive only in jars, where their remains are placed after the body had been cremated or decarnated by birds of prey. The custom is mentioned in all the major ritual books, such as those of Āśvalāyana, Kātyāyana, and so on, and the jar where the bones are placed is specifically called the *kumbha*. This corresponds to the later Ṛgvedic concept of death (i. 164.32, *sa mātur yonā parivīto antar bahuprajā nirṛtim ā viveśa*), namely return to the mother's womb, and is proved very clearly in the case of cemetery H by the crouched position in which dead infants are placed within the jar; apparently, the bodies of children

Fig. 2.9. Detail of painted earthen funerary urn from Harappa, Cemetery H.

could be sent back to the mother directly, without being stripped of later fleshy accretions by fire or carrion-eaters. Further guesses may be made that the star-like decorations on the jars are developed oculi, but this would need closer proof. Incidentally, we are in a position to explain one peculiar decoration in this later Harappan grave pottery, namely, the peacock (Fig. 2.9) containing a recumbent human figure within the disc that forms the bird's body. If the figure were sitting or upright, it might have been taken for some deity. The horizontal position excludes this, and a reference in the *Mahābhārata* (1.85.6) clarifies the situation. There, the dead are represented as having been eaten by birds and insects of various sorts, but specifically by peacocks (*śitikaṇṭha*), whence the figure within the peacock must be the dead man himself. The bird is not the common carrion-eater, so that he must have had a particular sanctity, which is confirmed by his being the companion and hence a totem of the river – speech – and mother-goddess Sarasvatī. With the particular name *śitikaṇṭha*, he is associated with the dread god Rudra-Śiva, and a *vāhana* of Skanda as well.

A little later, as in the *Śatapatha Brāmāṇa* xiii. 8.3.3, the Earth herself becomes the mother, into whose lap the bones are poured out from the *kumbha*, but clearly the original mother or at least her womb was represented by the pot. Therefore, it is clear that Vasiṣṭha and Agastya, in being born from the urn, are giving a good Aryan translation of their birth from a pre-Aryan or non-Aryan mother-goddess. The effective change is from the absence of a father to the total denial of a mother, a clear Marxist antithesis necessitated by the transition from matriarchy to patriarchy. After all, Aryan means a particular manner of life and speech, not a race. We may conclude, seeing that extended burial comes first, that the Harappan groups of Aryans had not the general habit of cremation, and that the later idea of a return to the womb is acquired from some of their former enemies whose remnants after the conquest were absorbed by comparatively peaceful means, unless, of course, it represents a second wave of invaders. We cannot prove directly that the manufacture of pottery was also a monopoly of women in the earliest stage here, or that Urvaśī Uṣas was a potter. But ritual pots continue to be made by the priest's hand without the wheel, as in *Śat. Brāh*. xiv. 1.2. 7ff., and the spade with which the clay is dug is to be formally addressed by the priest 'thou art a woman', as again in *Śat. Brāh*. vi. 3. 1.39. I think that this goes back to the period when both digging (for agriculture) and pottery were women's work. That the mother-goddess should weave the pattern of her son's fate and sew or embroider it (like Rākā in ii. 32.4 *sīvyatvapaḥ sūcycāchidyamānayā*) is most natural.

Another survival of the mother-goddess cult into later times seems quite clear from the story of Aiḷa Purūravas's parentage. He is the son of a prominent (for the Ṛgveda) goddess, Iḷā, and the Mbh says that Iḷā was both his father and his mother. The Purāṇic account then changes Iḷā's sex, Ila the son of Manu having become a woman by stepping into a grove sacred to the mother-goddess Pārvatī. In Mahārāṣtra almost every village mother-goddess has her grove, now usually dwindled to a thicket, though occasionally (as at Phāgṇe near Beḍsā) quite impressive; but there is no longer a taboo on male entry. Such places are to be found in other parts of the world, as for example, among the Attonga,[17] where any man who enters the sisterhood house even by accident is initiated as a woman and has to live as a woman thereafter. But this is not merely a later affair, for such initiation appears quite explicitly in the Ṛgveda, though its meaning has been obscured by mythological accretions (as perhaps with the Greek seer Teiresias). We have in viii. 33.19:

adhaḥ paśyasva mopari saṃtarāṃ pādakau hara
mā te kaśaplakau dṛṣan strī hi brahmā babhūvitha

"Gaze downwards, not up; hold your feet close together; let not your rump be seen; for thou, O priest, art become a woman". Nothing could be clearer than this, which shows (with the preceding *ṛks*) that a male priest has been initiated as a woman, and told to behave accordingly. And this cannot be Aryan for the mother-goddess plays no part in the warring life of bronze-age pastoral invaders and plunderers, whatever their past might have been. The conclusion is that the Ṛgveda shows the absorption of a pre-Aryan stream of culture, which goes into the very source and origin of Brahminism. Urvaśī's metamorphosis in Kālidāsa's drama is merely a late inversion of the original taboo upon male entry into the Mother-goddess's preserve. To this day women may not approach certain comparatively minor gods such as the Vetāḷa, Bāpūjī Bābā, and at some places Kārttika-Svāmin (Skanda).

The ṛk cited above occurs in the Kaṇva family book of the Ṛgveda. The Kaṇvas were demonstrably latecomers into the vedic fold, like the Kaśyapas, though the latter occupy a much higher position in later Brahmin tradition.[18] The Kaṇva Nārada is reported by several Purāṇas to have become a woman by bathing in a sacred pool; he regains his manhood by another immersion, but only after a considerable period as a woman. Nārada enjoys a very high position as sage, being quoted or addressed from the Atharva-veda down; yet he is still called a Gandharva in the epics. In Buddhist records, he and Pabbata are gods; a Nārada is a Brahmā, another a former Buddha! Most important of all, the Anukramaṇī makes him and his brother or nephew Parvata joint authors of *RV*. ix. 104, but with an alternative ascription to 'the two Śikhaṇḍinīs, apsarasas, daughters of Kaśyapa'. Referring back to the Bhīṣma story where that hero is killed by a Śikhaṇḍinī metamorphosed into a man, one may recognise traces of a very deep layer of myth regarding the tradition of mother-goddess cults, apsarasas, human sacrifice.

At the end of *Śākuntala* act v, the wailing heroine is taken by a shape of light which carries her off to the *apsaras-tīrtha*. At the beginning of the very next act, the nymph Sānumatī (or Miśrakeśī) comes from that sacred pool to spy upon the hero. She has just finished her turn of attendance upon men at the ritual investiture bath, '*jāva sāhujanassa abhiseakālo*'. Thus Kālidāsa balances the *Vikramorvaśīyam* with another play where the apsaras heroine (whose name makes her a bird-goddess) is rejected by the hero, directly inverting the original Urvaśī legend. The 'Great Bath' (Fig. 2.10) at Mohenjo-dāro, instead of being the 'hydropathic establishment' that Marshall calls it with consistent ineptitude, was probably the prototype of such tīrthas; consorting with the (human) apsaras was part of the ritual. This would be the Indus valley analogue of Mesopotamian ritual hierodule prostitution in temples of Ishtar.

Useful and suggestive parallels are to be found in Robert Graves's brilliant summary and interpretation: *The Greek Myths* (2 vol., Penguin Books, nos. 1026–7, London 1955). Though Hera was married to Zeus, the children of her body were not his. The Stymphalian bird-witches, the reality whose destruction underlay a labour of Hercules, were her priestesses. They provide a continuous chain through the bird-legged Sirens and the Harpies, to the owl-faced female on a stele at Troy I who had not yet become Hera or Pallas Athene. Hera was worshipped as Child, Bride, and Widow (like our Tulasī), and renewed her virginity by periodic baths in the springs of Canathus. This means simply ritual purification after the sacrifice of her earthly husband, presumably the temporary consort of her chief priestess. Aphrodite similarly renewed her virginity by bathīng in the sea off Paphos, while Athene and Artemis remained virgins. Nevertheless, a 'hụsband' was formerly sacrificed to Artemis in various places, boys flogged once a year till the blood drenched her image at Sparta; Actaeon was torn to pieces by his own dogs for having seen her naked. Anchises was

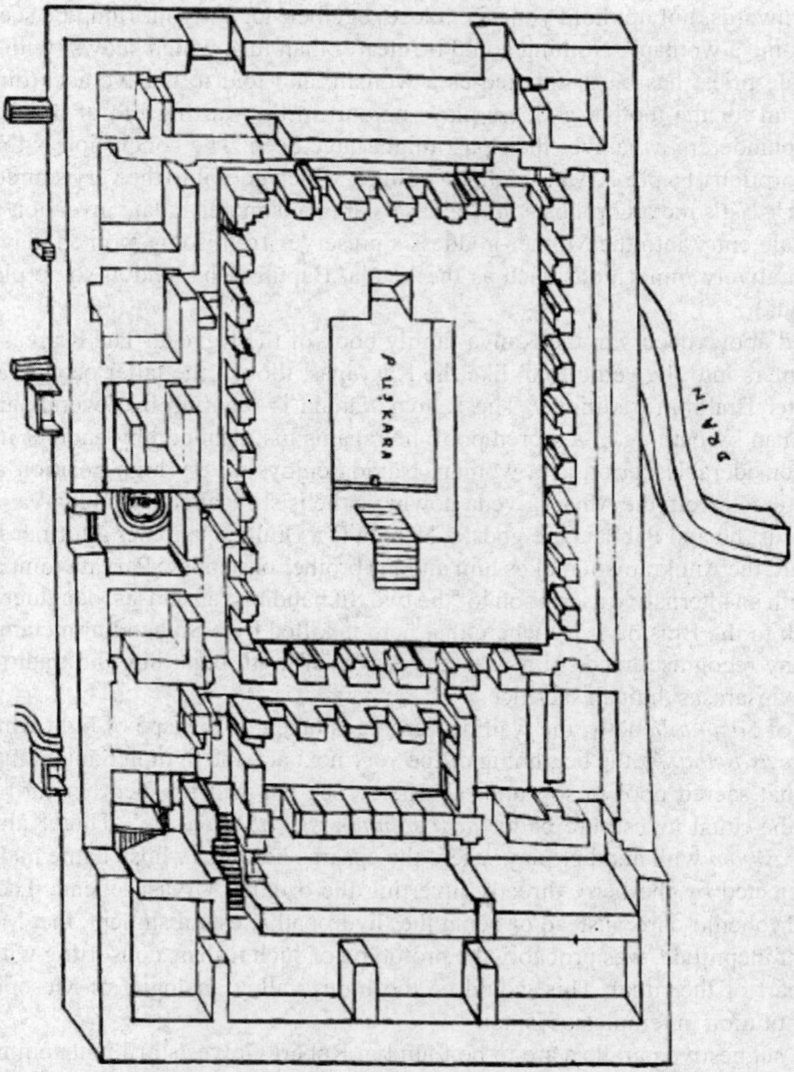

Fig. 2.10. The 'Great Bath', Mohenjo-dāro, a doubtful partial restoration; structure of one or more upper stories unknown; the *puṣkara* pool is 39′ × 23′.

horrified to learn that he had uncovered the nakedness of a goddess (Aphrodite) after a night of love, and begged her to spare his life. Precisely so did Purūravas beg Urvaśī to spare his life, while the *Śatapatha* legend merely inverts the original reason when it explains that he had broken the *taboo* by letting her see him naked. The primitive taboo can only have been against seeing the goddess in a state of nature. The transgressor would have to be punished; Purūravas, not Urvaśī, would be the person who had to vanish from the sight of men—by being sacrificed. The sacred pool is in evidence both in the *ṚV* and the *ŚB*, with Urvaśī's appearance as a swan reminiscent of the bird-goddesses. At Athens, the Vintāge Festival was marked by girls swinging from the branches of Erigone's pine tree on rope swings; this should explain how Urvaśī appeared to Purūravas as *antarikṣa-prā (ṚV*. x 95.17) just before the end. Her swinging high through the air was as much part of the ritual fertility sacrifice as the chant and the dance.

Nārada's metamorphosis into a woman by bathing in a sacred pool surely points to the renewal of virginity above. We still find living representatives of water-goddesses worshipped in the south, under the name *kannir-ammā* or *tannīr-ammā* among those who have not yet abandoned their old ritual for that of the brahmins. Patriarchal intrusion did not immediately abolish the sacred king's death by sacrifice, even in Greece. A surrogate was first sacrificed in place of the hero, and then perhaps symbolic puppets or totem-animals substituted. In some cases, however, the chieftain had to substitute in his own person for the displaced high-priestess as Hermaphroditus by wearing false breasts and woman's garments. So, Nārada may have been some such figure of the transition. The Greek myths do not show direct transference; there is no Indra, for example. Ouranos-Varuṇa are common, perhaps both masculinized from the original goddess Ur-anna, 'Lady of The Mountain'—a Mesopotamian equivalent of our Durgā which it is not possible to equate to Urvaśī. Eos seduces a suspiciously large number of lovers insatiably, in rapid succession (as did Iśtar): Orion, Cephalus, Cleitus, Ganymede, Tithonus, etc. Though etymologically comparable to Uṣas, Eos is a Titaness, hence pre-Hellenic; her fingers were only rosy, while those of our goddess must have been red with human blood. The Hittite Hepit was not elevated to the rank of Eve as in Palestine, but simply made Hebe, cup-bearer to the Olympian gods. Foreign deities adopted without the accompaniment of a substantial number of human followers generally receive a minor standing. The parallels we have pointed out above subsist only and precisely because the two societies underwent similar transition from matriarchy to the patriarchal form.

The origin of the much-discussed *satī* immolation of the widow with her husband's corpse now seems fairly obvious. The first widow in Greek myth to survive her husband and remarry rather than enter his flaming pyre was Gorgophone, daughter of Perseus. Widow-burning can only have developed from suppression of matriarchal tradition, presumably as a warning or precaution against its surreptitious revival. We must remember that the ordinary tribesman knew only group-marriage in both types of society, not the chief's hieros gamos. So, 'husband' denotes some chieftain or sacred king who gained his title to sovereignty (over the new society fused out of two distinct types) primarily by formal marriage to some local high-priestess or 'queen'. If, then, the husband died, there were ample grounds for suspicion that it was the wife's doing, a reversion to the old ritual. The *satī* custom would not only discourage this, but act like a curious inversion of the older sacrifice, and count further as provision for the departed leader in the next world. Yet, the *satī* is herself not on the same level as the dead hero's horse, bow, panoply and accoutrements immolated with him, for she immediately becomes a goddess, with her own cult. The ancient but still recited marriage hymn *RV*. x.85.44 admonishes the bride: *a-pati-ghnī edhi* = 'become a non-husband-killer'. This excellent advice is followed up with an invocation to Indra to give her ten sons and to make her husband the eleventh. This would carry the proper meaning only in a society which had not completely forgotten that the husband was once sent to the gods in sacrifice, but never the son.

The Urvaśīs faded away, but they are responsible nevertheless for the goddesses of the later pantheon that are married peacefully to the major gods. Their living representatives developed what became—with the rise of a trading society and cash economy before the Mauryan period—commercialized prostitution. Significantly enough, the older, superannuated, state-controlled meretrices of the *Arthaśāstra* (2.22, 2.27) enjoy the position of Madams and supervisors over their younger colleagues, with the title *mātṛkā* used for mother-goddesses. They are also responsible for the unholy institutions associated with temple-cults in the least Aryanized parts of India. Finally, they gave birth to two leading Brahmin clans, the Vasiṣṭhas and the Agastyas. When the jar-born sage Agastya 'nourished both colours', *ubhau varṇau pupoṣa* in *RV*. i.179.6 it cannot mean two castes, but both Aryans and non-Aryans, for he belonged to both, and his hymns show clearly the character of the compromise. Only intensive and systematic archaeology can decide whether the Agastyan penetration of the South is pure myth or has some connections with the great megalithic tombs of "saints".

NOTES TO CHAPTER 2

1. K. Marx *Capital* 1. 1. 4 "Value does not wear an explanatory label. Far from it, value changes all labour products into social hieroglyphs. Subsequently, people try to decipher these hieroglyphs, to solve the riddle of their own social product—for the specification of value is just as much a social product as language is"; cf. also J. V. Stalin (on Marxism in linguistics,) *Soviet Literature*, 1950, 9. pp. 5–31.
2. A. B. Keith: *The Religion and Philosophy of the Veda and Upanishads*. Harvard Oriental Series vols. 31–32, Cambridge, Mass, 1925; p. 183.
3. Max Müller. *Chips from a German workshop* (London 1868), Vol. ii, 2nd ed. pp. 117 ff, particularly p. 130.
4. In R. Pischel and K. F. Geldner, *Vedische Studien*, vol. I, Stuttgart 1889, pp. 243–295. Hereafter, Ṛgveda references will be indicated with or without the preceding abbreviation *RV*.
5. For the fire-drill as Urvaśī and Purūravas. cf. *Śat. Brāh*. iii. 4.1.22; for the fire-drill and any human procreation, Bṛhadāraṇyaka Upaniṣad vi. 4. 22, and other places.
6. Since the first publication of this note, certain other aspects have been pointed out which I cannot take seriously. A. Esteller S. J. tried to convince me in private discussions that the hymn had no mystery about it. Simple transposition of words, pādas and stanzas, with occasional emendations based upon Wackernagel's Dehnungsgesetz removed all difficulties. The reason Urvaśī left her husband was simply that he thrashed her thrice a day, a case of wife-beating not uncommon in India. I still prefer to take the unemended *RV* text. O. Herold, misquoting the title, regards it as a mere case of Aryan group-marriage, for which there might be no evidence but which apparently makes no difference to his judgment, being required by some (presumably Marxist) theory.
7. *RV*. x. 14.18 and 135 can only be meant to accompany various types of many-stage funerals. All the stages of a long and complicated marriage ceremony are followed in x, 85, and the whole of that late hymn cannot have been meant for recitation by any one individual inasmuch as the bridegroom has himself to speak some verses in the first person. As for dialogues, x. 10 (Yama-Yamī), x. 108 (Saramā and the Paṇīs) were almost certainly meant to be acted; possibly also iii. 33 (Viśvāmitra and the twin rivers), i, 165, i. 179, iv. 42, and a few others.
8. For the erotic significance of the waters, compare *tuñjāte vṛṣṇyaṃ; payaḥ paridāya rasaṃ duhe* of *RV*. i. 105.2. and Sāyaṇa on *yādurī* in i. 126,6; also the "Anna Livia Plurabelle" chapter in J. Joyce, *Finnegan's Wake*.
9. According to Mbh. 5.187.39–40, Ambā became a river with half her body. This river is given as flowing in the Vatsa country; a rocky tortuous stream filled with crocodiles, dangerous to pilgrims (*dustīrthā*). All these details seem to indicate an existing river, in the Gangetic plain above Allahabad which represented the mother-goddess Ambā. The moral is that getting any history out of the main episodes of our epics is less paying than, for example, writing the history of Charlemagne from the *Chanson de Roland* or of Rome at the time of Theodosius and Maximus from the *Song of Wayland*, or the *Dream of Maxen Wledig*. One may even conjecture that the basic legends come from the pre-Aryan Nāgas, and have been Aryanized along with the remnants of the people. For, Dhṛtarāṣṭra is only a *nāga* in Buddhist legend as elsewhere in Sanskrit, and the capital Hāstinapura is often called *nāgapura*. Sovereignty passes to Yudhiṣṭhira only after the jewel which Aśvatthāman (the ancient Indian king Spatembas mentioned by Megasthenes) bore in his forehead like any *nāga* of traditional myth and legend was torn out by force; the jewel is still associated with the fabulous sacred cobras.

10. The Bṛhaddevatā takes Suryā, Saraṇyu and even Vṛṣākapāyī as forms of Uṣas (Bṛd ii. 10, vii. 120–21). The speech-goddess Vāc there equated to Durgā, Saramā, Urvaśī, Yamī in the middle sphere (ii. 77) and to Uṣas in ii. 79–80. Urvaṣī is derived as *uruvāsini* (ii. 5.9). Making all possible allowance for the syncretistic tendency of such post-Vedic explanatory works, it is clear that these goddesses had something in common. This common factor can only have been their being mother-goddesses. For Saramā and all other goddesses whose names terminate in *mā*, we have the clear though late testimony of the Amarakoṣa 1.1.29: *indirā lokamātā mā kṣīroda-tanayā ramā*.
11. What Keith omitted from his reading of Tacitus is of particular interest to us, and I quote from H. Mattingly's translation in the Penguin Classics: "They are distinguished by a common worship of Nerthus or Mother Earth. They believe that she interests herself in human affairs and rides through their peoples. In an island of ocean stands a sacred grove and in the grove, stands a car draped with a cloth which none but the priest may touch. The priest can feel the presence of the goddess in this holy of holies, and attends her, in deepest reverence, as her car is drawn by kine. Then follow days of rejoicing and merrymaking in every place that she honours with her advent and stay. No one goes to war, no one takes up arms; every object of iron is locked away; then and then only, peace and quiet known and prized, until the goddess is again restored to her temple by the priest, when she has had her fill of the society of men. After that, the car, the cloth, and believe it if you will, the goddess herself are washed clean in a secluded lake. This service is performed by slaves who are immediately afterwards drowned in the lake." In comment, Nerthus is equivalent to the Aryan Nirṛti, a death-goddes; the sacred grove, the sacred lake and sacrifice of slaves are significant; locking away all iron objects would probably indicate a stone-age or bronze-age cult, probably the former. "Rejoicing and merry-making" would mean at least communal dances, and perhaps some orgiastic features as well in the Nerthus-Njord festival.
12. In *RV*. iv. 2.18, the Urvaśīs must be the multiple Usās, as is shown by reference to these dawns in the imbedding verse, particularly 16 and 19.
13. That these *suparṇāh* are not the sun's rays as Sāyaṇa and so many casual translators take them is clear from the sequence, for the sun does not rise till the next *ṛk* only the successive dawns can be meant.
14. *AV*. xiv. 2,14 clearly supplements the Ṛgvedic ceremonial, in the direction of group marriage: "in her here, O men, scatter ye seed"; the 17th ṛk hopes that the bride would be 'not husband slaying', and the next that she would be *devṛkāma*. The collective evidence is overwhelming.
15. Iśtar may not be the lady of the lake like an apsaras; but she is, like Uṇas, the great mother, an eternal virgin, as well as a hetaera. Her symbol, the eight-pointed star, associates her with the rising and setting sun as the 'morning star,' the planet Venus which is male in Sanskrit. The red oxen (v.80.3) that draw the wagon of Uṣas might be more than a figure of speech for the dawn colours, if it is accepted that Iśtar's ceremonial cart was hitched to red oxen in Babylonia. Both are immortal goddesses, but there is no reference to 'former l'śtars' as to former Uṣas. The Indian dawn goddess is born again and again, which seems to me to indicate a human representative, seeing that rebirth is inconceivable as well as unnecessary without death. This is not the equivalent of Iśtar's descent into the nether world, which is properly equated to the long stay of Uṣas in Varuṇa's realm (RV. i. 123.8 *dīrgham sacante varuṇasya dhāma*,) so fantastically twisted by Ṭiḷak to derive an Arctic home for the Aryans.
16. Other contents are limes representing the five Pāṇḍavas, some ordinary water, and some coconut water, both in small quantities. It seems curious that coconut water should be included and even more that the coconut, which cannot have been widely cultivated in India till after the time of Varāhamihira, should play an important part in virtually every Brahmin ritual today. Possible reasons might be the husked fruit's resemblance to a ritual pot, with its hair tuft, hard shell, oculi, contents of edible flesh so often divided and distributed as a sacrament, and of course the water. The multiple symbolism would be most suited to fertility cults after blood sacrifices went out of fashion. The Maoria visualize the coconut as the head of a slain lover [Peter Buck—Te Rangi Hiroa: *Vikings of the Sunrise*, (p. 312)]. The coir and the three black spots on the shell (of which one can be pushed through easily by the human finger, as by the growing coconut sprout) give an excellent representation of hair, eyes and mouth respectively, even in India.
17. R. Briffault, *The Mothers*, (London 1927) vol. ii. pp. 531–536, 550 *et. al*. Briffault's powerfully documented and inspiring three-volume work could not be used more directly here simply because archaeology now tells us

a great deal about the pre-Aryan element in what was once regarded as a purely Aryan Indic culture. The lack of historical analysis, for which Briffault's sources are far more to blame than he is, does not vitiate his main thesis, but does make it dangerous, on occasion, to carry some of his detailed conclusions over without close examination.

18. Though negligible in the Ṛgveda, the Kaśyapas had gained sufficient sanctity by the time of the Brāhmanas to rank high among their caste, and must have been specially prominent in U.P. and Bihār of the 6th century BC as is seen by the way they have managed to write themselves into Jain and Buddhist legends. Mahāvīra, who surely was a Ksatriya, is ascribed the Kaśyapa gotra. The three (supposed) Buddhas preceding Gotama are Kaśyapas (*Dīgha-nīkāya* 14). Asita Devala sheds tears over the infant Gotama in the prophet'e knowledge that he himself will not be alive when the child grows up to attain Buddhahood. At the level of tradition that is in all probability historical, we read of Pūraṇa Kassapa as a leading ascetic teacher at the time of the Buddha and king Ajātaśatru. The three Kassapa brothers had the greatest following among those converted by the Buddha himself. Mahākassapa convoked the first council after the Buddha's death, which gives him virtual leadership of the Buddhist monastic order.

3 At the Crossroads: A Study of Mother-Goddess Cult Sites

3.1. THE PROBLEM

The chain of incident and action in Śūdraka's deservedly popular drama *Mṛcchakaṭika* commences with a peculiar ritual on a dark night. The hero Cārudatta, an impoverished but virtuous brahmin caravan merchant, has just finished his evening prayers. At the beginning of the first act, he asks his clownish brahmin friend Maitreya to help in the consummation: *kṛto mayā gṛhadevatābhyo baliḥ; gaccha, tvam api catuṣpathe mātṛbhyo balim upahara*. "I have completed the *bali* (food-) offerings to the household gods; go thou, offer (this) *bali* to the Mothers at the crossroads". This simple request leads to rescue of the heroine Vasantasenā from abduction. Here we leave the development of the plot, to investigate the ritual.

The *bali* destined for the anonymous Mother-goddesses was a ball of cooked food. It had to be offered at the beginning of the night, but the actual deposit at the crossways need not be made by the same person who offered the prayer; another could place it on his behalf. The context shows, however, that the crossing of two city streets would not serve. The locus had to be some crossing on a highway (*rāja mārga*) outside the town. That this was an ordinary performance at the time of the play is clear from the absence of comment either in the play or elsewhere. The period is in some doubt, but the first four acts of the *Mṛcchakaṭika* are borrowed closely from the fragment (*Daridra-*) *Cārudatta*, ascribed to Bhāsa. This earlier play supplies the essential (and doubtless original) detail that Cārudatta was performing his divine worship on the sixth day of the (dark half of) the lunar month: *saṭṭhī-kida-devakayyassa*. In both plays, the moon rises a little later, at the end of the first act—just in the time to light the heroine on her way home when the hero discovers that he has not even oil for a lamp in his poverty-striken home. The *Mṛc.* reading is printed as *siddhī-kida*, but the commentator Pṛthvīdhara reports a variant to mean *ṣaṣṭhī-vrata-kṛta-*. The instruction *catuṣpathe mātṛbhyo balim upahara* is identical in both dramas. So, we are justified (without joining in the Bhāsa controversy) in the assumption that the custom antedates the Gupta period. It was widespread and generally understood. It is, therefore, surprising that the particular ritual occurs nowhere in the brahmin scriptures, which are otherwise so meticulous over every detail of any household cult.

The *Manusmṛti* (3.81–92) describes the daily Vaiśvadeva food-offerings in full. One of the food-balls is specially offered to the *pitṛs*=the Fathers, taken to mean the souls of departed paternal male ancestors. The last in the series is to be placed on the ground for dogs, outcastes, and wretches afflicted with incurable disease in punishment for some transgression in a previous birth. There is no mention of the group of Mothers, not even to accompany the Fathers; and nothing whatever about the crossroads. P. V. Kāṇe's compendious *History of the Dharmaśāstra*[1] gives full details of the evening *bali* food-offerings (2.745ff.), without reference to this particular rite; the Mothers and their *bali* receive perfunctory mention in 2.217–8, in keeping with the author's general disregard for anthropology.

Literary sources will obviously not help us much. That some rite like Cārudatta's was still current and familiar in the early 7th century should be inferred from Bāṇa's casual phrase: *niśāsv api Mātṛ-bali piṇḍasy eva dikṣu vikṣipyamāṇasya* (*Harṣacarita*, NSP. ed. p. 223). No mention is made of the crossroads; the *piṇḍa* to the Mothers is to be scattered into the outer darkness in all directions. Varāhamihira's *Bṛhatsamhitā* gives full details about iconography, prognostication, and divination, without bringing us any enlightenment upon the point in question. He says (*Br*. 58.56) only that each of the mother-goddesses should be given the attributes of that god whose name she translates into the feminine; this is in the vedic-patriarchal tradition, where the mother-goddess is but a shadowy consort for the male god. Special priests (*Bṛ*. 60.19) knew the rites of the Mothers' Circle, *maṇḍala-krama*. That such circles had a physical existence may be learned from the *Rājataraṅgiṇī* (1.122, 333–5, 348; 3.99; 5.55; *cf.* also 8.2776, *mātṛgrāma*). The crossroads, according to Varāhamihira, bring evil repute upon any house situated near the junction (*Bṛ*. 53.89). In *Br*. 51.4, the location is listed among inauspicious places, below the cemetery and the deserted temple.

3.2. THE MOTHERS

In spite of Kāṇe's silence, there is a rite which antedates the dramas cited above, and seems to be connected with the one in question. In Keith's[2] words, "A very odd rite is prescribed by the Mānava school, for the evening before the last Āṣṭakā: at the crossroads the sacrificer kills a cow, and dismembers it, and divides the flesh among the passers-by."

The Aṣṭakās are domestic funerary offerings, three or four in the whole year. As would be expected from the general tenor of Āryan ritual, the Fathers are the main recipients. The Mothers seem to have crept in as consorts, though assigned a separate direction of the compass. The significant point is the unique Mānava ritual, which would come about the 6th-dark lunar date. Why this was at the crossroads, and to whom the sacrificed cow was dedicated whose flesh was to be shared by every passer-by is not explained. It could not be for evil spirits, or goblins; nor is Rudra, who also haunted vedic crossways, graveyards, waters &c. as chief of ghosts, named. For that matter, the *Śatapatha Brāhmaṇa* (2.6.2.9) invites Rudra at a crossroads sacrifice: "graciously accept it together with thy sister Ambikā"; the conjoint nature of the offerings is emphasized, and 'explains' their name *Tryambakaḥ*, though Rudra is himself Tryambaka. Ambikā means 'little mother', and is elsewhere one of three sisters, jointly mothers of Tryambaka! The presumption is strong that the Mānava sacrifice was for the Mothers, not as mere ancestresses, but as separate goddesses in their own right whom it was necessary to appease, although vedic practice did not openly enjoin this. It will be made plausible in what follows that this practice was borrowed from the 'non-Aryan' element in India. This would account for the recipients of the crossroads sacrifices not being named explicitly, and for the rite becoming standard without benefit of the *gṛhya-sūtras*, as brahminism accepted more and more aboriginal practices. Finally, it also accounts for the crossroads, as will appear in the penultimate sections of this note.

The Mothers could not have been simple Aryan ancestresses, as dissociation from the Fathers shows quite clearly. There is, moreover, an ancient tradition[3] of mothers-in-common that cannot be reconciled with vedic father-right. It would be difficult to explain Pāṇini 4.1.115 unless mothers-in-common were taken for granted by the master grammarian. *Tryambaka*, later explained away as 'with three eyes' means 'with three mothers'. Though this appears physically impossible to us, the legends of Jarāsaṃdha born of two, and Jantu born of a hundred mothers-in-common show that there was an undeniable tradition of many mothers with equal status, even for a single child. These legends were meant to explain the record away when society had changed to the extent that the original concept seemed fantastic. Jarāsaṃdha was almost certainly a historic king of Rājgīr. However, several mothers who equally bear a child-in-common (without any particular father) is a primitive concept in some kinds of pre-patriarchal society, and the inexplicable notion is present, surprisingly enough, even in the Ṛgveda. But the *piṇḍa* offered to such Mothers would not have to be at the crossroads, because the domestic offerings at eve are for the special deities and ancestors of the family. The Mothers of the two dramas were independent deities of some sort.

They were, however, mother-goddesses in a group, without proper names. The *Amarakośa* 1.1.37 does say that they begin with *Brāhmī*, but commentators do not agree either as to the names or the total number, which seems to have increased well beyond the vedic, whether three as for *tryambaka* or the seven never-resting (? *yahvī*) mothers of truth (*ṛta*), or sixteen in another early list. Two stages are combined in the Skanda myth, the theme of Kālidāsa's unfinished or incomplete *Kumāra-saṃbhava*. The young god was born (by intermediacy of the river Ganges) jointly of six mothers-in-common (the Pleiades) with a separate head to suckle each. (Parenthetically, this might explain the three heads of Śiva *tryambaka*, whose image goes back to the three-faced god on a Mohenjo-dāro seal, and who must originally have had three mothers rather than three eyes. Several confluent rivers could account for the many 'mothers' as well as the polycephaly). Skanda (like his prototype Marduk in Babylon) was assigned the function of killing a troublesome demon Tārakāsura, and recruited his army from goblins. He was also joined by the Mothers—not the ones who bore him, but thousands of others, of whom some 192 are named in the 46th chapter of the (Vulgate) *Śalya-parvan* of the *Mahābhārata*. Three of the names are specially interesting. One companion-Mother is *Catuṣpathaniketanā*, "housed at the crossroads'; another is named *Catuṣpatha-ratā*, enamoured of the crossways. Even more remarkable is Pūtanā. A demoness by this name was killed by the pastoral child-god Kṛṣṇa whom she tried to nurse with her poisonous milk. The name cannot be a mere coincidence[4], for these Mothers-companion are described as with horrifyingly sharp teeth and nails, protruding lips &c, all standard terms for demonesses; and simultaneously as beautiful, eternally youthful women. THEY SPOKE DIFFERENT LANGUAGES—clear sign of varied tribal origin. The cults were therefore undoubtedly pre-Aryan, though in process of assimilation. It would appear that the Mothers were easier to control through their child Skanda—invented for that special purpose—than by the imposition of violently hostile patriarchal cults.

There is still not enough to account for the crossroads in all this. Any explanation must take that location into consideration, as also the great increase in the number of the Mothers, with or without names.

3.3. INFORMATION FROM FIELDWORK

It would be a simple matter to go through Bāṇa, the *Kathāsaritsāgara* &c to show the increasing strength of the Mother-goddess cult. It seems to me that this would not explain the rite in question so efficiently as investigation in the field. The examples given here are from Mahārāṣṭra, for it has not been possible to cover sufficient ground elsewhere with the same detail in inquiry. Similar information on the essentials should be available in many other parts of the country, and it is to be hoped that some readers will gather it.

The mother-goddesses are innumerable; many come only in groups without individual names. The most prominent are the *Māvalāyā*, which are water-deities, always in the plural, spread over the two tāluqās of Māvaḷ and Paün Māvaḷ. The name means 'the little mothers' though the termination *āyā* reduplicates "mothers". It is known in the region for over 2000 years, for *Māmāla-hāra* and *Māmāḷe* are inscribed on the façade[5] of the Caitya cave at Kārle in a Sātavāhana charter, so that the country name Māvaḷ in fact derives from the cult. They have no images in iconic form, being represented by numerous shapeless little stones daubed with minium, or by red marks on the sides of a tank, or on a rock, or on a tree by the water. They become *sātī āsarā*, 'the seven Apsaras', beyond the two *tāluqās*, though the number even then need not actually be seven. Similarly, the goddess Lakṣmī-āï in many villages is a whole set of shapeless red-coated stones, apparently having nothing to do with Lakṣmī, the beautiful consort of Viṣṇu. This is not a cult degenerated from that of Lakṣmī, who is called Rakhumāï in Marāṭhī, and represented in temples by carved images paired with her husband Viṭhobā or Pāṇḍuraṅga. It is significant that at Paṇḍharpūr, the leading spot of the Viṭṭhala cult, she does not share Viṭhobā's temple, but has a separate temple and worship of her own. The legend given for the separation is late, while the economic reason of two separate cults supporting more priests than one cannot be the initial one. She must have had a separate cult from the very first, as the mother-goddess (as the termination *āī* shows) without a consort, originally worshipped at Paṇḍharpūr, before the male god came upon the scene, probably from Kanarese territory, to become identified later with Viṣṇu. Similarly, the temples of Khaṇḍobā, a leading rustic god in Mahārāṣṭra and his terrifying 'wife' Mhāḷsā are generally separate. It is not difficult to prove that such divine couples are sometimes composed of deities which were actually hostile at an earlier stage, as representing the cults of two distinct kinds of society. The food-gatherers worshipped a goddess, while the god first appeared on the scene with pastoral life. The marriage of these Mother-goddesses is a phenomenon of the later conjoint society, as for that matter are those forms of human marriage without which individual maternity and paternity would be meaningless.

Every village in the region has at least one mother-goddess cult. Often, the deity is simply called *Āï*, the Mother, without any other name. Sometimes, she is named Ambā-bāï, 'Lady Mother', which is a step higher, and nearer to the classical nomenclature; so also for Lāḍubāï = the Dear Lady, and Kāḷubāï = the Dark Lady. Beyond these, however, there are fantastic local names not to be found elsewhere (though later identification with Durgā or Lakṣmī is sometimes made under brahmin influence)! For example, Tukāï (Koṇḍaṇpur) is comparatively rare, though she does turn up in more than one place. Tukārām was named after her. Jākhamātā should be the same as Jokhāï, with whom some people link her; the name has clear etymological connections with *Yakṣī*, and *ḍākiṇī*. Women who have died in childbirth or drowned themselves are sometimes given this cult as having turned into such a spirit or vampire. In such cases, the establishment of a cult depends upon its being demanded by the defunct, who shows the desire by appearing in some villagers' dreams. A crude, red-daubed, female relief at the end of the rifle range (beyond the Sholapur road, just outside Poona) represents such a funerary cult of a nameless *telī* woman accidentally killed by a stray bullet, who would not let her relatives in the oil-vendors' caste sleep in peace till a monument and worship was given her; recent as the event appears to be, the annual *pālkhī* procession used to stop at the place on its way to Paṇḍharpūr and perform the *āratī* lamp-rite as a matter of course, till the route to Sāsvaḍ changed to the easier Divā pass. A remarkable but not unique case of absorption may be seen a mile beyond Maḷavlī, near the village of Devaleṃ. The mother-goddess in her thicket is (as usual) several lumps of stone, coated with red, but her name is *satī-āi*. Fifty feet away is the actual *satī* monument to an unknown widow of the feudal period who immolated herself on the spot; but that is now called *gopāḷa-porā*, the shepherd-boys' dancing-post, because of the custom the lads have of dancing there in a group on certain days. The primitive goddess has become identified with the *satī*, and the cults have coalesced. A human *satī* may be forgotten altogether as such, though the monument remains identifiable by the customary (though not obligatory) bent-arm-and-hand with open fingers. If I am not greatly mistaken, two breast-like humps (fig. 3.1) on top of a *satī* stone would indicate *sahogamana*: that the widow immolated herself on the same pyre with her husband's corpse; a single hump would mean that she followed her husband into the next world some days after his cremation, on a separate pyre: *anugamana*. Such memorials exist at Bolāī, as elsewhere in our villages. She may be only just remembered but receive nothing beyond a sporadic coating of red and an occasional flower, as at Devghar and Ambarnāth. She may be regarded as special protectress of the village even though her name be forgotten as usual. This last is to be seen at Pimpḷolī, where a coconut is broken before her uncovered *samādhi* stone every Sunday, and the meat distributed as sacrament. Mr. N. G. Chāpekar in his *Badlāpūr*, (Poona 1933; p. 320) reports of crossroads cult for a man of the Mahar caste supposedly killed by some feudal member of the Kuḷkarṇī family. The spirit demanded the particular location, and receives the regular sacrifice of a goat, formerly of a buffalo bull-calf, from the Kuḷkarṇīs.

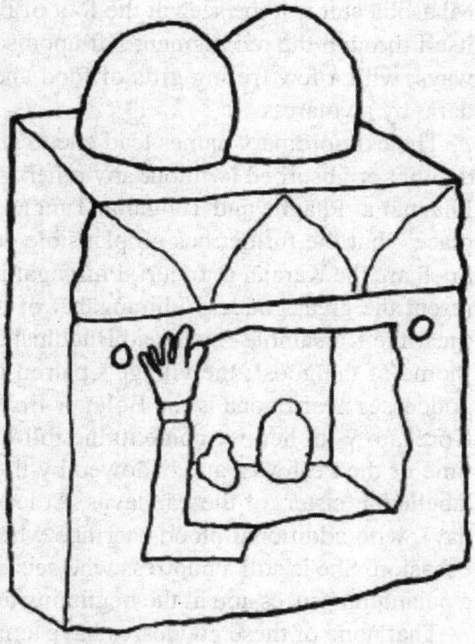

Fig. 3.1. Satī monument at Ambarnāth; height about 45 cm.

The *satī* and the *Sātī-Āsarā* should not be confused with each other nor with a remarkable, primitive, and dangerous mother-goddess Saṭavāī, or Saṭavī. The last is now also a term of abuse in Marāṭhī for an unpleasant harridan. The word is derived without question from Sanskrit *ṣaṣṭhī*, 'the sixth' whatever her original name or names were. The goddess Saṭavī is to be propitiated on the sixth night after the birth of any child, with a lamp burning through the night, and certain other articles (every one of which becomes the perquisite of the midwife at dawn) laid out for her. Among them may be the saddle-quern with its muller stone, but writing materials are always included. The goddess comes in person that night to write the fate and character of the child on its forehead in invisible but immutable words. This is brahminised as the *brahma-likhita*. Men have nothing to do with this ritual, though the power of the goddess is unquestioned. She is herself also the sixth date of the lunar month, which is her special worship day. Skanda, so peculiarly connected with the Mothers, is *ṣaṣṭhī-priya*, and the late *Devī-Bhāgavata Purāṇa* personifies Ṣaṣṭhī as his wife. Finally, though Ṣaṣṭhī (or Saṭhī, Saṭavī) has also been identified with Durgā, she remains unmarried in popular belief: "Mhasobā has no wife, and Saṭavāī no husband (*dādalā*)". Though a Mother, the goddess tolerates no consort. Mhasobā is the buffalo-demon Mahiṣāsura killed by Durgā-Pārvatī, but still regularly worshipped as a god, at times near her temple. The best example is in Poona, where a live

Mhasobā cult is to be seen at the foot of Parvatī hill-temple. Saṭavī worship occasionally manifests itself through the red pigment left upon some out-of-the-way rock, often by the road or at a cross-ways, with a few trifling gifts of food and a lime cut open. The rite is generally performed in the dark, by a votaress.

The extraordinary names lead one to suspect connection with some diminutive tribal group now defunct or absorbed (without any other trace) remain connected with the name of the village, *e.g.* Phāgṇāï at Phāgṇe and Tuṅgāï at Tuṅgï village, of which the latter may be explained as "the high place", but the former has no plausible etymology. Others come from still more obscure sources. Such are the Karajāï at Induri, Phiraṅgāï in the old Buddhist caves near Nanolī, (apparently to represent the great goddess Phiraṅgābāï of Kurkumbh), Warsūbāï beyond Junnar, Udālāï of Neṇavlī (near the Karsamble-Sudhagaḍ Buddhist caves), Surāḷāi at Bhājā (though *surāḷa* = *surālaya* means 'home of the gods'; the village's patron goddess is Jākhamātā). The most famous of such unique goddesses near Poona is the Bolāï or Bolhāï a mile from the village Vāḍeṃ-Ghoḍeṃ, not far from Koregāo. With her, we come to the full-blown primitive stage, for in spite of a temple built in the time of the Peshwās, and endowed by the Gaekwārs, she has not been brahminised beyond being labelled a 'sister' of the Pāṇḍavas. At least one goat is sacrificed to her every Sunday (her special day), with additional blood-sacrifice which some devotee might consider necessary on any other occasion. She is still a huntress who sets out on a two-month hunting tour in winter, symbolised by a palanquin procession at the beginning and the end.

That none of these goddesses have a male consort or 'husband' proves their antiquity. The reaction whose beginning is reflected in the Mhasobā cult came with the full development of a pastoral society, as is further shown by the rare male god Bapūjī Bābā, who is specially a god of the cattle, but whom women may not even approach without grave danger. One shrine is beyond Ahīre in the National Defence Academy area, and serves five surrounding villages in common, apart from casual help to people from a greater distance; similarly near Khānāpur on the other side of the lake. Others are: in the northwest corner of the walled enclosure of the crumbling Viṣṇu temple at Ākurḍī; on the Central Railway line near Maḷavlī; between Induri and Mahāḷunge; and the Bāpdeo at the top of the old pass between Koṇḍhwā and Sāsavaḍ is presumably the same god. The much more popular Vetāl, demonstrably later than the goddesses, is equally shapeless. He is a Scythianedapped head at Chinchvaḍ (fig. 3.2) and at times simulates Śiva's phallic symbol (fig. 3.3) into which his stones can be shown to have developed in certain cases. In general, he is also not to be approached by women. If really orthodox, his male worshipper will avoid the touch of a woman or sound of a woman's bangles before worship. Slightly more tolerant is the related monkey-faced god Hanumān or Māruti, who is incurably celibate (though a powerful god among the peasantry as the Maruts were in the days of the later vedas); but women are allowed to worship him. The child-god Skanda, so obviously devised to bring the Mothers and their cults under male control, has not escaped this masculine tradition. When worshipped in Mahārāṣṭra under the name Kārttika-svāmin, women are forbidden to approach him. This seems to contradict the Purāṇas, but it might be remembered that the nymph Urvaśī, heroine of Kālidāsa's

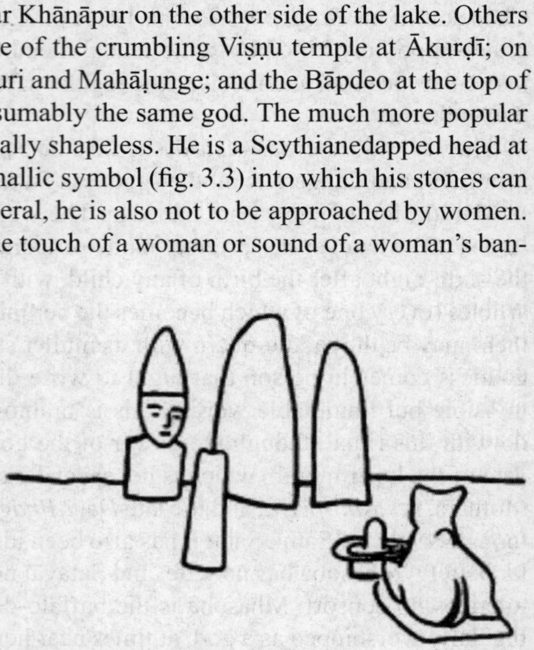

Fig. 3.2. Vetāī at Chinchvaḍ.

Vikramorvaśīyam, was metamorphosed into a vine for trespassing into a grove sacred to the god, and hence forbidden to women. We shall prove again, a little later, that this marks a forgotten stage in the development of Skanda, and that the original taboo was quite different, as was the forbidden grove.

The goddesses are Mothers, but unmarried. No father seemed necessary to the society in which they originated. The next step is shown by marriage to some male god. Jogubai has a 'husband' Mhātobā at Kothrūḍ and Vākaḍ. The extraordinary feature of this marriage is that Mhātobā is really Mhasobā = *mahiṣāsura*, while the wife Jogūbāī is Yogeśvarī = Durgā, whose most famous act was killing the buffalo demon. This is by no means an isolated case, for Mhasobā is again married to Jogubāī at Vīr, under the name of Maskobā. In both cases the slight change of his name is made apparently to permit the nuptials. The Vīr god was set up by immigrant shepherds, and still goes in procession once a year to a hillock adjoining the one on which his cult is located. The hillock is still called Tukāī's pasture and her little shrine there contains a crude red-daubed relief which shows the goddess crushing a tortured buffalo—*Mahiśāsura-mardinī!*

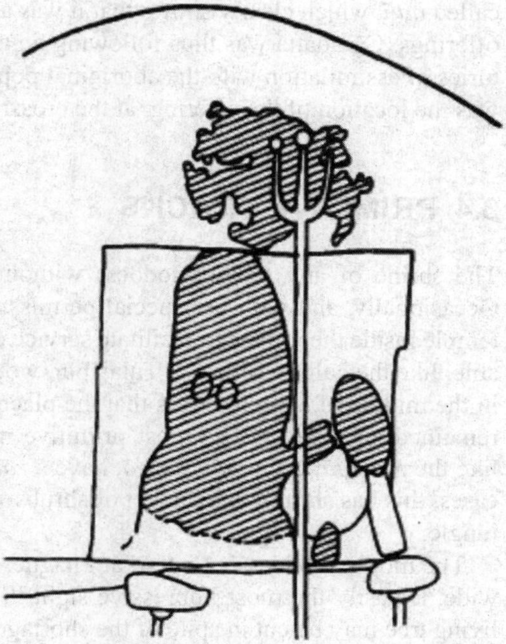

Fig. 3.3. Vāghobā (Tiger-Lord) of Pimpḷoli Bedsā pass; red pigment shaded. Note limes impaled on trident.

These gods are death-gods too, and the goddesses also deal out death if not placated. They preside over epidemic disease. Devi (goddess) is simply the name for small-pox. Marī-āī has to be worshipped to prevent death from cholera, Sītalādevī is the particular goddess that can protect little children from small-pox, Gaurābā from measles. The goddesses are all usually worshipped in the towns by women (though the priests may be men) during the nine days of the *nava-rātra*, beginning with the month of Āśvin (October new-moon). It is difficult to connect these 'nine nights' with the harvest; the real harvest festivals are nearly a month later. Moreover, most of the goddesses are given special offerings. In the villages, there are obligatory blood sacrifices, unless the cult has been brahminised by identification with some purāṇic goddess, in which case the sacrificial animal may be shown to the goddess but has to be cut up at some distance. Rarely, a bloodless offering may be substituted. Finally, the *ṣaṣthī* and no-moon nights are also special in the worship of the goddesses, as the latter with Vetāḷ; blood-sacrifices have clearly been demanded (in fact are still occasionally made) on such nights. A reflection of this custom is to be seen in the case of the greater Jogeśvarī of Poona, the seniormost goddess of the city, whose image is clothed for the day and a silver mask put on, early every morning, with one exception. The exceptional date is that of the no-moon, on which *tithi* the primitive, stone-relief image underneath is left visible, and has to be given a fresh coating of red (minium in oil) pigment—itself clearly a derivative of a still earlier blood-rite.

The famous stanza *limpatīva tamo'ṅgāni* emphasizes the pitch dark, which is indeed essential for the various incidents that follow in the *Mṛcchakaṭika*. But a no-moon night could not have brought out the hero's desperate poverty. The ball of food that Cārudatta offered on the 'dark-sixth' was called *bali*, which clearly shows that it was a substitute for blood-sacrifices as were his Vaiśvadeva offerings. Cārudatta was thus following an ancient custom that had been taken up during the centuries of assimilation with the aboriginal population. The only feature that remains to be explained was the location of the offering, at the crossroads.

3.4. PRIMITIVE TRACKS

The shrine of any mother-goddess without an *identificatio brahmanica* is outside the village. Occasionally, and with her special permission, a representative stone may be brought into some temple inside the village to facilitate service during the rains. Only if it should grow widely fashionable, like the cult of Tuḷlajā at Tuḷajāpūr, would a settlement develop. Otherwise, finding the shrine in the middle of a town means that the place has grown from economic causes while the cult-spot remained unchanged. The most primitive mother-goddesses, excepting specialized water-deities like the *Māvalāyā* and *Sātī Āsarā*, have a *rāna*, literally 'forest' about the aniconic image. In most cases, this has shrunk to a thicket of shrubs worthless as fuel; but occasionally, the grove is quite a jungle.

The mother-goddess's 'forest' at Phāgṇe, about three hundred metres long by fifty to a hundred wide, is easily the most impressive sight in the middle Paünā valley. Not a single branch of any living tree may be cut in spite of the shortage of firewood; the goddess has consistently refused her permission to those greedy timber contractors who sought to placate her by sacrifice of a goat and offerings of clothes, coconuts, and ornaments. The Phāgṇe elders, mostly Muḷūt by surname, have a tradition that they were immigrants from Muḷe in Bhor state. They believe that Phāgṇāī came with them, and that her 'brother' Khaṇḍobā than appeared in the river-bed (now silted up by a change of course, but the locus is still carefully marked off). Excellent microliths are found on the eroded hillside and ridges just behind and on either side of the grove, which leads one to think that some primitive goddess must have occupied the site before the immigration. It is extraordinary that during *Navarātra*, all women are excluded from the grove and the vicinity of the temple, a guard being set for the purpose. This is a general rustic *tabu* for the 'nine nights' not observed in city temples. The Ila-Ilā myth shows that such jungle groves were primeval, originally never to be entered by men, under penalty of transformation into a woman. Inasmuch as men have usurped the priesthood, this tabu has been inverted here. But the Sisterhood, the sacred grove, tabu on male entry, and punishment for a transgressor by his immediate initiation into the sisterhood and necessity of living thereafter as a woman all exist in parts of Africa (as among the Attonga). At Phagne, women may occasionally take a short cut across a corner of the sacred grove, but the tabu is generally observed at all times, and has obviously been inverted from an original tabu upon male intrusion.

The magnificent grove at Phāgṇe inevitably draws the minds to the classical *nemus* of Diana at Aricia which formed the starting point of Frazer's *Golden Bough*. Peculiarly interesting for us is the epithet *Trivia* of that goddess in the Aeneid (7.774, 778), Diana of the crossways. Quadrivia would have been the precise equivalent of the Sanskrit, but European mother goddesses were triple, so that the forked junction suited their physiognomy better. Phāgne, it should be pointed out, is actually at the join of two major ancient routes. One leads up the Paünā valley, the other crosswise from Bhājā past Tikoṇā to Chāvsar. Before the Muḷshī dam was built, it was the route to the mountain passes of Ḍerā, Vāgjāī and Savāsaṇī, still the best in the region, and formerly important enough to be dominated by the forts of Sudhāgaḍ and Korīgaḍ, as well as flanked by the enormous, ruined Buddhist cave complexes of Karsambḷe and Ṭhāṇāḷā. The survival of the grove proves the existence of a vast primeval forest that stone-age man could not have cleared with his tools, nor by fire. The low spur, now stripped bare except within the goddess's preserve, shows an indefinitely long track (microlith) along its exposed surface. Excellent microliths are found on the other patches of comparable high ground in and near Phāgṇe, also by the riverside; but no larger tools have come to notice as yet, nor prehistoric pottery, in that locality.

The primitive origin and nature of the extant cults is shown by the injunction (as also in the case of Vetāḷa) that the stone must be open to the sky. Roofing it over brings grave misfortune upon the misguided worshipper, but the goddess's consent is generally obtained when the villagers become sufficiently wealthy. Therefore, the cults go back to a period before houses were in fashion, and when the 'village' was on the move. But the grove could not be moved, so that the site must have been chosen for other reasons than proximity to a village. What reasons?

The more fashionable cult-spots are visited by a number of people out of all proportion to the population now resident in the vicinity. Bolāï, Āḷandī, and Paṇḍharpūr are such examples. These local cults were, presumably, at or near places from which colonization occurred. But the colonization was not haphazard, and these places lie demonstrably on routes of considerable age. In the beginning, these must have been the ways for the seasonal transhumance ('boolying') of men and herds. Even now, sheep-herders from Ahmednagar district trace such a drovers' round of about 400 miles on foot every year, with their flocks. The routes, however, have now been modified because of extensive farming, and the herders are paid in measures of grain by the peasant to fold the sheep on given plots of land for a night or two, thus fertilising the impoverished soil. The route of pilgrimage connecting Āḷandī and Paṇḍharpūr is still followed seasonally (beyond the time of pilgrimage) by a considerable vagrant population, partly because of the numerous intermediate cult-spots it links up, which make begging easier. A little investigation shows that many of the stopping places have marked deposits of late stone-age tools, and that the route is clearly prehistoric. Bolāï certainly was on such a route, now but little frequented because the present Poona-Ahmednagar road passes through the next parallel valley. The natural caves at Kesnand near Vāgholī are also on the abandoned trade-route, which, connects them with Bolāï. Theūr was on a prehistoric route and important river-crossing, and has one of the eight autochthonous *aṣṭa-vināyaka* Gaṇeśa images that rank over all the other Gaṇapatis in Mahārāṣṭra at least. Phāgṇe is on the Paūnā valley trade route (leading past Tuṅgī to the Sudhāgaḍ passes and Chāul harbour) that touched the Beḍsā and Śelarwāḍī caves (locally, Ghoravḍī caves). Similarly for the other examples I have given.

It is possible to go much further in this direction. My fieldwork showed an unexpected number of cult-spots on gentle hillside slopes, nearer the valley-bottom than the top of the hill, but at a considerable distance (1 to 2 miles as a rule) from the nearest village and from present sources of water. They could not have been near any village when the land had been cleared and plough cultivation came into general use. Nevertheless, the cult is kept up under difficulties, even when there is no shrine. Whether a temple has been built or not, these isolated cults show one remarkable feature: the location always yields a considerable number of microliths in far greater concentration than any other locus near by. There are virtually no larger stone tools. Among handy examples is the Ambābāï stone, aniconic and red-coated as usual, by the crossing of the Bombay-Poona road and the Central railway, on the track leading to the pass for the Beḍsā caves. Another is a funerary *samādhi* temple near Rāyarī, by the Dehū area. There are plenty of others. They are not all mother-goddesses now, but without going into detailed argument, there is reason to believe that even some of the male gods have been converted into their present form from obliterated Mother-cults.

The microliths have more than local importance, being identical in size, type, material and technique of manufacture with those discovered by A. C. Carlleyle in South Mirzapur caves, and reported in 1885. They are known in other countries as well (V. A. Smith: *IA*. 35. 1906, 185–95), and precede the age of metals. Tumuli in the nearby Gangetic plain yielded pottery, large stone tools and microliths, but never any metal. The Vindhyan caves and rock-shelters above do not show even the other stone tools, while their meagre pottery seems unassociated with the microliths. Lumps of haematite found with the tiny artifacts were used to draw pictures on the cave-walls which show that the toolmakers possessed bow and arrow. The chains or rather tracks of microlith sites await competent field archaeology to trace them southwards from the Gangetic tip of the great Deccan route. However, this tip can hardly have been at Mirzapur, for the region under the name of "southern mountain" (*dakkhiṇāgiri*) was opened up not long before the Buddha. The hostile, Aryan raiding charioteers drawn by the cave-users must have represented the spearhead of a search for iron and other cres, which led to the settlement of Rājgīr and eventual hegemony of Magadha.

The cult sites are not the only places in the Mahārāṣṭra districts considered where microliths are found concentrated. The find-spots follow about the same level along the foot of the hills. The tools are not accompanied by any pottery, and there is not enough soil left to construct a stratified sequence in most of the places. Following these microlith groupings along the hill, however, one conclusion is unavoidable. These tools represent the pre-metal and pre-pottery stage when the valley bottom was not cleared of jungle. The whole assemblage is characteristic of what might be called Mesolithic cultures in the older nomenclature, with herds and a little sporadic cultivation to eke out considerable food-gathering, and some hunting.

Such a population had to shift from place to place. Permanent settlement could not come before the day of cheap metals, i.e. of iron. It is difficult to imagine the use of iron as common anywhere in the Deccan much earlier than the Mauryan conquest. There are no convenient deposits of copper ore within easy reach of this region, and the *Arthaśāstra* does not know of southern iron. The natural route of the savages before the swampy or forested valley bottom was opened for cultivation would go precisely along the level indicated, not as a thin foot-track but as a broad though irregular band with the passes as fixed points. The annual 'crossing the boundary' just after the 'nine-nights' festival surely marks the commencement of a primitive booly.

The groups that moved along these tracks could not have been numerous. There was no question of their possessing land, for land-ownership is not a primitive concept. Fixed plots are meaningless till the plough has conquered the soil. For this, the fertile bottom lands have to be cleared for forest, and kept clear, which is not possible in our monsoon country without iron tools in plenty. Land to the savage is territory, not property. It seems to me that the still remembered Mahārāṣṭrian custom of *gāṃva-saï* goes back to pre-settlement times. This used to be the propitiation (at such date as the *bhagat* might set) of all local deities, spirits, and goblins. The impressive feature is that every human being had to go to live beyond the village (residential) limits for seven or nine days, during which the place would be completely deserted. After living in the fields or under trees for the period, and performing the required worship and blood-sacrifices, the inhabitants would return with the assurance of greater crops, less illness, and augmented general well-being. The ceremonial of return is conceived as a resettlement. The fixed cult-spots for pre-agricultural people would necessarily be those where their regular paths crossed, places where they met for their pre-barter exchange with the ceremonial and communal ritual that always accompanied it, or where several groups celebrated their periodic fertility cults in common. *Thus, the crossways are logically the original sites for the mother-goddess cults.*

3.5. THE TRADE ROUTES

This can be taken beyond the realm of mere conjecture. If the prehistoric tracks ran as outlined above, it would be logical to find some of them developing into later trade-routes, and into modern roads. The last is not an absolute necessity, for settlements moved down into the valley, by the riverside, as land-clearing progressed. This shift makes definite proof rather difficult. However, we have enough in common between old tracks and new, particularly the passes, to prove the thesis. The great Buddhist cave monasteries (all near mountain passes) at Karsamble, Thāṇaḷā, Bhājā, Kārle, Beḍsā and Junnar fix the main trade routes without any doubt, particularly when smaller intermediate caves are linked up. It is logical to expect merchants to go along the tracks most frequented by whatever people lived there before the country was settled by fixed, plough-using villages. The Buddhist monks, not mere almsmen but expert food-gatherers (cf. *SN.* 239 ff. and many *Jātaka* stories), who penetrated the wilderness to preach *ahiṃsā* and peaceful social behaviour would initially follow the same tracks, in order to reach the greatest number of savages. Their religion insisted upon the cessation of blood-sacrifices, and the cult-spots were the most likely places for their preaching. Therefore, these cults and the major Buddhist caves which are obviously at the junctions of great trade-routes should have some demonstrable connection, never completely obliterated by the change of routes after food production became general. In fact, this is just what we do find.

The goddess Yamāï has a shallow relief image (fig. 3.4) carved into the Beḍsā Vihāra cave. A goat is sacrificed to her in front of the cave in *navarātra*, once a year.

An occasional fowl, or more commonly coconut repays a vow or assures tranquillity to the villager whose sleep Yamāï is sure to disturb—if neglected too long—by a nightmare. Yet she has no temple in the village, which would have been much more convenient in the rains; the village does have temples to more civilized and commonly worshipped deities. At Kārle—again in the caves, but not the villages below—she is the traditional family goddess of Bombay Son Koḷī fishermen, who come all the way to make their vows, pay her worship, and to dedicate their children. Inasmuch as the goddess (locally named Ambā-bāï and Veher-āï = Mother at the caves) has only a relief image in the shrine just at the Caitya entrance, the ritual circumambulation is done about the great stupa and not Yamāï's 'representative' in front. The Koḷīs take the stūpa as the goddess herself, though unable to explain this; the child for whose birth vows are invariably made to Yamāï is 'shown' to the stupa without fail. It is natural, as has happened in other cases, to take a stupa (trimmed suitably, if necessary) as Śiva's phallic symbol; but to take it as a mother-goddess is extraordinary, to say the least. There is no cult in the caves at Bhājā, because the little village has moved down into the lowlands about 50 years ago from a site on the slope. A little further along the route, we find Tukārām's caves at Bhāmchandar, originally natural caves but now extended by hand in most cases, generally to make temples. No attention is paid to the fact that the mother-goddesses of the village two miles away near the river are still located here, and given their coat of red. The next hill, Bhaṇḍārā, (where Tukārām also meditated) has a good microlith site, with Buddhist caves and a stupa, which have passed without notice by The Gazetteer and by archaeologists. Tukārām and his special deity Viṭhobā have pushed out any earlier cult that might have existed, but the microlith track is very near. The cave-temple on the grounds of the Fergusson College, Poona (shown on the wrong hill in the old district *Gazetteer*), was originally a set of monastic cells, almost certainly Buddhist Just above is a tiny shrine to Hanumān, originally a cult-spot for a "Pensioners' Vetāḷa". By this shrine are found microliths in plenty, and below the caves, much better ones in great numbers. In all these cases, however, it is difficult to PROVE the quite plausible existence of the cult before the monasteries were carved out.

Fig. 3.4. Yamāī of Beḍsā *vihāra* cave; note earlier relief at upper left.

The most interesting complex is at Junnar, where many trade routes met. There are four major groups of caves about the decaying city. Of these, the Gaṇeśa Leṇā group has some minor goddess, overshadowed by the modern shrine of the elephant-headed god (one of the autochthonous *aṣṭa-vināyakas*) built into one of the larger caves. Gaṇeśa was, after all, admitted into the Mahāyāna pantheon, so that it would not do to insist that the caves were an older cult-spot in spite of the special importance given to this Gaṇeśa. The Tuḷajā caves have a modern image of the goddess Tuḷajā similarly inserted. But on Mānamoḍī hill, we find the unique and primitive goddess Mānamoḍī being worshipped in one of the caves, and we do know that the name is at least as old as the caves. One of the inscriptions mentions the Order resident at *Mānamakuḍa*, which is Mānamoḍī, when it is remembered that *ka* would be softened to *a* in the prakrit style of pronunciation. The goddess, unlike Tuḷajā and Gaṇeśa, is not found elsewhere, in any context. The actual worship to-day is offered simultaneously to three post-Buddhist images identified by the authors of the *Gazetteer* as those of the Jain *tirthaṃkaras* Ádināth, Nemināth, and their attendant goddess Ambikā. All three together are called Manamoḍī (sometimes Ambikā), and so worshipped without distinction by the villagers. The name has the literal meaning 'Neck-breaker, and is reminiscent of the goddess Kavaḍadarā ('Skull Splitter') eight miles away in the adjoining Ār valley.

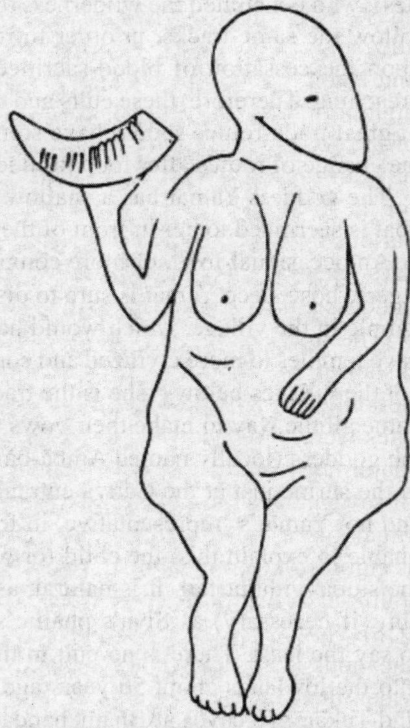

Fig. 3.5. Red-coated relief of Mother-goddess (Les Combarelles, France).

Even more interesting is the fourth major group at Junnar, of the caves that run along the side of the cliff topped by Śivanerī fort. The stronghold derives its name from Śivābāï. a primitive goddess in one of the former Buddhist caves (close to a dining hall donated by or for the Yavana Ciṭa) within the outer fortifications. The very popular local goddess is alone, without a consort. Her modern (Buffalo-demon-trampler) image might have been modelled after a human stage-actress, but for the supernumerary arms. The original aniconic image, red-coated and painted with oculi, was smashed by some bigoted vandal one night in 1947, but is still duplicated in flour. The Sanskrit word *Śivā* denotes more than one plant, among them the sacred *śamī* tree; it also means 'jackal'. Though the priests I met were aware of no connection with Śiva, the *Amarakośa* 1.1.39 does give Śivā, or Sivī as one of Pārvatī's names. The connection is less logical than would appear at first sight, as the stanza also calls her Bhavānī, Śarvāṇī, and Rudrāṇī. The vedic Rudra = 'dreaded' perhaps grew later into Śiva which means 'blessed'; but Bhava and Śarva are two other quite distinct vedic gods. The primitive goddess of the high place was variously assigned as wife to more than one Aryan god, and then the 'husbands' were identified with each other. Had the cult been set up by Pāśupatas, who broke into north Indian Buddhist monasteries, the male god would have had an image, and even the goddess a better one than a shapeless lump of stone. These caves enter modern history in 1629–30. A Marāṭhā noble, engaged in the dangerous game of trading allegiance between the Muslim kingdoms of Ahmadnagar, Bijāpūr, and Delhi, left his pregnant wife at Junnar to look after herself. The high-born lady, too proud to go back to her own people and conscious of the husband's cooling sentiments (he took another wife a couple of years later) took refuge in the fortress, and prayed to the goddess for the birth of a second son. The answer to the appeal made in such parlous times was a son named, as the *bakhars* tell us, after the goddess—the famous Marāṭhā king Śivājī. Bhavānī remained his patron goddess for life, presumably after the brahminical identification of the '*Amarakośa* with *Śivā*.

Fig. 3.6. Stylized Mother-goddess, engraving on bone; European stone age.

The monastic caves were mostly patronized and liberally endowed by merchants, many from distant places, as we learn from their inscriptions. In fact, they were, in the days of their glory, not only very important customers, but also great banking and supply houses for the traders. Their sites were located according to the junction of primitive tracks, which became crossways on the major trade routes. A further incentive for the monks to choose such a location was the proximity of savage cults, because it was a principal mission of the Order to put an end by persuasion to all ritual killing. This is very neatly brought out by the archaic Buddhist *Suttanipāta* (*SN*). The monk is enjoined not to enter a village or town except to beg his food. His stay for the night should be on a hill, in a cave, under a solitary tree outside the village, or by a corpse-enclosure (*susāna;* cf. *SN* 958). Now these were precisely the places where the most gruesome rites were practised. Indeed, the monk is explicitly warned: "He should not be frightened by those who follow strange cults, even when their most dreadful practices are witnessed. These and other perils should be sustained by one who pursues the beneficent way" (*SN* 965). The Buddha himself set the example by spending nights by the cult-spots and converting bloodthirsty cacodemons to whom sacrifices were made (*SN* 153–192), while the economic success of early Buddhism was due to its successful protest against the vast, ever-increasing vedic animal-sacrifices. The primeval cults returned when the caves were deserted. In some cases as at Mānamoḍī, even the original name of the goddess is recognizable. The mark of Buddhism was not erased completely, however. The two special goddesses in the Junnar caves tolerate no blood-sacrifice watever. At Kārle, the sacrificial beast may at most be shown to the goddess Yamāī's surrogate, but the actual killing has to be done at a considerable distance.

The Order introduced fundamental economic changes. Indian Buddhist monasteries were responsible for agrarian settlement (as was the case in parts of China) whether directly or through the merchants associated with the cave monasteries and the trading tribal chiefs who turned into kings. But it will not be denied that the monasteries remained tied to the specialized and concentrated long-distance 'luxury' trade of which we read in the *Periplus*. This trade died out, to be replaced by general and simpler local barter with settled villages. The monasteries, having fulfilled their economic as well as religious function, disappeared too. The people whom they had helped lead out of savagery (though plenty of aborigines survive in the Western Ghāṭs to this day), to whom they had given their first common script and common language, use of iron, and of the plough, had never forgotten their primeval cults.

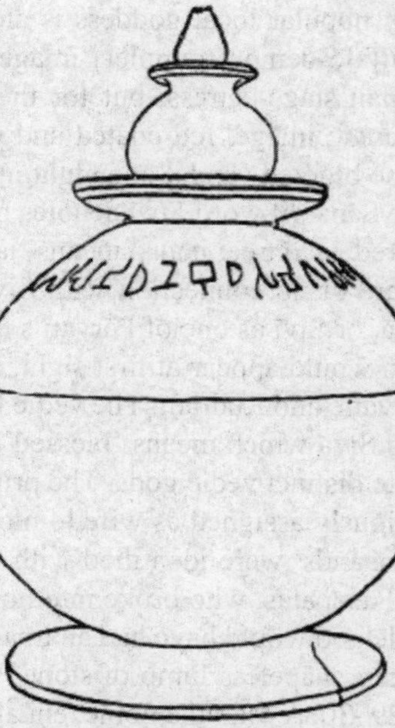

Fig. 3.7. The Piprahvā vase, presumably containing relics of the Buddha at Kapilavastu.

We may take one more example from a different region. The Buddha's birth is reported in Pāli literature as having taken place in a sacred *sāla* grove called *Lumbini-vana* (*Jātaka, Avidūrenidāna: Luṃbini-vanaṃ nāma maṅgala-sāla-vanaṃ;* the translation 'garden' is unjustified). His mother was then supposedly on her way to her parents' home at Devadaha from Kapilavastu, which latter town must be placed at Piprahvā on the Nepāl frontier because of the find of the famous relic casket (fig. 3.7) in the Sākyan stupa to the Buddha. The Asokan pillar found near Paḍariā inside the Nepāl frontier excuses the *bali* tax to Luṃmini village because 'Buddha Sakyamuni was born here'. The nearest modern village is over a mile from the site, though there is no question of hill and valley in the wide alluvial plain, and no reason for the village to have moved. The locality is still named Rummin-deī, the termination being the shortened form of *devī*, 'goddess'. The little shrine by the Asokan pillar wherein Māyā was depicted at the time of the nativity was attributed to Rummindeī by the villagers. So the Buddha's mother was worshipped even at the turn of the century as the goddess Lumbini or Ruṃmini, with the red pigment and occasional blood sacrifices that disgusted pious Buddhists, my father among them. The picture is quire clear, knowing what we do. Māyā made for the grove of the goddess, which was on the main route (from Sāvatthi or Devadaha to Kapilavastu and ultimately to Kusinārā, Vesāli, Paṭnā, and Rājgīr). It was, moreover, at the crossing of two routes the other going to the chief Koliyan town Rāma-gāma nine *yojanas* to the east, as Fa-hsien reported. She must have felt her time coming on, went to pay homage to the goddess, and to receive her special protection. The protection turned out to be inadequate, for Māyā died on the seventh day after giving birth to her incomparable son; but she was herself identified with the goddess and receives her worship. The parallel to the Satī-āī and Jākhāī above is clear, while the mother's death is suspiciously close to the perilous sixth night after the child's birth. The commentary *Papañca-sūdanī* on *MN.* 101 reports that Devadaha was the village adjoining the Lumbini grove, and was in fact so named because of the lotus-pond used for Sakyan consecration ceremonies. The tradition is uniform and uncontested that Māyā bathed in this sacred *puṣkariṇi* just before her delivery—an act whose special significance now becomes clear.

3.6 THE JĀTAKAS

This section is devoted mainly to supplementary information from the Buddhist *Jātakas*, because the collation of literary sources with archaeological discovery and living tradition is a major purpose of the present note. The reason for giving the *Jātaka* birth-stories a separate section, rather than scatter the information as footnotes throughout the chapter, is their age and unitary redaction, older in any case and nearer to the life of the common people than the *Kathāsaritsāgara*, for example. In their present form—namely Fausböll's standard edition reference being made by the letter *J*, followed by the number of the *Jātaka*—these stories have apparently been retranslated into Pāli from a compendium of tales extant primarily in the Siṃhalese at that time. The source of the latter lies in northern documents brought to the south by the early monks. The later redaction is attested by reference to the coconut *nāḷikera* in *J.* 466,535, and 536. In the first and the third of these, it is mentioned among other trees as the sign of a fertile place. In the second, the useless wealth of the miser is compared to a coconut found by a dog. The nut itself was well known on the Andhra coast only by the 1st century BC, and on the western coast not later than 120 AD. The *Jātakas* may therefore be taken as influenced by conditions during the Śātavāhana period, and their historical detail infiltrated by such tradition as was then extant. Social conditions had changed considerably in some cases from the time of the Buddha; the rise of Buddhism is itself testimony for the change. In what concerns us, however, it will be possible to select fairly reliable details.

It is essential in each case to ask whether the particular detail is indispensable to the original story or not, and whether the setting is unmistakably southern, such as could not have existed at the time of the Buddha in Bihār. Whenever independent northern confirmation is possible, the tale may be taken as very old, and its nucleus pre-Buddhistic. Thus, for example, the late word *lañca* for a bribe taken by an official is specialized to the *Jātaka* complex; but bribes existed much earlier. Some of the observances that are 'explained' by the stories are certainly old. For example, the tabu on garlic for Buddhist nuns in the 'present' story of *J.* 136 could not have been imposed by the Buddha himself. The use of an Udumbara-wood seat at a royal consecration, with sprinkling by water out of a conch-shell could hardly originate in a boar's prowess and cunning, as in *J.* 281. Yet both customs existed. The *nāga* cobra-demon Maṇikaṇṭha of *J.* 253 reminds us of the Central Indian Maṇi-nāga cult which is found in numerous medieval copper-plates, and apparently still exists (even at Rājgīr); this is unlikely to have been a mere Ceylonese interpolation. Fa-hsien recorded the special respect paid to the patron *nāga* at the great Saṃkāsyā monastery (as at some others: fig. 3.8); the huge *nāga* himself appeared as a small white snake on certain special days to receive the monks' innocuous offerings. On the other hand, it is difficult to account for casual mention of killing monkeys and eating monkey-flesh, even by a brahmin (*J.* 528, *J.* 516, and *J.* 177), particularly as the well-known brahmanical precept *pañca pañca-nakhā bhakkhā* repeated in *J.* 537 would make monkey-flesh

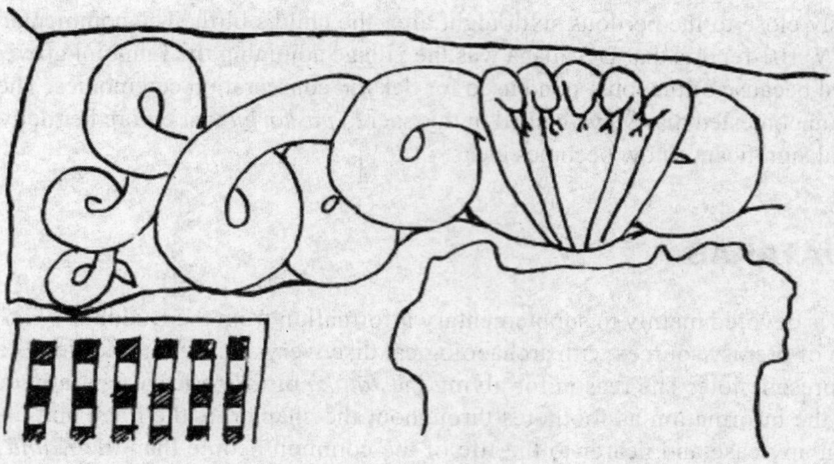

Fig. 3.8. Nāga above cell-door, Ṭhāṇāḷā.

tabu. The lowest Indian forest-tribes (including some Kāthkarīs). do kill and eat monkeys even now, while the *Jātaka* performance is reported as in outlying villages, *paccantagāme;* but the idea would horrify most Indians.

Traders setting out on their travels (*J.* 19) made animal sacrifices to some deity, and vowed to make more if the journey were profitable; the vows were regularly fulfilled. Apparently, such deities were associated with some tree outside the village, sometimes in a grove or the dense jungle. In *J.* 113, men make the sacrifices to the *yakkhas* at cross-ways (*caccara-racchā*) with fish, flesh, and wine in bowls or sherds: this resembles the sacrifice to Rudra and the goblins. (In *J.* 77, king Pasenadi of Kosala is terrified by sixteen ominous dreams in a single night; the brahmins advise him to make extensive blood sacrifices (*yañña*) at every crossways. The location is not specially prominent in this source, but major crossroads were most favoured for meritorious public works (*J.* 31), and sentenced criminals wefe flogged publicly at crossings). In fact, the *yakkhas* often ate human beings (among them unwary traders) who entered certain localities which Vessavaṇa as the chief of the demons had assigned to a particular *yakkha* or demoness. Many *Jātakas* narrate how the Bodhisattva converted such goblins to a simpler diet and kindlier way of life, which has to be interpreted to mean that human sacrifice went out of general fashion (except among forest tribes) before the time of the Buddha. The specially cruel warrior-king makes sacrifice of kṣatriya prisoners to a Nigrodha (*Ficus Indica*) tree's deity in *J.* 353 in order to take the besieged city of Taxila. The captive's eyes were plucked out, sides ripped open, entrails hung on the tree, blood to the level of five fingers poured out by the trunk (or five finger-marks drawn in blood like the 'Five Pāṇḍavas' of rustic shrines), and the five kinds of human flesh (organs) specially offered to the deity. In *J.* 537, the Nigrodha tree outside the market-town of Kammāsdamma received very similar sacrifice, but was afterwards railed off, with the right to simpler 'principal' offerings. The historical existence of this Kammāsadamma in Kuru-land (Delhi-Meerut) is attested by the Buddha Gotama's having preached there (*Dīgha-Nikāya* 15 and 22 as well as *Majjhima-N.* 75 & 106). This custom of establishing cults for tamed demons as senior recipients of reasonable sacrifices is further confirmed by *J.* 398 where *Makhādeva*, a demon of the same kind of tree, is set up to receive sacrifice outside the city gate; and similarly by J. 6, *J.* 155. &c. However, human sacrifice continued as a desperate expedient, obligatory for some purposes. The king in *J.* 481 orders a brahmin to be sacrificed at the foundations of a city gate—a custom which survived in slightly changed form to the 18th century. It is certain that the monks in the south knew earlier versions of these stories, which were further encouragement to preach against the animal-and perhaps the human sacrifices that were made to goddesses near cave-sites. But the deity would be given a less gruesome cult, not far away, like Fa-hsien's *nāga* at Samkasyā.

Professional armed guides who could be hired to see the caravan through dangerous wilderness still existed when *J.* 265 was drafted. This is in the tradition of the *Jaiminīya Brāhmaṇa* 2.423–4, where such guides over limited stretches of territory are mentioned (cf. W. Rau: *Staat und Gesellschaft im alten Indien;* Wiesbaden 1957, p. 30, p. 52). Among the various low professions that contemporary brahmins followed (*J.* 495, stanzas 255–6), is that of convoying the caravans, arms in hand: *asi-commaṃ gahētvāna khaggam paggahya brāmanā/vessa-pathesu tiṭṭhanti, sattham abbāhayantica.* They are called *samā gopa-nisādehi*, which passed the commentator's and translators' comprehension, being equated to 'shepherds and barbarians'. The actual meaning is quite clear from the *Jaiminīya Brāhmaṇa* passages; these brahmins are like those who guard (caravans) against the forest-savages'. The caravaneers ran the danger of attack in the wilderness, from brigands whose presence would be later discovered by the *pāsāṇa-muggara* that they had abandoned (J. 76, 83, 414). The word is taken as a compound for 'sticks and stones', but *ayo-muggara* means iron mace and *pāsāna-muggara* must denote (as probably in *J.* 220 also) 'stone-headed mace', say the hafted celt whose use by jungle folk was still known or remembered when the *Jātakas* were first set down, but apparently forgotten by the time of the revision, and certainly unknown to the commentators.

This last has some interest because of the missile discus (fig. 1.17) depicted in the Carlleyle-Allchin caves (*MAN* 58. 1958, 207; pp. 153–5) in Mirzapur. Among unusual weapons, the *Jātakas* report the axe-adze (*vāsi-pharasukam; J.* 186), and take-down models of the sword and of the compound ibex-horn bow (*J.* 181). The 'razor-edged wheel-weapon' *khuradhāraṃ cakkāvudham* occurs in just two places: the preamble to all *Jātakas* where the Adversary Māra (equated to Namuci in *J.* 536; *SN* 439, and "Kṛṣṇa" too as "dark demon") hurls one at the Buddha about to reach enlightenment; it turns into a flower garland without causing hurt. Secondly, we find it in the Vāsudeva-Kaṃsa story, *J.* 454. Otherwise, the sharp wheel is barely mentioned, and then only as a magic instrument of torture, e.g. *J.* 104, where it revolves upon the head of some overgreedy wretch. Inasmuch as the Mirzapur charioteer as depicted holds the wheel he is about to throw by its rim, it follows that the whole rim was not sharp; on the other hand, its revolving painfully upon the head of the damned would mean that there were sharp blades along the spokes as well, whether or not any part of the rim had a cutting edge. The date of the cave-painting should be about 1000–800 BC, for the region was settled apparently under the name Dakkhiṇāgiri (*J.* 39, *J.* 268; *SN*. 4th *sutta*) by the time of the Buddha, who preached there.

This brings us to the question of Rummin-deī. P. C. Mukerji (*Antiquities in the Tarai, Nepal;* Arch. Sur. Ind. Imp. Ser. XXVI, pt. I, Calcutta 1901) made a careful report correcting A. Führer's supposed exploration (reported in: *Buddha Sakyamuni's Birthplace in the Nepalese Tarai*, Allahabad 1897, later withdrawn from circulation). He notes that the deity is a 'local goddess of some celebrity', which apparently means that the name occurs in several localities. His map actually shows another Rummin-deī in Indian territory, about 5 miles S. by W. of frontier post no. 66. (See also fig. 3.9). The shrine at the Buddha's birthplace (p. 34) received and perhaps still receives 'offerings of eatables, goats and fowls'. An alternative local name for the same goddess is Rūpā-devī, apparently in reference to her beautiful appearance. Though this is not found in the *Jātakas*, we do find there an obscure word *rummi* applied specially to the appearance of a grim ascetic (*J.* 488, *gāthā* 118: also Fausböll 6.194). The derivation might be from the Sanskrit *rumra*, but not from *rukmin.* So, there is an excellent chance of the name Luṃbini having originally been the adjective *rummini* for some dread goddess, gruesome and beautiful at the same time, like so many tribal Mothers. The *Suttanipāṭa* says that the Buddha was born 'in a village of the Sakyans, in the Luṃbini *janapada*': *Sakyānaṃ gāme janapade Lumbineyye* (*SN* 683). This line in the oldest surviving Buddhist document interchanges the names of the village and its *janapada*, but must be taken as it stands. The *janapada* undoubtedly continued to be named after the goddess Luṃbini in local parlance long after the Sakyans had been massacred by Viḍūḍabha. The parallel is with the county name Māval after the goddess Māmālā, seen in the Māmālā-hāra at Kārle from Sātavāhana inscriptions. The plural aniconic representation holds in both cases. The actual Luṃbini goddess 'is represented by a collection of broken sculptures of antiquity', apparently including fragments of the nativity scene (fig. 3.10). But Mukerji took the Buddha's mother Māyā as a Koliyan, presumably after the late *Mahāvastu* tradition. This is impossible, for the Sakyas were too proud to marry outside the tribe. They even fobbed off king Pasenadi's demand for a Sakya bride with the daughter of a slave woman. This deceit was ultimately to cost them dear. Māyā's sister Mahāpajāpatī Gotamī, the stepmother who reared the infant Buddha, has old *gāthās* in her name where she declares herself to be the daughter of the Sakya Añjana and his wife Sulakkhaṇā.

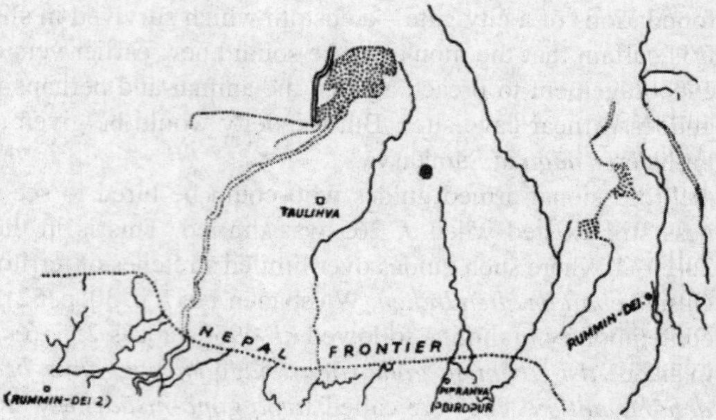

Fig. 3.9. Sketch map of Sakyan territory; note two Rummin-deī shrines.

Fig. 3.10. Fragments of relief sculpture showing the Buddha's Nativity.

At the time of the older Pāli tradition, and certainly at the time of the Buddha, the Koliyans were just emerging from their primitive tribal stage. Some were followers of the Buddha, and received a share of his relics. Theirs was the only original relic-stūpa that remained undisturbed by Ajātasattu and Asoka, according to Buddhist legends. Yet, a *gāthā* at the end of the *Mahaparinibbāṇa-sutta* says that their share of the Buddha's ashes was worshipped at the Koliyan headquarters Rāma-gāma by the Nāgas, so that some Koliyans remained aborigines. The site of Rāma-gāma could be located not more than 45 miles eastwards from the Rummindeī pillar, probably in the foothills; but that needs some careful archaeology, above the relic-hunters' level. The *Jātakas* tell us of a quarrel between the Sakyas and their Koliya neighbours over diversion of river-water (*J.* 536). Once, the Sakyas even poisoned the water, a practice then regarded as a sin not permissible in warfare among civilized people. The mutual reproaches in *J.* 536 are quite clear. The Koliyans taunted the Sakyas of having intercourse with their sisters, like dogs and jackals. The legend of brother-sister marriage among the Sakyans is sometimes dismissed as a bit of southern rewriting. Older Aryan tradition permitted such marriages, *e.g.* among the Persians, as the story of Cambyses reported by Herodotos shows. Moreover, a man's female first cousins would on occasion count as his 'sisters'. On the other hand, the Koliyans seem to be accused by the Sakyans as still keeping to their tree-totem (Koḷ = *Zizyphus jujuba*), without a real chief (*anātha*) and living more like animals than (food-producing) humans. In any case, Māyā could not have been on her way to Koliyan territory, so that Lumbini was on a road crossing.

The name Māyā cannot be translated as "dangerous illusion" in this case. A second meaning is "love", particularly a mother's love, while Mahāmāyā as the great universal Mother-goddess (*Kālikā-purāṇa* 6.62–8.74) is sometimes identified with Durgā. The two other meanings are easily explained if, at some archaic period, men were lured to their destruction by the priestess who represented or even personified the goddess, but whose male consort had regularly to be sacrificed in some fertility rite. Queen Māyā now being worshipped as the mother-goddess is not so incongruous as it might appear to those who think only of Buddhism's benign message. Mahāyāna Buddhists paid homage to Hārīti, originally a child-eating demoness. In I-tsing's time, she was depicted near Buddhist monastic kitchens; it should be noted that the Śivābaï shrine at Junnar occupies what used to be the kitchen of the cave-group, being adjacent to the dining-hall.

Just one more item from the *Jātakas* is of interest. In *J.* 510 and 513, the demoness who eats little children almost immediately after birth is supposed to have been a former co-wife who made the dying wish against her rival, 'may I be reborn (a demoness) to eat your children'. The implication is that she did not die a natural death, but is likely to have committed suicide in her rage. This is parallel to the Jākhamātā tradition. Whether the temple of Māyā was originally a cultspot for her having died so soon after childbirth is not clear; the structure excavated at Rummin-dei commemorates the nativity, not her decease.

3.7. CĀRUDATTA'S SACRIFICE

We are now in a position to answer the query with which this note began. The crossways were, from the stone age, places where the Mothers were normally worshipped by savages whose nomad tracks met at the junction. The food-*bali* replaces their blood-sacrifices, particularly on dark-sixth and no-moon nights. Cārudatta was the son of a *sārthavāha*, and resident of the merchants' quarter. As such, he must have known the travelling merchants' custom (followed to this day by the few remaining caravaneers) to salute and, if possible, sacrifice to deities passed en route. The most prominent of these wayside cults would naturally be of the Mothers at the cross-roads. Presumably, the ritual propitiation was carried out by pious caravan merchants even when they remained at home. However, nothing prevented any brahmin's adopting it in the manner of the Purāṇas, which have been specially written to justify and even to glorify so many primitive autochthonous rites. This was a regular mechanism for assimilation, and acculturation.

NOTES TO CHAPTER 3

For the background: V. S. Sukṭhaṇkar, *Studies in Bhāsa*: Memorial Edition (Poona, 1945) Vol. II. pp. 81–183 and 347–352; (or *Q. J. Mythic. Soc.* 1919, and *JAOS*. 42.59.74); chapters 2 and 8 of my *Introduction to the Study of Indian History* (Bombay, 1956).

1. P. V. Kāṇe: *History Of The Dharmaśāstra* (Poona, Bhāṇḍārkar Oriental Research Institute); particularly Vol. 2, 1941.
2. A. Berriedale Keith: *Religion And Philosophy Of the Veda*; Harvard Oriental Series, Vols. 31–2 (1925); p. 428; see also pp. 145, 239, 322, 414 and 426 for passing reference to trifling magic rites at the crossways, the haunts of evil spirits occasionally of their leader Rudra.
3. D. D. Kosambi: *The origin of brahmin gotras: JBBRAS*, 26, 1950, 21–80, particularly the final section on survivals of mother-right in the Ṛgveda.
4. The gloss *pautana: Mathurā-pradeśa* proves that Pūtanā was the special goddess of the Mathurā region.
5. D. D. Kosambi: *Dhenukākaṭa: JASBom* (= *JBBRAS*) 30.1956.50–71, and for the water-goddesses, *Urvaśī & Purūravas, ibid*. 27.1951.1–30.

4 Pilgrim's Progress: A Contribution to the Prehistory of the Western Deccan Plateau

Fieldwork based upon Poona leads to the conclusion that certain rustic traditions and observances in Mahārāṣṭra have their roots in the late stone age. Many nameless village gods have risen from gruesome origins to identification with some respectable brahmin deity. A transformation of the cult seems clearly to reflect a change in its human worshippers, from the food-gathering savage, through pastoralist, to agrarian food-producer. The development was not continuous, nor always in a direct line. Conflict between the gods generally reflects human group-conflict. Divine marriages, acquisition of a family or encourage, and successive incarnations are theological manifestations of social fusion. Such parallel changes in society and religion were repeated in different localities. The apparently senseless myths so illogically put together in our Purāṇas have a peculiar basis in reality. The villagers continue to live under conditions much nearer to those when the traditions and legends were formed; certainly more so than did the brahmins who recorded a fraction of local myth to synthesize it for their own profit.

The continuity of certain cult-spots does not mean that descendants of the original prehistoric tribesmen continued to worship the same god at the same place with, at most, a change of name. Not only ceaseless nomadic movements but famines, migrations, feudal warfare and epidemics confuse any regular sequence. Nevertheless, some continuity of tradition often remained. If the same people failed to return to their previous range, their successors were not too different. It was known that cults had existed in certain places; their restoration in some form was a simple insurance against natural disaster, even when the new immigrants brought their own gods. Newer forms of production, the spread of a money economy, rapid transport, education and growth of employment at distant centers—all these work more effectively to erase the marks that survived millennial development. Nevertheless, some traces are still legible. This attempt to read them before they are completely obliterated may not be without value.

4.1. THE END OF PREHISTORY IN THE DECCAN

By prehistory is generally meant pre-literate history, events which have to be reconstructed without the aid of coeval written documents. Because episodes are not to be reconstructed in the present case, we consider primarily the change from a predominantly food-gathering economy to food production by use of the plough in settled villages. THIS MAY BE DATED FOR OUR REGION TO THE 6TH CENTURY BC.

The *Suttanipāta* (*SN*) is shown by its archaisms to be the oldest surviving work of the Pali Buddhist canon. It contains all identifiable *Discourses* of the Buddha mentioned by name in Asoka's inscriptions. Omitting quite obvious text-criticism, *SN* 976–978 says: A Kosalan brahmin (named) Bāvari came down 'The Southern Trade Route' (*Dakkhiṇā-patha*). He dwelt on the bank of the

Godāvarī river, at the junction with the Mūḷā valley, in the domain of 'The Horse Tribe' (*Assaka*). He and his little group of disciples lived by food-gathering from the ground (*uñcha*, here tubers, mushrooms &c.; later to mean 'gleaning after harvest') and from trees and shrubs (*phala*, in the sense of nuts, fruit, berries). Eventually a considerable village came into being in that locality, and Bāvari was able to perform a great brahminical fire-sacrifice (*mahā-yañño*) with the surplus he could gather from the settlement.

It is obvious from this passage that regular food-production and durable, plough-using village settlement was only beginning to spread in the Deccan at the time. Being too old to go back himself, Bāvari sent his best pupils north to ask deep questions of the Buddha in Upaniṣadic style. The Buddha's reputation had just reached him. The answers were so satisfactory that Bāvari became a convert without ever having seen the Teacher; old Buddhist tradition labels him the most distant follower during the Buddha's life-time. It was reasonable to deduce from this that the emergence of the Western Deccan from prehistory must be placed in the second half of the *6th* century BC.

The Assaka people may be identified with early Sātavāhanas; not then the dynasty but still a tribe. It is known[1] that the horse is connected in some totemic sense with the dynasty. Further information is derived from the route (*SN* 1011 *ff.*) followed by Bāvari's questing pupils. They started from Paiṭhaṇ "of the Assaka" (which lay to the south-east of their hermitage); crossed the Narmadā at Maheśvar, to Ujjain, Gonaddha, Bhilsā, Kosambī (on the Jamunā), Sāketa (Fyzābād, the older Kosalan capital), Sāvatthi (Seṭ-Maheṭ, the contemporary Kosalan capital). Thence they turned eastwards through Kapilavastu (Piprahvā), south to Pāvā, Kuśinārā, Vesālī (Basārh) and the Magadhan capital (Rājgīr), where they found the great Teacher. From Śrāvastī, they obviously followed the principal trade-route of their day, the very track along which the Buddha preached most of his new doctrine. The presumption is therefore strong that they accompanied trade caravans over the entire circuitous route, and that Paiṭhan was the southern terminus. This city was a Sātavāhana capital in historic times. Moreover, *Asaka* was in the Sātavāhana domain, as proved by the Nāsik inscription of Balasiri.[2] Whether or not the Pitinikas of Asokan edicts are 'The Men of Paiṭhaṇ' or the Sātiyaputas the Sātakaṇis does not concern us here.

Brahmins were most generously rewarded by Sātavāhana kings for their fire-sacrifices, as we learn from the long Nāṇeghāt inscription.[3] Bāvari started a tradition that grew. Indeed, the stretch from Tokā-Pravarāsaṅgam to Nevāsā remained a peculiarly sacred region for brahmins throughout history. Excavations[4] at Nevāsā and opposite Maheśvar prove some interrupted occupation from the early second millennium BC, but nothing to indicate steady growth towards extensive food production. The first Sātavāhana rulers could hardly have been worthy of any royal status or title before the second century BC. The point is worth developing in some detail.

A piece of wood from the ceiling beams of great Caitya cave at Kārle was dated[5] by the British Museum's radiocarbon laboratory at 280 BC with a standard deviation of 150 years in either direction. This means a chance of less than one in forty that the woodwork is later than 20 AD; any possible effect of fungus growth and damp further reduces the probability for a late date. The 3rd century BC is the most likely period for Kārle; the caves in the portion now collapsed may even have been a century earlier. Stylistic arguments do not affect this, for pillars were often roughed out. to be finished later as donations became available (*e.g.* the Pāle caves near Mahāḍ, and the pillars behind the Kārle Caitya); the richer donors could have whole new cells added. The first known royal donation[6] to the Order at Karle (by Uṣavadāta) is dated approximately 120 AD. This means that the great wealth represented by the cave monasteries derived from traders and from the highly profitable long-distance trade in special commodities from the north. The Greek settlement at Dhenukākaṭa[6] and an unmistakable sphinx on the right 13th pillar (fig. 4.1) indicate some overseas connections at about the beginning of the Christian era. This trade may have come through the west-coast harbours (Broach, Sopārā, Kalyāṇ, Thāṇā, Chãul, Dharamtar) but the goods had to be carried into the Deccan proper by pack-animals. Coastal forests, the sheer Deccan scarp and rugged valleys interdicted bullock-cart traffic. The monasteries, as we know from Chinese records of the same sects (*e. g.* the Mahāsaṁghikas at Kārle), were not only important customers but acted directly or through associated merchants and guilds as major banking houses and supply depots. In spite of their location on the trade-routes, no cities developed in the immediate vicinity—with the exception of Junnar. This city, whose name is presumably corrupted from the epithet *jūrṇa-nagara* = 'The Old City', was probably the Tagara[7] of the *Periplus* and Ptolemy; its development as a convenient distribution center in the Deccan was made possible by the Nāṇeghaṭ pass and the narrow but easily cleared Kukḍī river valley.

Fig. 4.1. The Sphinx (on pedestal); rt. 13th pillar, Caitya cave, Kārle.

The monasteries were a main stimulus to local food-production, not just the end-product of the new mode. Under the conditions of the Deccan, which has neither a loess corridor nor a river flowing through some alluvial desert, agriculture on any considerable scale means knowledge of the cheap metal iron. The famous black soil is not amenable to cultivation without the heavy plough; the forest could not have been usefully cleared by slash-and-burn methods alone except for meagre patches high up the hills. Iron is found in plenty in Dharwar outcrops and near the coast, but the technique of reducing the ores and forging the metal came with the northern traders and missionaries in the first half of the first millienium BC. The oldest ploughs must also have come from the north. The model seen in Kuṣāṇa sculptures (fig. 4.2) is unquestionably the prototype of a plough; with curved yoke-pole, flat mould-board and vertical handle still to be seen in parts of the Deccan (fig. 4.3). This is so rare that it does not occur among the numerous types exhibited at the Agricultural College, Poona. The places where it is in use (Dehū-Cākaṇ; Junnar) were first developed under Buddhist influence; this particular implement survives only where the soil is not too heavy. Proper cultivation of the best Deccan soil needs eight to twelve oxen at the yoke, even with a modern steel plough. This is in strong contrast with the alluvial soil of the great northern river-valleys, and the loess areas in Gujarāt.

Fig. 4.2. Kuṣāṇa plough with vertical handle, curved yoke-pole, and flat mould-board.

To sum up: Food production became the dominant form in the Western Deccan during the second half of the 6th century BC. The impetus came from the North, whence was derived the knowledge of iron, of the heavy plough, and of useful crops. Kingship developed locally after penetration by trade caravans and Buddhist monasteries; indeed it was made possible only by changes in the instruments of production. Trade meant accumulation of new property which made the chiefs independent of the tribe. Metals enabled the king and his nobles to develop into a select class of armed warriors who entered upon a career of conquest. The brahmins, with their caste system and Vedic sacrifices, provided a new social theory which raised these warriors above the rest of the tribe, as a privileged caste. Finally, plough agriculture led to a vastly superior food-supply with a concomitant jump in the total population. Those who continued to live as food-gatherers were rapidly outnumbered, eventually to become low marginal castes unless they died out altogether. The generosity of the kings to monasteries and to the brahmins has a clear, logical foundation in the changed mode of production.

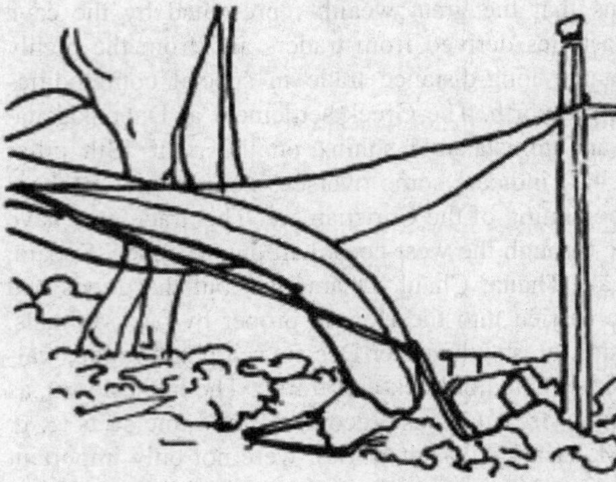

Fig. 4.3. Modern plough on Kuṣāṇa model, in use at Junnar.

4.2. CULT MIGRATIONS, THE GODDESSES AND MEGALITHS

Kāḷūbāī, The Dark Lady, is represented all over Mahārāṣṭra by red-daubed aniconic stones called *tāndaḷā* (shaped like a grain of rice) which do for any primitive deity without distinction. Accretion of wealth (automatically followed by brahmin priests) often transforms her into Kālikā, a form of Durgā. The center of the Kāḷūbāī cult is now at Māṇḍhardev, a peak on a high plateau nine miles south-west of Śirvaḷ. The annual fair in December attracts over 50,000 pilgrims in spite of distance, difficult access, and quite inadequate water supply. It has not yet been possible to explore the long, narrow plateau (which extends towards Wāī) for stone-age remnants. A temple in so high and distant a place is characteristic of cults that came into fashion in the high feudal period. The masculine god's name for the site may indicate a pastoralist phase.

The cult of Tukāī disseminates from a center at the village of Koṇḍaṇpūr, at the foot of Siṃhagad fort. Though the great village fair at Mārgasīrṣa (November) is well attended, the original cult-site is known to be a spring on the cliff Rāma-kaḍā about five miles away, beyond the village of Kalyan. The goddess came down with a devotee Hīrā-bāī, whose memorial at the entrance to the temple enclosure also receives some worship. The spring is regarded as the source of the water that flows from a rock just below the Koṇḍaṇpūr temple. The goddess is served not only by ordinary priests but also by *ārādhīs*, men who dress and live as women, though not castrated like the Pavayās, nor catamites. They attend upon her at Koṇḍaṇpūr and Rāma-kaḍā on special days, and carry her metal image (usually

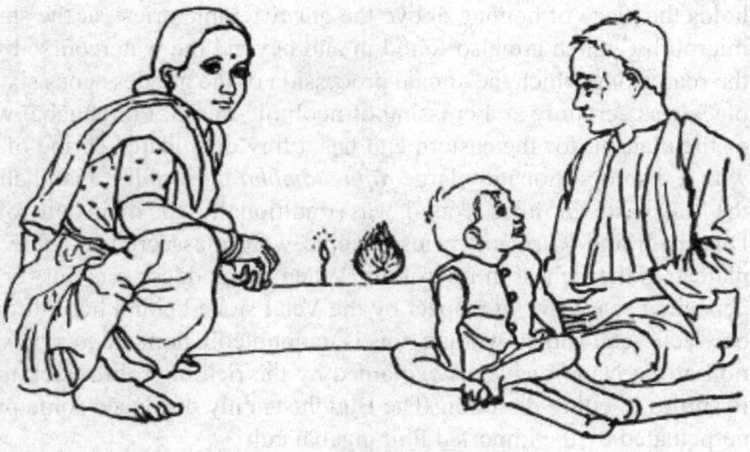
Fig. 4.4. Koḷī child being dedicated to the great *stūpa* as Yamāī, Kārle Caitya cave.

a mask) at Poona, or at festivals in honour of any popular goddess. The origin or motivation of this institution, so reminiscent of foreign cults in Asia Minor, Malta, and of the Mater Idaea at Rome, is not known. Though she is identified with Ambā-bāī, or made into a "sister' of the great goddess of Tuḷajāpūr upon whom well-developed Mother-goddess cults in this part of the world ultimately focus, it is notable that Ambābāī at Paṇḍharpūr (with a *Mahiṣāsura-mardinī* image) has female *āradhanīs*, who are also low-class prostitutes. They not only wait upon the goddess, but have an extraordinary torch-dance and are supposedly accompanied by the goddess whenever they dance along the via sacra, whether the image is taken out or not. On the other hand, male priest—chiefs among several tribe-castes (Pārdhīs, Tigaḷas, &c.) have to dress up as women for special worship. The oldest of our spring festivals, the obscene *hoḷī* saturnalia, generally included a *koḷīn*, a man dressed as a woman, among the dancers about the fire. Finally, elders from the first settler families of Koṇḍapūr still make an annual pilgrimage to their real patron goddess, the Navalāī located 12 miles up the valley from Wāī. This was the place from which Koṇḍanpūr was colonized at an unknown date, according to village tradition. This principal Tukāī cult was presumably absorbed with the aborigines near Rāma-kaḍā; a few Tukāīs (Ākurḍī, Roṭī, &c) are directly identified with the Great Goddess of Tuḷājapūr, for the local people have forgotten, or never heard of Koṇḍaṇpūr.

Yamāī is supposed by Mahārāṣṭrian peasants to have originated at Śivrī, four miles on the Jejuri road from Sāsvaḍ. The Son-Koḷīs of Bombay (coastal fishermen, not to be confused with tribal Koḷīs from the hills) pay their considerable, voluntary, annual tribute only to the Yamāī by the Caitya cave at Kārle. She is identified by these Koḷīs with the great Caitya itself (fig. 4.4), not with the Śivrī goddess—of whom the Son-Koḷīs have never heard. Several other Yamāīs in Mahārāṣṭra have local respect; the Yamāī of Kaṇesar near Pābaḷ is slightly better known. The minor goddesses Karajāī, Khokhlāī, &c. are also known in more than one village, but the connection between the places is usually obscure.

The goddess of Kurkumbh, Phiraṅgāī, whose representatives appear as far away as Hivre (above Sāsvaḍ) and in the once Buddhist caves at Nānolī beyond the military depot of Dehū, is one of three great 'Sisters' (the others being the Devī of Tuḷajāpūr, and the Ambā-bāī of Rāśīṇ). The Poona-Sholapur road leads to the medieval shrine in a rather neglected village. The original site of Phiraṅgāī's advent from Tuḷajāpūr was on the plateau back of the village, to which she accompanied a devotee of the barber caste. The grateful devotee had himself beheaded in sacrifice to the goddess on a spot which is still marked with his *pādukā* (footprints) and by a crude representation of the goddess. The cult-object in the later hill-top temple is a shapeless *tāndaḷā*. The barber caste still holds the place of honour, above the *gurav* temple priest, at the shrine. The plateau is littered with microliths, which are also found in and beyond the watercourse by the village, and by the side of the road along which the annual procession of the goddess goes six miles to the river at Dhoṇḍ. The place was certainly at a crossing of neolithic tracks. Phiraṅgābāī was not the first divine occupant of the plateau, for the eastern end has a tiny dilapidated shrine of the unusual goddess Jhanjhanī, with a disproportionately large *dīpa-stambha* light-pillar. Jhanjhanī, still worshipped by people of the Māḷī caste for miles around, was (traditionally) the main deity of two extinct villages just below: Dharmadi and Kurmaḍī, whose people were massacred in some forgotten raid. That end of the plateau is the richest in microliths. When the goddess sets out for the riverside, the *pālkhī* is first deposited as a mark of respect by the Vetāl stone behind her hilltop temple. In view of the enmity between Vetāḷ and all women, this is undoubtedly homage to a previous deity of the spot. The location of the Nānolī caves is explained by the rich microlith track that passes just below, extending for miles in either direction. The Buddhists only displaced some primitive deity whose memory is perpetuated by the imported Phiraṅgābāī cult.

The most interesting goddess Bolhāï of Vāḍeṃ-Ghoḍeṃ, shows the dangers of taking living tradition directly back into prehistory and illustrates the complex nature of prehistoric movements. The Vājī ('Horse') family of Pācaṇe-Pusaṇe west of the Paünā river claims and enjoys seniority among her worshippers, though the Khādves of Lohogāo and Magars ('Crocodile') of Haḍapsar have nearly equal rank. The Bolhāï cult is negligible at Pusaṇe and absent from Lohogāo, Haḍapsar or the Paünā river basin. The present 18th century temple of Bolhāī (built or rebuilt by the Gaekwars) has replaced some older shrine to other deities, as proved by discarded fragments of beautiful carvings. The primitive image of Bolhāī has terrifying inlaid eyes and bared teeth, but hardly any other features; the icon taken out in procession is a fine late-medieval Pārvatī in brass alloy. A previous temple is still on the hillside to the rear, with a relief in the form of *Mahiṣa-mardinī*. This location has neither microliths nor other marks of prehistoric occupation whereas the present temple settlement was on a great megalithic site, demolished by the modern construction, though a significant number of microliths are still to be found. The still earlier traditional site, Bolhāī's 'kitchen', shows a striking deposit of microliths; it lay at the junction of several prehistoric tracks which may still be traced. Bolhāī first appeared here, according to her priests, and was persuaded to move to the present temple by her 'brothers', the Five Pāṇḍavas. The main cult-object at the Kitchen is completely open, unenclosed, and difficult to associate with a purely mesolithic economy. This is the *ghat-śīḷ* = *ghaṭā-śilā* = *pot-stone*, a horizontal basalt slab (fig. 4.5) roughly 7′ × 4′ with an average thickness of two feet. Though regarded as natural, it has been brought from a distance, dressed to a certain extent (without metal tools) and mounted by human labour on a boulder of slightly greater size. On the northern face is an engraved double circle, about a foot in outer diameter and not perfectly drawn; this is still daubed with minium. Under a crude arched cavity in the cap stone is a rounded oval stone in a hollow made in the wedge which keeps the cap-stone in position. This stone, coated in red, is supposedly the original goddess. The slab has numerous fist-sized lumps of basalt placed about its rim, each in a hollow of its own. In the center of the top face is a much deeper depression about 18″ across holding a loose egg-shaped stone (fig. 4.6); another, slightly smaller, is on the south side, in the boulder used as base. These stones are smooth and rounded; all the 'cups' were made or at least enlarged to their present size by rolling the stones (and perhaps many predecessors) about, like a short, heavy pestle in its mortar. Bolhai's 'stove' some distance from the pot-stone, was at one time such a cup till the rim was broken away by accident or design. Many ovals surround the kitchen and megalithic piles stretch to the north.

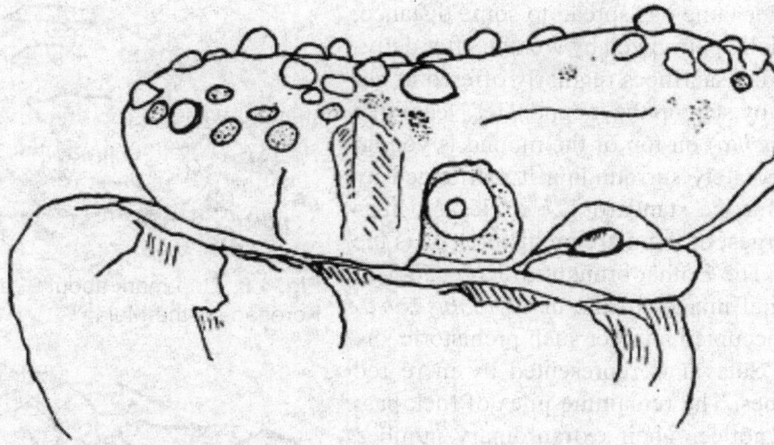

Fig. 4.5. The pot-stone, with original Bolhāī shrine under arch to the right.

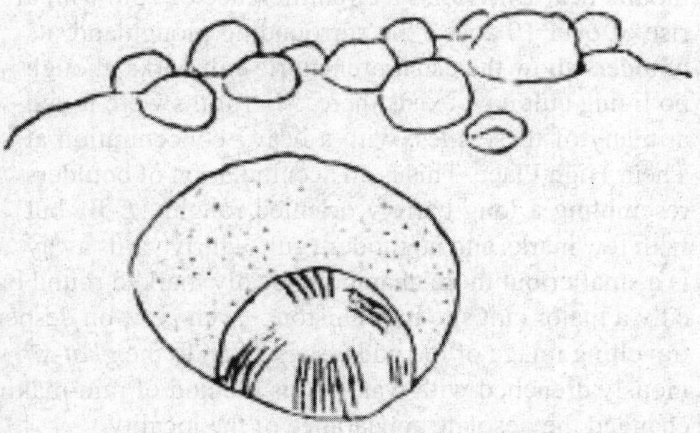

Fig. 4.6. Cup and roller, top of cap-stone, Bolhāī's shrine.

Bolhāī did migrate, though not with the Vājīs, whose seniority derives from their joining and reviving a cult long fallen into desuetude. The comparatively modern Bolhāīs set up at Poona and Sāsvad owe their transfer primarily to local butchers. But a few Bolhāīs are found along the old track which became a trade route, e.g Koregão-Mūḷ and Corācī-Āḷandī. (This continues into the Karhā valley, where megaliths are scarce; but the goddess Borzāí occupies a megalithic site on the margin of that valley above Sonori and below Malhārgaḍ, whether or not related to Bolhai or to the original migration). Tumuli piled with large basalt rocks are feature of this route; several dozens lie on the south bank of the Muḷā. Though in disrepair, and not recognized by the peasants as the handiwork of human beings, these mounds are clearly artificial. Dolmens (fig.4.7) with cap-stones, cup-marks (the largest at Nāyagão 2′ 10″ × 1′ 10″) no longer containing the pestle-stones (fig. 4.8); engraved ovals sometimes six feet on the longer diameter (fig. 4.9) and often of several lines one within the other that run over two or three faces of a boulder—these are all unmistakable signs of prehistoric superstition, completely forgotten by the peasantry. Neither the graven lines nor such boulders or slabs as have been dressed show any mark of metal tools, with the exception of the few recently broken up for dykes or building materials. Wherever a strong modern cult survives at such a locus, it is of a mother-goddess. The best known after Bolhāī is the Saṭavāī in the area of

Fig. 4.7. Dolmen, Nāyagão; cap-stone nearly 4′ in length.

Theūr village. Her fame has spread to some distance, and she is especially patronized by women after delivery. Blood from the sacrifices regularly offered to her is sprinkled step by step up the mound. Her Neem tree (a *Melia azadirachta*) on top of the mound is young, the stones immediately surrounding it rearranged by the peasantry. But the standard 12″ circle and lines graven on the largest of them are prehistoric, as is the whole megalith. The Bolhāī brought to Koregāo-Mūḷ with modern relief images of the usual *Mahiṣāsura-mardinī* type reoccupied another such prehistoric site while inconless Satavāī is represented by mere red spots on the stones. The remaining piles of rock pass without cult or notice. Their extraordinary number, even more than their shape, is reminiscent of the the round barrows on Salisbury plain. An impressive mound near Bhivri has a circumference of 250′ with a rise of over 10 above the surrounding ploughland; its boulders show the usual prehistoric cultmarks, though no living cult now exists there. Microliths were found at many of these sites, with a heavy concentration at Theūr High Place. This is an accumulation of boulders resembling a long barrow oriented roughly *E-W*, but with few marks and no modern cult. Thirty yards away is a smaller but more characteristically marked round boulder-pile. Bolhāī's Kitchen was undoubtedly a major cult site in prehistory. Even now, on desperate occasions when the monsoon fails, the travelling image of the goddess is taken to the *ghaṭ-śīḷ*, worship offered, and the cap-stone ceremoniously drenched with water. This method of rain-making, though claimed to be infallible, has not changed the desolate appearance of the locality.

Fig. 4.8. Cup-mark about 9″ across, at Koregāo-on-the-Muḷā.

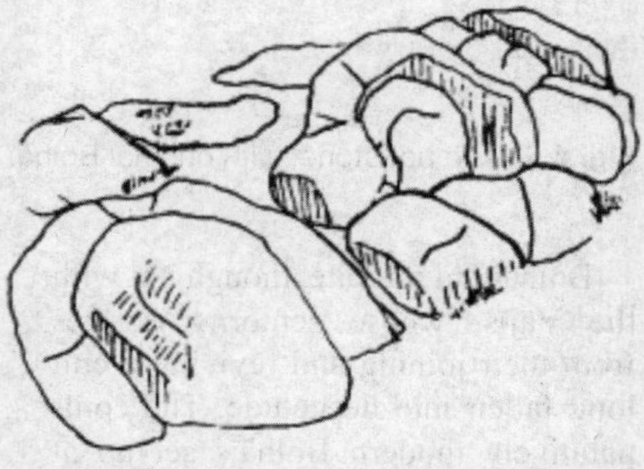

Fig. 4.9. Deep-graven ovals; Theūr khiḷā.

The cap-stone of Bolhāī's first altar, being a basalt slab of high quality supported only at a few points of contact, rings like a clear bell when struck. The bell-tone issues also when any of the pestle stones on this slab is rubbed around in its cup. Tradition has it that the ringing sound was heard not only from the *ghat-śīḷ* as at present but issued simultaneously by the goddess's image a mile away, whenever the main pestle-stone was rolled about in its large cup at the center of the slab top. This was the signal that the goddess allowed her worship to begin. That the miraculous transfer of sound no longer takes place is ascribed to the prehistoric altar having been defiled by the touch of some unknown woman in her courses who thus broke the menstrual tabu. However, the explanation that the cups are substitutes for bells cannot be accepted. The large cup-and-pestle at the *SE* end of the bed-stone does not give out any such sound. The many boulders elsewhere which show the cup-marks are all likewise dumb. The cup and pestle are unlikely to have been a kitchen implement. The *ragāḍā* now used in Mahārāṣṭra does resemble this, but is known to be a comparatively recent import from the Southeast (Āndhra and Karnātaka). The original significance of the cup ritual has now been forgotten.

The patron goddess of Theūr is Mhātryāī='The Aged Mother', whose temple is at the river's edge. She came, according to the oldest peasant women of the village, 'from a long distance, behind the plough'. That her real dwelling is not her shrine, nor any of the old mounds but a natural rock island in the river without ovals, circles or cup-marks seems to prove her late advent. 'Vessels used to appear mysteriously from the river, near that rock', goes the report; this, as well as a similar legend about the Kuraṃjāï of Īnduri may indicate traditional finds of prehistoric pottery looked upon as sacred by the villagers. Curiously enough, a powerful Gaṇeśa cult, one of the eight autochthonous *aṣṭa-vināyakas* of Mahārāṣṭra, sprang up within hail of the High Place, and still attracts numerous pilgrims to the impoverished hamlet. The present Gaṇeśa temple was built or rebuilt by Mādhav Rāo Peshwā; he died at Theūr in 1772, to be accompanied into the next world by his widow Ramābāī whose *satī* monument in tasteless modern style disfigures the riverside. Theūr exemplifies a prehistoric holy locality without continuity of the actual cult. The ruined *khiḷā* to the west of the village Khaṇḍobā has ovals or circles engraved on almost every stone. A casual Mhasobā near the river occupies one of the finest megaliths of the hundred or more in the vicinity of Theūr, through the actual pile is now dilapidated by stone-robbing for the adjacent dyke.

4.3. CULT MIGRATIONS: THE GODS

Three at least of the principal deities worshipped in Mahārāṣṭra go back to pre-Buddhist or early Buddhist times, apart from the Mānmoḍī at Junnar and the Māvalā-devī near Kārle. The *Mahāmāyūrī Mantra*[8] gives a long list of the patron *yakṣas* for various localities. Among them occur at least three names still familiar to Mahārāṣṭrians: Nandī (without Śiva) at Nandikeśvar; Vīr in the Karhāḍ region, and Khaṇḍaka of Paiṭhaṇ. Caravans of Kanarese showmen still travel in old style through Mahārāṣṭra to show off sacred Nandī bulls, slightly trained to perform and at times to help in divination, but without any Śiva image. Khaṇḍaka has undoubtedly grown into Śiva at Paiṭhaṇ proper, but the cult of Khaṇḍobā spread in the Middle Ages, absorbed many others, and is now most concentrated on the mountain at Jejuri, high up the Karhā valley. There are many rival Khaṇḍobās, as at Pāl. The location, and the peculiar worship given to the Khaṇḍobā by the Dhangars will appear in the sequel as of special interest. He has two 'wives', neither of whom normally shares his temple. Of them, Mhāḷsā is still a frightful demoness as well as goddess: the other, Bāṇāi or Bāḷāī, may preserve the memory of the Bāṇa tribe and dynasty known in the 4th century to the early Pallavas and to Mayūraśarman.[9] She is peculiarly a Dhangar deity, as is Khaṇḍobā's 'Prime minister' Hegaḍī. Vīr or Birobā has many temples in Sātārā district and wherever Dhangars have had their seasonal resting places (*vāḍī*) for a long time: *e.g.* Pāṭas and Nātepute. He should be distinguished from the Māṅg-Vīr cults set up by people of the low Māṅg caste to placate the spirit of some dead adult, just as their Ceḍā is a boy's ghost that refuses to be laid unless given a cult. Vīr worship centers somewhere in the Sātārā district, and clay images of this god were and probably still are buried with the Dhangars in western Sātārā.[10] This sheperds' god has not the complexity of Khaṇḍobā, whose cult has the peculiar *Vāghyā* priest, frenzied *Murcḷyā* women attendants, and many other intrusive elements assimilated over the centuries. However, the Vīrabhadra of some Purāṇas, supposedly a general of Śiva's army in battle, may reflect the Vīr cult.

One major shrine of Vīr is at the village of that name, now being flooded by a new dam on the Nīrā river. Curiously enough, the principal god of the village is not Vīr but Mhasobā, often pronounced Maskobā. Published tradition[11] indicates that the settlement developed with the god's advent in the company of immigrant Dhangar herdsmen from Sonārī in Beḷgaum district, via Kharsuṇḍī near Mhasvaḍ and up the Nīrā river valley. Three distinct stages in the god's progress at Vīr proper are marked by separate temples and their accompanying myths. The main (and final) temple, which received donations in the 18th century from the Marāṭhā king Śāhū, is some three miles above the original site of advent. The real image of the god is still a red-coated *tāndaḷā* stone. The Dhangars gather in great numbers at Vīr, twice a year, to worship their Great Lord: at *Dasarā* for commencement of the annual transhumance with their sheep; and for ten days in *Māgha* (February) when a tremendous slaughter of sheep and goats terminates the principal festival. Village clans, however, gained their seniority by sacrificing a boy each to the god. The place of this human sacrifice is still marked by a monument and by a cult, though the sacrifice has been moderated by the addition of a legend that the god obligingly brought the children back to life. The special prerogative of *śids* (*siddhas*) chosen from these privileged families is the right to undergo the ordeal at the Māgha festival. This consists of slashing themselves with sharp swords. No blood is supposed to flow unless the celebrant has been defiled by some forbidden, sinful act. When genuine inspiration is proved by such immunity, the *siddha* has prophetic insight for a brief spell. One leading family has a further privilege, namely of having its principle male swung around the special post (*bagāḍ*) by sharp hooks; these are no longer passed through the muscles of the loins, but slipped under the sash.

The published account of Maskobā's travels and settling down at Vir relates nothing about his being accompanied by Jogūbāī. Nor is anything said as to how and when they came to be married. Maskobā, Bhairav, Khaṇḍobā, Vetāl, Mhātobā are all equated or related to Śiva in various mutually contradictory ways. The fact that Tukāī, to whom Maskobā has to pay annual homage, crushes Mahiṣāsura-Mhasobā on the adjacent hillock has passed without comment. Moreover, the villagers to whom this is pointed out profess themselves unable to see it, though the relief image shows the buffalo-demon being quite unmistakably crushed. The few microliths at Vīr are by Tukāī's shrine; the trade route from the port of Mahāḍ could not have been properly developed till the Gupta-Vākāṭaka period. Maskobā is a comparatively recent intruder.

The Mhātobā of Kotharūḍ village (now swallowed up by Poona city) has also Jogūbāī for his wife. His original locus is shown as a red-daubed boulder over two miles away, on the hill-top. There he rested, having come with "herdsmen" from Vākaḍ on the Muḷā river. The people of Vākaḍ have a temple to Mhātobā-Jogūbāī (older than 1678 AD) but recognize the seniority of Hiṃjavaḍī village a mile further. Hiṃjavaḍī has a tiny Mhātobā shrine, with a relief of Bhairav type on horseback, on a little knoll at the foot of which are found microliths of good quality, almost the only such deposit in the whole area. Remarkably enough, the Hiṃjavaḍī Mhātobā has no consort at all! This premier Mhātobā came from the Koṅkaṇ. He caused some virgins to be drowned in a deep pool of the river, near a spot now marked by a little temple close to the boundary of the two villages. Then he was obliged to invite the junior Mhātobā (his double) from Cās Kamān to the north (six miles from Kheḍ) and to set him up at Vākaḍ. The wood for the hook-swinging post and beam, however, has still to be brought from Bārpe, higher up in the Muḷā valley, presumably on the senior god's route. Jogūbāī has obviously been accepted as substitute for the pre-Mhātobā goddess of Hiṃjovaḍī.

Formerly, two human victims were offered to the god every year, at Caitra (April, full moon). The honour was shared between the Jāmbhūḷkar clan of Hiṃjavḍī and the Māṅg caste of the same village; each group selected one representative for the purpose. The place of decapitation and the two slabs where the heads were exhibited and worshipped are still shown. The god had to be taken in procession over the heads. The sacrifice was commuted by the god who appeared in a dream to the last male survivor of the Māṅgs. Now, the Jāmbhūḷkars retain the prerogative to the *bagāḍ* hook-swinging, the hooks still being passed through the loin muscles. The Māṅg representative is honoured by having his thigh slit open. The blood from this operation is used to place a mark upon the god's forehead; the flow from the wound is then magically staunched by charcoal powder and ashes from the altar. The honour of sacrificing the first goat at the annual festival goes to the Muḷūk ('Original') family of Cās-Kamān. Their version is that the 'seven' girls drowned at Vākaḍ were of the Muḷūk clan, kidnapped from Cās-Kamān by Mhātobā himself. The god had come to Cās-Kamān from Vākaḍ for a while, and still has a shrine there by the decayed Muḷūk house. He saw the maidens when they went to pay homage at the spring festival to the Nāga whose shrine still exists by the riverside. The party was visible till Kaḍūs, but disappeared thereafter till Mhātobā reached the pool at Vākaḍ. We may note that the Tyche of Cās-Kamān is still Kuṇḍ-Māūlī, 'Little Mother of the Pool', two furlongs down the river from the Nāga shrine. Her principal worshippers are the semi-aboriginal Koḷīs and she clearly derives from some megalithic deity who might or might not be connected with the rape because of which the Muḷūks derive their seniority. Mhasobā, in front of the shrine, is her 'cart-driver'!

The Vākaḍ-Hiṃjavaḍī god overthrew some Mother-Goddess cult violently, perhaps drowning the priestesses in the river pool. The memorial shrine is known as that of Hirāī-Sitāī, but the supposed number of the College of virgins, seven, is less than the actual number of unshaped stones representing them. That the patron god was really a Mhasobā is proved by several Mhasobā cults (without changed name, or Jogūbāī) set up in their individual fields by farmers of Hiṃjavaḍī and Vākaḍ three of these are close to the temple of the drowned maidens. Mhātobā's second advent with a wife was obviously due to the local demand for a goddess; the pre-Mhātobā people had not been wiped out.

The story of the Umbare Navalākh migration is more straightforward. The patron god Bhairav, called simply Nāth (The Lord) came from the Koṅkaṇ via Ḍhāk near Karjat. The first settlement was on top of the hill back of the village, a long plateau which holds water for at least six months of the year, and where the village cattle still graze. The original Nāth shrine is near the top, above a saddleback pass. The village then moved down to the bottom of the hill; the site is marked by the older Hanumān temple. The final move was a mile further to the riverside, where the village remains to this day about the main Nāth temple. Five hundred years ago, this Umbare was the principal city of the whole region, second only to Junnar. All trade from the Kusūr pass, Bhor Ghāṭ and the passes further down the range enriched it with tolls in transit. No less than twelve stone-built temples survive, plus a large Īd-gāh and a mosque of about the 15th century. The feudal governor's palace has disappeared, except the main gateway; other ruins, never properly investigated, serve to emphasize the full cycle of decay, caused by the nearest road now being six miles away, with a river and several ravines in between. The villagers still make the difficult annual pilgrimage to the impressive cave of Bhairav above Ḍhāk, which takes two complete days each way. Umbare is not a microlith area like the next village Nānolī. There could have been no question here of displacing a strong Mother-goddess cult. Had the place been of any importance as a trade center in the 6th century AD, one would expect to find Buddhist caves in the locality, which is otherwise eminently suitable.

Many other villages besides Umbare show a trend which continued well into historical times, and may be extrapolated with due caution into prehistory. The formation of many villages, let alone their progressive descent to the riverside, could not have been feasible before the iron age in this region. The lowest land was covered by forest and swamp. On the other hand, without an ample supply of metal and a considerable number of villages, no powerful kingdom could exist. The Sātavāhana standing army—strong enough to raid the country as far north as the Gangetic basin, and for constant warfare with neighbours on all sides—implies a regular and ample food surplus from extensive agriculture. Agriculture is now along the river, at the bottom of the valley; but terraces, visible all over the region under discussion, go high up the mountain, often on a slope of more than 30°. Expert handling of the plough is needed here, if indeed the plough can be used at all; but the yield is not, and could never have been, heavy enough to justify the labour. The standard crop on these high 'demarcation terraces', as distinct from the 'levelling terraces' further down, is some coarse grain like *nācṇī* (*Eleusine coracana*), *varī* (*Coix barbata*), the millet *sāvā* (*Panicum frumentaceum*) and the like. These can be cultivated and are still cultivated wherever possible, by slash-and-burn methods, and planted or transplanted into holes punched with a digging stick (*ṭhombā*). The modern chest-high *thombā* is too heavy to need further weighting, but annular stones labelled 'mace-heads' by our archaeologists[14] are undoubtedly prehistoric digging-stick weights. *Sāvā* is the *sāmāka* of *SN* 239, which then grew wild, and could be eaten by the more austere food-gathering ascetics who regarded themselves as above begging alms. Mostly, the high demarcation terraces are under hay. The lower terraces, which often continue the upper without interruption, are level, and under steady cultivation of food grain, normally rice in the wetter regions, and wheat, *jvārī (Holcus sorghum), bājrī (Holcus spicatus*) otherwise. The particular cereal depends upon local conditions, while irrigation (begun mainly in feudal times) makes more than one annual crop possible, with systematic rotation.

4.4. MICROLITH TRACKS

Inasmuch as microliths have often come to light near primitive cult sites, the distribution of such artifacts would be of prime importance for our reconstruction of prehistory. It is remarkable that the loci could not, for the greater part, have been cult-sites or even occupation sites. The best microlith sites form a continuous track with many branches, or several intersecting tracks. Of these, it has been possible to study closely (fig. 4.10) a stretch of about 8 miles near Poona, and selected though interrupted stages over two further ranges: one (nearly to Paṇḍharpūr) about 130 miles to *SE* others about 35 miles to the *NW* and 45 to NE from Poona proper (fig. 4.11). In addition, a long plateau at Poona adjoining the track but about 300 feet higher also yielded microliths, in lesser number, of cruder fabric. We may call this the 'highland' culture, as distinguished from the 'lowland' track. One feature of the lowland tracks is that the surface finds show only microliths without pottery or larger stone tools. As one goes further down the river valleys, the average technique improves; many of the specimens are works of art, some as delicate as fine surgical tools. Excavation and erosion show enough of the underlying soil to prove that there are no occupation layers, nor other artifacts such as pottery. A track normally runs along the bottom of the hill at the margin of the river valley. For the Indrāyaṇī and the Bhīmā, where there is a considerable meander with high ground in the middle of the valley, the track finds a corresponding extension. From Bhaṇḍārā with its stūpa and Buddhist caves favoured by Tukārām, past Nānolī (Phiraṃgāī Buddhist caves) the track is marginal; but its continuation through Sāṅgvī to Kāmbare and Govitrī is on the middle high ground. Theūr with its great river bend and deep pools seems to have been—as it is to this day—a fishing camp as well as cult site, not on the main track. Other fishing camps may be seen, at Kumbharvaḷaṇ on the Karhā and by the burial ground near the Poona Mental Hospital, where a small tributary joined the Muḷā-Muṭhā river. Fishing certainly provided an important supplement to primitive diet.

The shrunken rivers with their silted pools are now so badly overfished as to provide little more than sprats. Yet a look over the bridge at Dehu, where the fish in the deep pool are protected and sometimes fed as sacred, shows that the rivers can still produce Mahseer three to five feet or more long, in large numbers.

However, fishing could not have yielded the lowland microlith culture's principal food supply. The Poona microliths reach their maximum concentration at certain favoured spots, clear of the forest but conveniently near a former

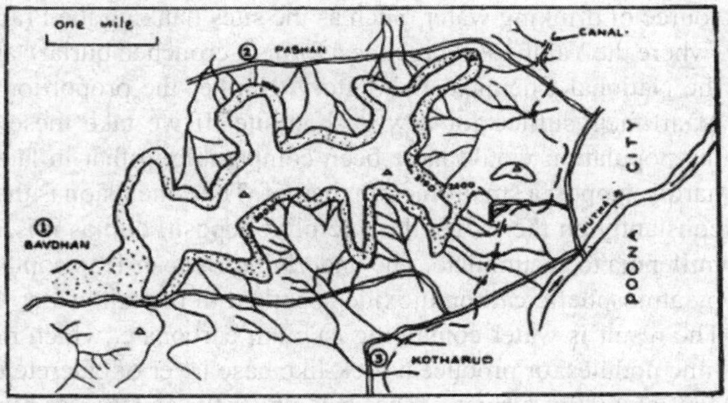

Fig. 4.10. Highland and lowland tracks at Poona. Contours at 2000′ and 2150′ above sea-level shown. The lowland track parallels the former. Triangles mark megalithic sites where modern cults exist.
The above figure is for representation purpose only.

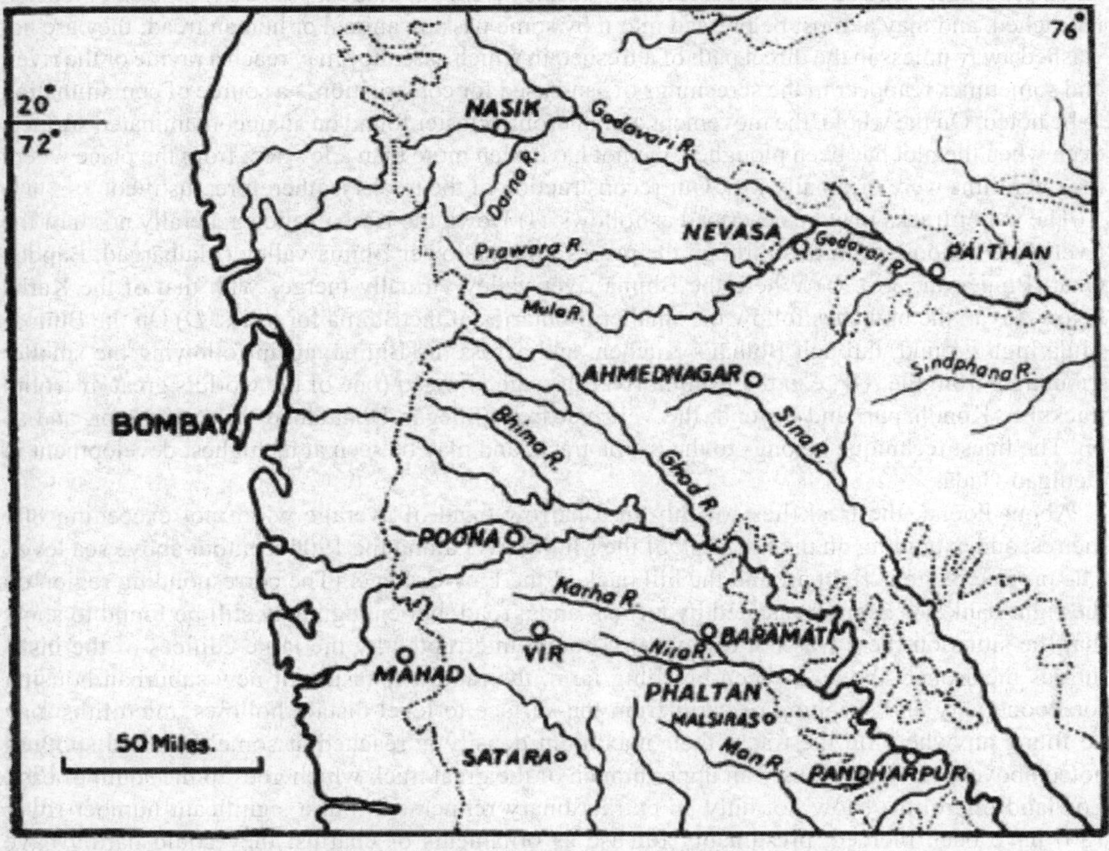

Fig. 4.11. The main area of fieldwork for this chapter. The dotted line gives the 1650′ contour, and closely parallels the great Deccan scarp on the west.
The above figure is for representation purpose only.

source of drinking water. Such as the sites flanking the Prabhat film studio, Vaidvāḍī burial ground (where the Vaidūs still practice a form of crouched burial), and two old springs on the hillside facing the National Chemical Laboratory. Neither the proportion of cores found nor the actual number of artifacts suffice for a workshop site. If we take these places as permanent occupation sites, the population would have been comparable to that in later times, whereas food-gathering could hardly support a small fraction thereof. The conclusion is that these are camp-sites. The people were constantly on the move; the microlith deposit, thin as it is, must have taken not only centuries but millennia to accumulate. The underlying Deccan Trap contains calcium silicate which is acted upon by atmospheric carbon dioxide absorbed in the rain water that percolates through the basalt strata. The result is water containing calcium carbonate, which may deposit lime encrustations, or form lime nodules, or produce a rock-like base layer of calcrete under favourable inundation. Most of it goes along the surface of the rock, under the soil, to rise by capillary action. The lime-impregnated soil thus produced is whiter in colour than the upper layer, and corresponds in its own way to the breccia layer in limestone caverns. With deforestation and negligent farming by a progressively impoverished, demoralized peasantry (both processes became serious at the beginning of this century), the upper soil is washed away, exposing the white earth which resists erosion even when wet and discourages vegetation. Any artifacts above this layer sink gradually down till the calcified soil is reached, and may at most be pressed into it by some passing animal or human tread; they are not washed away unless in the direct path of a freshet, in which case they may reach a ravine or the river, and sometimes reappear in the screenings of sand used for construction—a source of contamination to be noted. On the whole, the movement of a microlith cluster found on an uncontaminated surface, even when the plot has been ploughed, cannot have been more than a few feet from the place where the microliths were originally lost. Our reconstruction of the tracks is, therefore, justified.

The major tracks may be described as follows: *A*) Down the Karhā valley generally north of the river. *B*) Offshoots from this through the passes into the lower Bhīmā valley (Malhārgaḍ, Bāpdev Ghāt, Bhuleśvar, &c). *C*) Where the Bhīmā river valley virtually merges with that of the Karhā below Yavat, the branches follow the smaller tributaries of the Bhīmā for miles. *D*) On the Bhīma-Muḷā high ground, through Bolhāī's Kitchen, and across the Bhīmā, again following the smaller tributaries from the *NW*, e.g. the Kāminī river through Nimgão (one of the world's great microlith tracks) to Koṇḍhāpurī and beyond; the Veḷ river from Taḷegão-Ḍhamdhere up to Kaṇesar, and so on. The finest technique belongs to the Karhā track, and may be seen at its highest development in Deuḷgão-Gāḍā.

About Poona, the track lies roughly in a narrow band of average width not exceeding 800 metres, and extending on the left bank of the Muṭhā river along the 1900′ contour above sea level. The precise range is right around the hill back of the Law College. (The corresponding region on the right bank has been devastated by a canal and a road, but enough may still be found to show that the situation there was not different). Though interrupted by the large edifices of the institutions mentioned above, a sheep-breeding farm, the rapid expansion of new suburban housing for Poona City and stripping of earth from the surface to level distant hollows, microliths may be found anywhere on the track; their maximum density is reached at some favoured spots as noted above. This is obviously an upper branch of the great track which goes to the south of east. Lowland microliths show not only an extraordinary refinement, but a significant number (over 150) have been pierced, presumably for use as ornaments or charms; they could hardly have been drilled through for ease of transport, being so few (about 6 per thousand) and so ordinary.

Every advantage was taken of natural pits, flaws and softer material imbedded in the chalcedony, in boring the holes. If metal were available at the time, one would expect to find beads, or better-shaped microliths. The drilling was presumably accomplished with fine rock points, or bone points with fine sand as abrasive. The largest holes are about 3.5 *mm* in diameter; the smaller (which can only be threaded by a stiff hair or fine wire) need a fine needle to clean, and are often bored through from both sides, to meet at an angle in the middle. A curious circular patch 4 *mm* or so in diameter may be observed about the hole, when the material is translucent chalcedony; the optical index is apparently changed by the heat generated in boring. So far as I know, this is the first time such finds have been announced. They show that the users had an advanced technique, complete mastery of their material, a delicacy of touch that any lapidary would envy, and knowledge of the bow-drill, hence of the bow.

The beautifully made microliths, which often look like scale models of flint tools from other countries, show considerable sophistication. Most of them are standardized parts of compound tools, such as arrowheads, harpoons, sickles; some are delicate knives for gelding and burins for working bone. Many show deposits of foreign matter *after* the tool was made; this would not adhere to the smooth chalcedony without some bonding agent. Tree gum or even better, a mixture of unslaked lime and fresh blood[12] would be ideal for the hafting of such tools, or to build up larger tools from them. The ensemble indicates considerable advance in dressing hides, presumably for containers in the absence of pottery. Not only would the skins be fleshed carefully, but the fibres on the underside would have to be broken without cutting through the skin. This amounts to buckskin tanning without chemicals. Microliths which could split sinews and others which are unquestionably awls are present in sufficient number. Baskets were, presumably, also made with the withes split by microlith tools. This would solve the main problem of any food-gathering economy—the problem of food storage. Hunting, fishing and the harvesting of edible wild grass seeds would supplement the diet. Any agriculture must have been trifling; if they pastured animals of their own, the beasts could not have been larger or more thick-skinned than sheep.

To this day, the Dhangars favour the Karhā margin. They remain only for four months of the monsoon in any fixed place, in small units (*vāḍī*) of a dozen human beings with up to 300 sheep. The *vāḍī* moves on after the rains, and may follow a drover's round of as much as 400 miles, till the next monsoon sets in eight months later. Even then, the herders need not always return to the original residence. The Dhangars preserve one mesolithic custom: they still use flints for gelding their rams. The selected nodule of chalcedony (now of grainier rock) is placed on a basalt anvil, hammered with another heavy lump of basalt, and the sharper fragments, if large enough to be gripped securely by hand, used at once to castrate the rams. There is no retouching of the edge which gives the old microliths their utility; nor are the pieces mounted or hafted. A flint knife thus made has to be boiled with the testicles and thrown away. None are ever kept beyond the first brief period of use, but they are much too large and too crude to contaminate the genuine, beautifully faceted stone-age artifacts—which no Dhangars (or any other rural inhabitants) can recognize as tools or even as artifacts. The process survived (as did the use of flint knives for circumcision among the Jews) simply because the wounds are sterile where metal knives used in the same way mean serious infection.

The Dhangars do not use stone tools for any other purpose; their gods on the march are represented by wands (*kāthī*) topped by coloured strands of wool, stuck in the ground by the camp and worshipped each morning before the sheep are driven out to graze. The actual paths followed by the herds have been shifted by the current agrarian economy. The herders are paid by the farmer in grain or cash for penning the sheep for a night or two on plough-fields, for the valuable fertilizer provided by the droppings. This means a considerable deviation from the original pastures, intensified because of erosion, desiccation, overgrazing and replacement of good fodder grass by spike-grass. Though the caste produced such generals as Malhār Rao Hoḷkar, no professional Dhangar now does any hunting, or uses weapons; their flocks and camps are amply protected by ferocious watchdogs. The wool clip is now sold, whereas they used formerly to make rough blankets (*kambḷī*) out of it, carding, spinning and weaving the annual clip themselves.

The Dhangars whose *vāḍīs* lie nearest the Western Ghāṭs (*e. g.* Jāvaḷī in Sātārā district) move eastwards down the river valley soon after the monsoon sets in. The reason is that excessive damp will rot the hooves of their sheep. From about 100″ near the scarp (and over 200″ on the scarp itself), the precipitation decreases to 12″ or so below Vīr, or the corresponding site in any parallel valley. This means that the original Dhangar life was of ceaseless movement; only land clearing by the peasantry made the four months of fixed residence possible for later sheep herders.

4.5. HIGHLANDERS AND LOWLANDERS

The great annual pilgrimage of the western Deccan is to Paṇḍharpūr. There are really two pilgrimages every year for the *Vārkarī* believers. The first, now the main effort, is on the eleventh day of the waxing moon in *Āṣāḍha* (July); the second on Kārtika (October-November) *ekādaśī* is really the return pilgrimage supposed to start on that day from Paṇḍharpūr. The intervening four months of the rainy season are the Hindu *cāturmāsa* lenten season when travel would be interdicted by strict brahmin precepts. Therefore, the celebrations must have their origin in a pre-agrarian society, for the farmers could not possibly afford to be away from their plough-lands during the early monsoon, when basic farm operations are in hand. Moreover, the Viṭṭhala cult[13] which is the ostensible object of the pilgrimage, is comparatively recent. Jñāneśvar, who went on this pilgrimage in his brief lifetime, nowhere mentions Viṭhobā.

The pilgrimages were originally the seasonal movement of prehistoric lowlanders. The rains set in well before Āṣaḍha *ekādaśī*, so that water and pasturage are available even on the drier parts of the route. On the western range, sheep would be affected by the rot in the heavy rains which would even otherwise make non-agricultural life rather difficult. Deer and other small game would certainly move down the valley, while fishing camps would be useless on flooded streams. Similarly, the return journey from the dry lower reaches of the main river valleys would be pleasant as well as obligatory after the last rains had passed, about a month after *dasarā*. At the upper reaches, grazing and water would be plentiful, the summer heat tolerable, and salt from the seacoast within reach. The prehistoric trade in salt would account for the few coastal microlith sites[14], though this is again my own interpretation. The western coast did not come into its agricultural development till the coconut (of Malayan origin) was introduced, probably late in the first century AD. Salt continues to be a valuable commodity of export from the Koṅkaṇ, to the present day. It is still brought by Lamāṇ pack-caravans up the old roadless passes, to the hinterland.

Apart from the microlith tracks and Dhanger customs, there is considerable support for this reconstruction. Some fifty odd *pālkhī* processions constitute the essential part of the pilgrimage. The palanquins are taken out in the name of various local saints, from as far away as Paiṭhaṇ

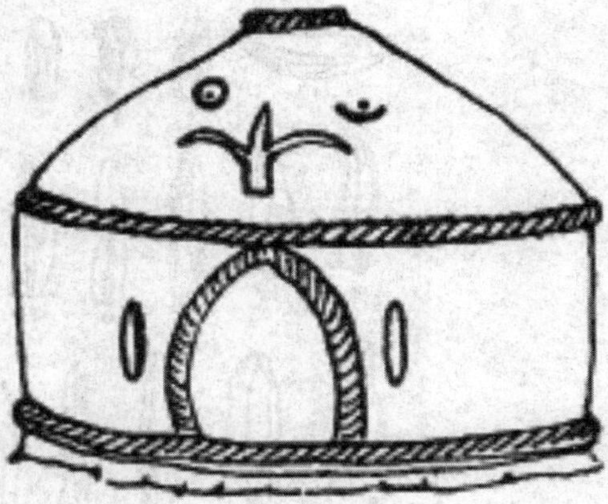

Fig. 4.12. Terra-cotta shrine of Vetāḷ, about 75 cm across, shaped like a soul-house (Barāḍ). Made in the traditional form by some potter, about 50 years ago.

(Eknāth); the organization in this form seems to date from Haibat Bābā at the beginning of the last century. Pilgrims may and do go individually by train (Bārsi Light Railway) or bus (Sholapur Road), or on foot; but the merit is far greater if they join one of these *pālkhis*. The main palanquins from our region are three: that of Jñāneśvar from Āḷandī, Tukārām from Dehū, and Sopān from Sāsvaḍ. The first has been displaced by the change of roads and no longer passes over Bāpdev Ghāṭ, for example. It meets the microlith track at Phaḷṭaṇ, after which the artifacts become common as far as Nātepute. The region known as Sāt Māḷ (between Māḷśiras and Veḷāpūr) again shows microliths. It is notable that all the processions, and not only these three, meet at Vākharī four miles away from Paṇḍharpūr, have their celebrations, and merge into one great parade in order of seniority to the city of Viṭṭhala on the Candrabhāgā river. The real terminus is clearly Vākharī. The other common point for the three main western palanquins is Sāsvaḍ on the Karhā. The *pālkhī* taken in Tukārām's name follows the great microlith track most closely: Sāsvaḍ Ekatpūr, Kothāḷe, Āmbī, Jaḷgāo, Bārāmatī, Saṇsar, Lāsurṇe Reḍ, Sarāṭī, Āklūj, Borgāo, Kuravḷī, Vākharī. Each of these unequal stages takes a day; the whole march lasts a fortnight. The track which shows microliths of the finest technical perfection (fig. 4.13) in great numbers passed approximately five miles to the north through Rūī, between Barhaṇpūr and Gojūbāvī, past Paḍvī, Devaḷgāo-gāḍā and Pārgāo.

Another relic of ancient days may be seen by the pilgrims at Barāḍ, or Khaṇḍāḷī, on the Sopān route. Terracotta shrines (fig. 4.12) to Mhasobā (Khaṇḍāḷī) or to Vetāḷ (Barāḍ) have the form of 'soul-houses' in other countries. No house or hut of the peculiar bell-tent shape is now known in the territory under consideration. The central smoke hole and the two levels of stitches on the wall indicate a movable wigwam structure of some sort, rather solidly constructed. The rolling terrain of the Sāt Māḷ. though under the plough, is clearly fit for nothing but pasturage; its litter of microliths indicates its use as such in prehistory.

If only the pilgrimage from Āḷandī or Dehū to Paṇḍharpūr were the main objective, the logical and easiest route to follow is the Poona-Sholapur road, which passes within sight of the megaliths and up which the goddesses came from Tuḷajāpūr. That no *pālkhī* of any importance takes to this, and that the upper Nīrā valley is poor in microliths shows that the Karhā valley high ground formed the main route of the prehistoric booly, joined by numerous tracks from all directions. There is a good reason for this. The Karhā ground (really a plateau) is higher than the corresponding terrain in the Muḷā-Muthā valley by at least 400 feet, and would therefore be better pasture land on the whole, less dangerous to flocks, and at the same time well watered though better drained. The microlith sites on the right bank of the Muḷā-Muṭhā-Bhīmā complex lie on secondary tracks branching off from the great Karhā track, and overlap the megalith region.

The nearest considerable deposit of hand-axes or large stone tools lies further to the south, near Badāmī.[15] It may be noted in passing that the change of tools corresponds also to that from basalt

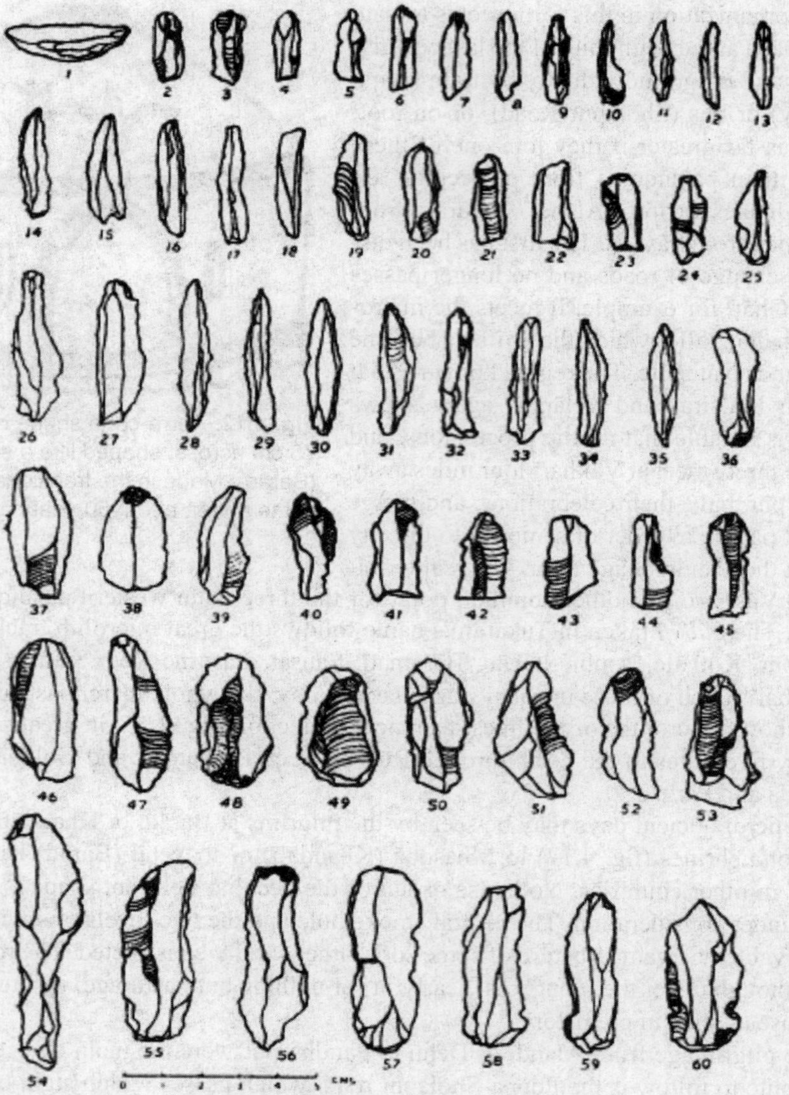

Fig. 4.13. Lowland microliths from the Karhā-Bhīmā divide, near Supā.

to granite for the underlying rock and from an Aryan (Marāṭhā) to Dravidian languages (Kanarese or Telugu). The one carefully investigated site abroad where microliths are found in considerable numbers without pottery or large tools is Jericho.[16] The pre-pottery Jericho *B* stratum which comes closest to our lowland culture goes back apparently to the eighth millennium BC (by C_{14} dating). The *Terī* sand-dune culture on the east coast of India, also purely microlithic and pre-pottery, has reasonably been assigned a date not later than 4000 BC. The Deccan culture described above could have flourished to the iron age, seeing that neither copper nor bronze could have been of much importance on the Karhā track; but then, one would certainly expect to find pottery and larger stone

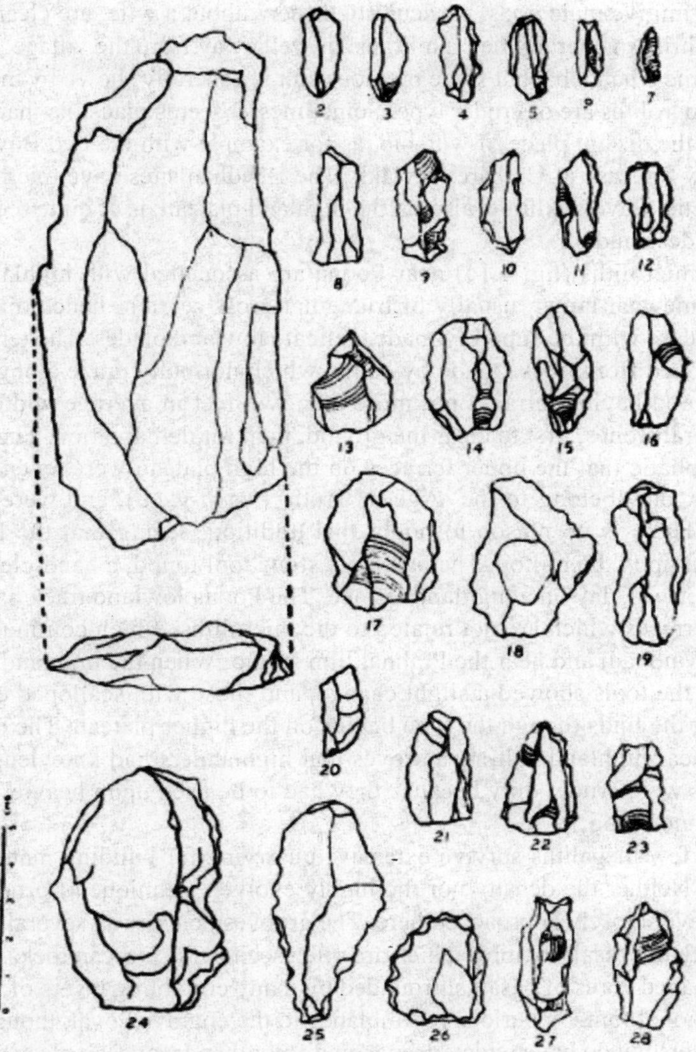

Fig. 4.14. Highland tools from the megalithic plateau on Vetāḷ hill, near Poona. No. 24 is a drilled specimen. Scalloped edge of 26 made by pressure-flaking.

tools. Hence, 4000–8000 BC would be a suitable period, at a rough guess. In the food-gathering stage, a great concourse in Āṣāḍha would have been impossible. With sheep and digging-stick agriculture to supplement the gathered food, the natural limit of the annual monsoon shift would be the rolling pasture lands of the Sāt Māḷ, never under heavy forest. A great modern pilgrimage implies the regular production of a food surplus. The system of agriculture that made this possible would also mean gradual displacement of the people towards good soil and the rivers—hence Paṇḍharpūr.

The Dhangar worship of Mhasobā is a considerable change from the mesolithic. The real deity of the original lowlanders would be the mother goddess, *āī* under whatever name, as for food-gatherers in general. The primitive male gods, particularly those without a wife, are clearly of late highland origin, and their shrines generally lie on hilltops, or well away from the village. They may often be identified with some Khaṇḍobā, but some previous cult is generally shown by microliths at the site. These highland microliths are of cruder type. Sometimes, it seems plausible that the original pastoral village lay by the distant place of worship, as for example with the two Bāvdhāns near Poona, and as was clearly the case at Umbare Navlākh. The Bāvdhān sites have microliths. A Phiraṃgāī cult set up within the Bāvdhān limits also on the highland plateau, is cf quite recent origin, and fell immediately into desuetude.

The highland microliths (fig. 4.14) near Poona are associated with highland terraces. These microliths are somewhat larger, usually of triangular cross-section, hence thicker and with less facets than is the case with the superbly made, delicate lowland blades. The terraces may in some cases have developed from tracks made by cattle, which normally graze along a contour. A little trimming gives good haying terraces not more than two feet in average width. The next step is shoring with natural stones, first to clear the ground, then for demarcation. The oldest peasants at Kotharūḍ are emphatic that the upper terraces on the high plateau were, even when level, never under the plough; they belong to the 'Age of Truth' (*satya-yuga*), and were made by pastoral people (*gavaḷī*). There is no reason to doubt this tradition, seeing that the Kotharūḍ god was originally resident upon the hilltop. The one large stone tool found, a hand-cleaver or chopper of chalcedony (4.14, no. 1) lay on a highland terrace. The Poona lowland track has been interrupted by more recent terraces which are not related to the microliths, which continue beyond the ruins of a terrace as at Vaidvāḍī and near the Prabhāt film studio. When the highland terraces gradually moved downhill, the tools showed a slight change, and those with scalloped edges are specially prominent among the finds though the type begins on the higher plateau. The occasional delicate microlith found near highland cult-sites proves that highlanders had knowledge of refined technique. Their tools were cruder only because they had to be used upon heavier material, presumably cattle hides and wood.

The ruins of a few megaliths survive extensive quarrying for building materials on the Poona highland plateau. Neither the density nor the highly evolved technique of grooving that one sees about Theūr was ever closely approached here. The grooves do exist on several stones, and are not to be confused with the basalt 'bombs' which are often seen in the Deccan rocks. The latter are generally hard egg-shaped cores of basalt surrounded by many crumbling layers of softer rock; weathering gives the whole 'bomb' a curious resemblance to the engraved oval, though the latter do not have the softer layers but do have wider, deeper, and smoother grooves in place of the narrow interstrata lines. The 'bombs' may have supplied the models for primitive megalith builders' marks. At Poona, the Kotharūḍ-Pāṣāṇ hill-top Mhātobā (without Jogūbāī; an immigrant from Vākaḍ) was part of such a megalith, now mostly smashed to pieces. About fifty cairns nearby re-use megalithic boulders, are on soil soft enough to dig, and may represent a necropolis. The whole complex seems to denote a megalithic site reoccupied much later by pastoral immigrants. The range of megalithic remains can be traced at least to Pābaḷ 40 miles north of Poona, but their density is very low, and they make more frequent use of natural outcrops than at the center of this particular culture, namely the Theūr-Khāmgāo region on the south bank of the Muḷā.

The relationship between the builders of our newly discovered megaliths[17] in the Muḷā-Bhīmā lowland and the people of the Karhā microlith track is still obscure. The reversal of the highlander-lowlander altitudes found near Poona is due to the lesser rainfall, and probably later migration along the lower valley. The movement of cults from Kanarese territory in historic times along much the same route has been noted. Iron-age megaliths are well known in the South, particularly on granite rocks. Though the concentration from Khāmgāo to Theūr (over 100 megaliths) seems greater than elsewhere, the megaliths can be followed down-river to the tri-junction of Poona, Sholapur and Ahmadnagar districts at the village of Khānoṭā. Here, the boulder piles seem smaller than up-river, but the Bhoī fishermen of Khānoṭā worship the goddess Mahāmāyā at a spot in the river bed where the exposed rock still has prehistoric Mother-Goddess ovals, one about 15 feet long. No large stone tools have been found among these particular megaliths. Long slabs are much more difficult to carve out of black basalt than from granite, and crack or crumble more readily; hence the difference of construction. The absence of pottery is harder to account for, but no opinion can be given without excavation. That the megalith builders attached some special importance to chalcedony nodules imbedded in the basaltic trap-rock is proved by the numerous pits left on the removal of these nodules; by the existence of fractured nodules still *in situ*, but with a deep groove about the inset, showing that the laborious attempt was finally abandoned, and by the use of such nodules to center grooved circles (fig. 4.16). There is a strong possibility that the pierced microliths were made from such imbedded nodules, which would then give another point of contact between highlanders and lowlanders.

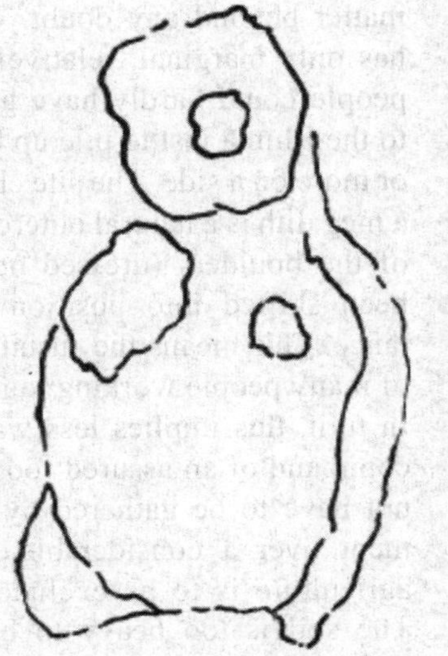

Fig. 4.15. Megalithic rock-engraving on Vetāḷ Hill, Poona, height 16″.

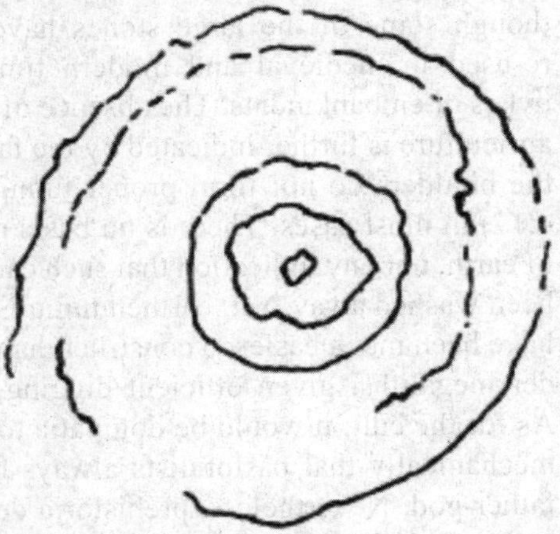

Fig. 4.16. Megalithic circles, centred on a chalcedony nodule and deeply engraved on bed-rock; Vetāḷ Hill, Poona diameter 15″.

I suggest that the people who piled up the megaliths were an early, transient merger of cattlemen with nomads of the microlith track, the latter element still dominating the religion. In the first place, the territories overlap to some extent, especially where the two river basins merge below Yavat. Secondly, the Poona highlanders used larger and thicker artifacts; those found in the Bhīmā-Muḷā megaliths are barely to be distinguished from the delicate Karhā type. That Poona highlanders were associated at one time with megaliths is clear from lines (figs. 4.15, 4.16) carved on boulders atop the Law College Hill plateau, up to within 50 metres of the Great Vetāḷ. On the same hilltop plateau, a flat knoll 1000 metres to the west is rimmed with the remnants of smashed megaliths, and completely encircled with '*satya-yuga*' terraces, though no cult of any sort survives here. The stones have been wrecked by extensive quarrying for rubble and stone blocks, and the cup-marks are hardly as much as two inches across, but enough remains to put the matter beyond any doubt. The Karhā valley has only marginal, relatively few megaliths; people could hardly have gone down thence to the Bhīmā just to pile up boulders four feet or more on a side. The site chosen as a rule for a megalith is a natural outcrop. Even so, many of the boulders (dressed or not) have often been shifted into position from some distance. This means the sustained heavy labour of many people working together at one time. In turn, this implies less wandering and fair command of an assured food surplus that did not have to be gathered by ceaseless movement over a considerable distance. Plough agriculture is to be excluded at this period. The soil is too heavy to be properly tilled before the iron age, and would not be sufficiently productive with slash-and-burn alone; but the land was excellent for cattle-grazing, before agriculture. There are no terraces, though some of the large stones have been re-used in medieval and modern times for dykes or embankments. The absence of heavy agriculture is further indicated by the fact that the boulders do not form proper tumuli (fig. 4.17) in most cases. There is no basic mound of earth, nor any indication that such earth has been washed away. Yet, earthen tumuli would have been much easier to construct than boulder megaliths, given efficient digging tools. As for the cult, it would be dogmatic to insist mechanically that pastoralists always have a father-god. Nevertheless, prehistoric deposits in Raichur district and elsewhere to the *SE* show engraved bulls, bull's head puppets, the horn design, or a male deity. Here, we have an entirely different set of marks: large ovals, small circles, and sometimes the two close together in the form of a limbless body with head. That the nearly perfect circles should all be about 31 *cm* in diameter shows that they must have been drawn by similar methods, probably by using the thumb and a finger of the adult hand for compasses. Ovals may go to two metres or more and often show a high, swollen interior. Peasants recognize and sometimes use rectangular arrangements of large boulders on the ground (*vāḍā, vādagē*) as cattle-enclosures, the low walls being supplemented by thorny branches whenever cattle are to be kept from straying at night. A complex enclosure of this type at Koregão-Mūḷ is still in excellent condition. It is all the more remarkable that the same villagers should not know the function of the boulder-piles, or even recognize them as artificial. The Marāṭhi name for such a pile or cairn (often made as a funerary monument) is *khiḷā* if of

Fig. 4.17. Dolmen, Theūr-Nāyagāon. Cap-stone nearly 4′ high. The foundation is solid rock, without space for a burial.

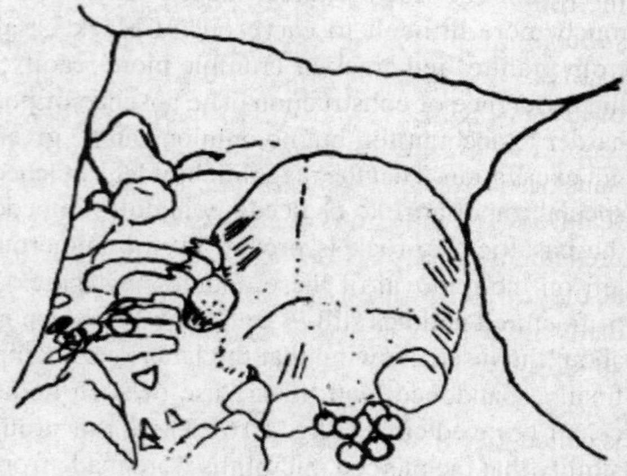

Fig. 4.18. Māndhrāī shrine under capstone, Varvanḍ High Place. Limes in the foreground, votive wooden cattle at left, and bangles (left) were recent offerings.

large irregular boulders; also *varaṇḍā* in the Koṅkaṇ, and *varvaṇd* in the region under discussion. It cannot be a mere coincidence that a village named Varvaṇḍ lies where the finest Karhā microlith deposits approach the megaliths. Varvaṇḍ has a spectacular High Place which is still a place of worship. The cult object here is in a hollow under a four-foot rock which has been carefully propped up. The bulge in the base stone underneath which represents the goddess is coated in red minium, and worshipped by the villagers under the name Māndhrāī (fig. 4.18) Wooden votive cattle, limes, and women's bangles are placed before her in the deep cave-like hollow. (Normally, such votive cattle would be deposited before some father god like Gavaḷūjī Bābā, Bāpūjī Bābā, or Vetāḷ, often a deity not to be approached by women. The Tyche of Kesnand village, Jogūbāī, has such cattle placed in front of her shrine near the village boundary with Loṇī Kand, but they are actually in a little enclosure above which a Vetāḷ presides, and do not form an exception to the general practice). Single and double ovals, cup-marks and the rest of the insignia are to be seen on other boulders, while the High Place is flanked by several other megaliths, some of which show the rough arched hollows under which major cult-objects once lay. The larger 'cups' are called *sāḷuṅkhā* in Marāthī, a term which also designates the *yoni* socket in which the phallic emblem of Śiva is fixed. The sexual symbolism is unmistakable and generally admitted, without benefit of Freud. The *liṅga* would presumably have developed out of the pestle-stone rolled about in the 'cup'; the original stone may have been the homologue of a foetus rather than of the phallus. The Sanskrit word *śālāṅkī* means puppet or doll, though there may be no etymological connection. A feature of the megaliths at and near Varvaṇḍ is that sockets have been made in some of the rocks, presumably for wooden flag-poles. The biggest (at Varvaṇḍ) is 27 *cm* deep, an oval 12 × 14 *cm* at the top, tapering towards the bottom, and seems too irregular to have been made by a metal drill. Sometimes, as between Koregão-Mūḷ and Theūr, innumerable megaliths follow a pattern so closely as to confuse the visitor, who feels that he has been going round and round in a circle.

A curious survival may be seen at Khāmgão, at one end of the local megalith tract. This locality is called *gāḍe-moḍī* after the legendary disappearance of a whole wedding party, bride, bridegroom, company and the bullock-carts into the ground. The reason is not given, but the tradition is interesting as the only reference to any human burial under the megaliths. The carts are represented by a fractured stone wheel lying flat on the ground, made with metal tools in modern times. This is worshipped, and there are several minor cults nearby among the boulders; of these, two are of Māva-lā-devī. The modern stone wheel seems to have replaced the flat circles and ovals of the megalith period in other localities as well. The patron deity of Cākaṇ is the god of the Wheel', *cakreśvar*, who has given his name to the town and made his appearance in the form of "a wheel of the chariot of king Daśaratha". This extraordinary shape is easily understood when one sees that the temple appears at the end of what was once the High Place, now sadly ruined by quarrying and stone-robbing. A dolmen and the oval marks are still visible among the boulders between Cākaṇ fort and the god's temple by the stream. Even more significant is the appearance of a goddess under a huge boulder at the temple end of the megalith. This deity, variously called Añjinā Khāparāī (Mother of the Slab), Khajurāī (Mother of the Date-Palm), or just Devī, has now the usual *Mahiṣa-Mardinī* relief, though her prehistoric ancestry is not to be doubted. The Wheel of Cākaṇ was supposed to have dropped off at Kaṇesar and been brought to the tank in front of Cākan temple—which does not contain any such wheel. The patron goddess of Kaṇesar is a well known Yamāī, and the local inhabitants know of the legend without being able to point to any spot where the wheel might first have dropped off. The presumption is strong that the supposed wheel was also a Mother's Circle on bed-rock.

The megaliths, at any rate, cannot all have been crossroads cult-sites. The complete survey of their full range, and the excavation without which little definite can be said about their age or purpose, are both well beyond my own means. However, their number and concentration makes it most likely that they were funerary monuments of some kind. The dead clan-chief, or medicine-man, or 'saint' could have been sent back to The Mothers entire, or only his decarnated bones or cremated ashes deposited at the site. Possibly, the cairns commemorate a *hieros gamos* and double sacrifice, *e.g.* the Khāmgão legend. Digging might prove or disprove this and also tell us something about the tools and pottery—if any—used by the prehistoric builders; the chances are poor, because the megaliths are on solid rock. The gravid oval under a little arch so painfully hammered out of the upper stone at Bolhāī's Kitchen is a small-scale predecessor of the Buddhist *stūpa* in its cave. The name *dhātugarbha* (relic-womb) applies to the type of *stūpa* (as at Junnar and Pitaḷkhorā) which has a reliquary concealed somewhere in the face of the dome. We have noted that the great *stūpa* at Kārle is regarded as the goddess Yamāī. The *Śatapatha Brāhmaṇa* 13.8.1.5 and 13.9.2.1 refers to round funerary barrows of the Asuras, which should mean pre-Aryan structures not later than the 7th century BC. perhaps tumuli like those at Mirzapore. There is a direct line of descent to the great northern *stūpas*. The most that can be said here is that surface finds show no sign of conflict between the megalith and the microlith people of the Poona district, nor is there any surviving tradition to that effect. Whoever piled up the rocks did so before the later aggressive Highland pastoralists with their herds, Father-gods and rougher tools, began to expand and turned aggressive. Mahiṣāsura-mardinī belongs to this period. Such a change would, in all probability, be connected with the first proper use of iron in food-production. The date of this important change in the means of production would be early in first millennium BC.

The evolution seems about as follows. The highlanders were later intruders who, in several waves, occupied territory of little use to the lowlanders. They pastured cattle. Land-clearing for agriculture begins with their terraces. As their cleared lands moved downhill, a permanent fusion became necessary. The union of the two cultures and of the two sets of people is represented by the ultimate marriage of the Mother Goddess to the Father God of the pastoral immigrants. Even to this day, Bāpūjī Bābā' (Father Lord) is "dangerous to women" but peculiarly a god of the cattle. He is located well outside the villages for this reason. Vetāla, born of Śiva and Pārvatī in human form (according to the *Kālikā Purāṇa* (52) is also not to be worshipped by women; his devotees try to avoid the sight of woman or sound of a woman's bangles on the mornings when they do homage to Vetāḷ. The most prominent of these cacodemon cults near Poona is on the highland plateau at the junction of five village boundaries and has been mentioned above and is known as the Great or Elder Vetāḷ.

4.6. LATER DEVELOPMENTS

The next stages are still visible in places of worship near Poona. The 'Younger Brother' Vetāḷ is on the lowland track near the State Sheep-breeding farm, thus located to save devotees the long climb uphill to the Elder Vetāḷ. However, two reliefs of nameless many-armed goddesses lie nearby and male worshippers worship both Vetāḷ and Devī without regarding them as related; the women do not offer to the Vetāḷ. Still nearer my house, a set of crude stones represent a Mhasobā slightly displaced by modern buildings; some of these stones, without distinction, also represent Lakṣmī-āī (not uncommon as a consortless Mother-goddess) in spite of the male god's avoidance of women. The terracotta soul house at Barāḍ contains two aniconic stones, whereas only one should be the Vetāḷ occupant. Next to the shrine is a larger masonry structure for Vāgh-jaī, one of the rustic 'Seven Sisters'.

The *Kālikā Purāṇa* passage cited above narrates also that Vetāla and Bhairava were incarnations of two of Śva's goblin followers, and that the god and goddess incarnated themselves so as to have these two for human sons. Yet the curse that was adduced as reason for this coming down to earth resulted in Vetāla and Bhairava being born monkey-faced. Vetāḷ's birthday still coincides with that of Hanumān. However, Hanumān may be worshipped by women though he remains celibate. The syncretism, advanced a stage further by this Purāṇa, continued its logical course among the peasants, who further take Śiva, Bhairav, and Vetāḷ as of the same substance, and at times change one cult into the other. Chapter 93 of the *Kālikā-purāṇa* says that Vetāla fell in love with the wish-fulfilling cow Kāmadhenu, upon whom he begot the great bull Nandī who is now Śiva's mount. From this bull and the cows of Varuṇa came all the best cattle, thus descended from Vetāḷ and Nandī. This fiction is surely based upon the identity of, or at least the connection between Vetāḷ and Bāpūjī Bābā. The conflict between the god and the goddess was not always easily smoothed over by the Purāṇas. A copper plate charter of the 10th century at Sañjān (*EI 32*.1957. p. 60, lines 34–47) gives a decision of the god of Bhinmāl, who had been brought to Sañjān and found himself in conflict with the adjacent goddess Daśamī (Tenth). The goddess's devotees were to pay a quit rent, to encroach no further upon the god's precinct, and to bear the entire sin thereafter should any of them commit suicide or self-mutilation in rage against the god. Sañjān at the time had a Muslim governor appointed by the Hindu king, and a settlement of Zorastrian (Pārsī) refugees from Iran, who solemnly witnessed this rigmarole.

A little earlier than the quarrel at Bhinmāl, two beautiful temples of the Yādava or Western Cālukya period were being constructed at Parḷī, a village six miles from Sātārā, at the foot of Sajjangaḍ. The high fort is popular with brahmins and middle-class pilgrims for its shrine of Āṅgalāī founded by Śivājī's preceptor Rāmadās, and for relics of that saint. The Parḷī temples are to Mahādeva. Local tradition has it that they were built in that great age when day and night each lasted for six months. The Five Pāṇḍavas set out to make a complete replica of Kāśī during a single night. The goddess Jogāī interrupted the work, out of sheer jealousy, by taking on the semblance of a cock to crow untimely as at the approach of dawn. This induced the Brothers to stop their work, never to be resumed. When the cheat was discovered, the evil-plotting female was seized by the foot and hurled across the river. Thus, her original shrine by the greater Mahādeva temple stands empty—a simple affair of four undecorated stone pillars without walls, supporting a massive but now ruined slab roof. The decidedly better stone temple built where Jogāī landed seems to have been of the late Yādava period, but collapsed many years ago during a hurricane. The present image of Jogāī is a black basalt relief of a goddess on the warpath. Next to her is a male image of a 'brother', Bāḷ-Śīd. A third, older image of a gowned female has been damaged, but is still worshipped as Jakhāī, which should mean *yakṣī*; this may have been the original goddess tossed out a thousand years ago and now called Jogāī. A stone's throw away, three or four natural stones under a banyan tree are the otherwise unknown and rarely worshipped god Tiḷavlī. In spite of her troubles, and notwithstanding the proximity of more fashionable temples on the fort and in the village, Jogāī attracts pilgrims from the peasants as far away as Khānāpūr. Parḷī village honours all its gods and goddesses regularly, but the village elders have, remarkably enough, to pay annual homage to a Ghāṭāī (Mother of the Pass) some eight miles to the west of Sātārā.

One local tradition has it that the image of Āṅgalāī set up by Rāmadās on top of Sajjangaḍ was found in the river, whence this may have been the mother-goddess supposedly thrown across the river. The whole myth as preserved by the last immigrants shows conflict between some original Mother goddess and Śiva which could not be resolved by marrying off the two deities, though the name Jogāī (*Yogeśvarī*) shows that the possibility was at least considered. Nor could her cult be suppressed altogether as may have been the case at Ambarnāth, 34 miles from Bombay, where an ornate Śiva temple dated 1060 AD still exists. For, Ambarnāth is not a corruption of *Amaranātha* (The Immortal Lord), but of *Amba-nātha* or *Āmba-nātha*, according to an inscription formerly inside the northern doorway. This would make him a 'husband' of the original mother-goddess, who has been eliminated altogether.

4.7. TOWARDS AGRICULTURE

The microlith track at Poona bears direct witness to some of these changes. The lowland track passed through the high ground at the foot of the hill, behind the cricket field of the Fergusson College. Microliths of excellent quality are found just above this, on both sides of the water reservoirs of that college. But a few yards away, the hill slope is bare of artifacts, and a trifling climb brings us to a small plateau which now houses a shrine to Māruti (Hanumān). This was built and rebuilt after World War II, but for many years the college authorities carried on a struggle against the devotees of a Vetāḷ to whom no shrine existed except a miserable cairn, but whose worshippers persisted in coming from the city to sacrifice at the spot. The cause is obviously ancient, for small microlith fragments of the cruder highland type are deposited in good concentration at this cult spot but nowhere else on the hill nearby. The existence of some powerful prehistoric cult is proved also by the caves on the ground of the College (shown on the wrong hill by the *Gazetteer*). The main cave now houses a heterogenous collection of Hindu deities, including Śiva, Nandī, Gaṇeśa, Pāṇḍuraṅga and Rakhumāī, with a Hanumān carved in the portico over an older monkey-god. That the cave was not meant to be a temple is shown not only by this motley combination but by its facing north, whereas the eastward orientation of a normal temple could have been achieved by a little shift in location. The northern exposure, four other caves which have survived blasting for rock, and a considerable water cistern (now dry) prove that a small Buddhist monastery existed at this point. Just above the caves are four square sockets for the pillars of some vanished structure; a fifth cave lower down was sometimes used as a temple by the low-caste people settled below. This adjacency of lowland and highland microlith deposits, which approach closer at this place than usual (though with clear separation), is undoubtedly related to the cult spot and to the monastic caves. Hillside cisterns on the same level near the Catuḥśṛṅgī temple, and carvings on the black basalt rock that has crumbled away from the hill may indicate the beginning of another monastic establishment less than a mile away, above the same microlith track. The temple at Catuḥśṛṅgī dates from 1786, but some local goddess must have received earlier worship at the same place. Bāṇere, five miles away, has the next artificial but definitely post-Buddhist cave, which houses funerary steles as well as a Yamāī and a Mahādev. A Tukāī resides just above, in a shrine of her own at the top of the hillock. Bāṇere is close to Vākaḍ, on the other side of the Muḷā. The terrain and season were both unsuitable for microlith hunting.

The early trade routes did not follow every microlith track. The moment village settlement based upon the plough and leading to the formation of kingdoms came into its own, the microlith tracks in the untouched pasture lands were useless to the northern or overseas trader, and doomed to extinction. The *Periplus*[18] gives some identifiable harbours on the west coast below Semylla (Chāul). The first is Mandagora: the mouth of the Mandā river by Kuḍā, which contains some beautiful Buddhist caves difficult of access by road. The region seems to have been occupied by tribal people whose probable name was Mandava. A Mandavi princess Sāmaḍinikā dedicated a water cistern at Beḍsā; the royal house patronized Kuḍā, and the root *man* is prominent in place names of the locality. Some of the numerous old cairns between Taḷe (with fort and caves, hence on the trade-route) and Kuḍā might be worth investigation, though not recognized as graves by the local people today. There is no specially convenient pass, so that the distant trade went by sea, or to Junnar through passes at the head of the Muḷśī valley. The next port is Palaepatmae, which can only be Pāle near Mahāḍ, close to the Sāvitrī river which still constitutes an important coastal port for country vessels. The road to Bhor from Mahāḍ is late, though the difficult pass was in use much earlier. On the saddleback at the head of the pass, some 17 miles from Mahāḍ, a microlith site is found—unique for the route. The place has a cult to the god Kāḷsarī and lies within the village limits of Umbarḍe (less than two dozen families). The village god is Kāngrūmal, also unknown elsewhere. The most logical place for microliths on this trade route (which runs to Paṇḍharpūr and across the whole Peninsula) should have been the Copālā (fig. 4.19) near Śirval. This mortarless 'Hemāḍpantī' structure has a classical balance and harmony reminiscent of temple 17 at Sāñcī which should date it to the Gupta-Vākāṭaka period. It lies at a crossroads, for the road to Vīr and Phaḷṭaṇ branches off road from Poona to Sātārā near this

Fig. 4.19. The Copāḷā, near Śirvaḷ.

Fig. 4.20. 'Cell-doorway in Śirvaḷ cave, showing sockets for door-frame, grilled window, and arrangements for locking; the cell must have housed valuables.

point, a good track leads to Māṇḍhardev, and another Buddhist caves. Nevertheless, the building is not a temple; it contains nothing but a stone platform into which two large stone jars are sunk. These containers resemble the much larger stone jars at both ends of Nāṇeghāṭ pass traditionally depositories for the tolls. The Copāḷā apparently collected gifts for the Buddhist cave monastery (fig. 4.20) about three miles away, behind the village of Śindevāḍī, on the old route to Mahāḍ. Nowadays, those peasants of the neighbourhood who cannot go all the way to the 'Five Pāṇḍavas' in the caves offer a coconut at the empty Copāḷā and feel that their homage has reached the deity of the caves. Yet, no attempt is made to set up a cult at or near the Copāḷā.

Below Mahāḍ, the *Periplus* gives a Melizigara whose location might have been on the creek to Chipḷūṇ, or on the next creek to the south. Here the cave monasteries of Karhāḍ furnish some indication of the route. Like Kuḍā and Mahāḍ these are late, post-Sātavāhana in any case. "Byzantium" should be a corruption of Vejayanti, Banavāsī in North Kanara—another creek port. The others are doubtful.

Portions of the lowland track served the earliest hardy pioneers who explored the wilderness to climb the Deccan scarp in search of trade. Once the earlier Buddhist monasteries were established, there was no reason for immediate penetration into the Karhā valley, where agriculture would not have been so profitable as in the richer black soil of the parallel valleys. Junnar microlith finds cannot be compared to those of the Karhā region. A solitary though excellent microlith found below Mānmoḍī, another beautiful piece near the Tuḷajā caves, and some decent specimens on the saddleback at Āptaḷe (the logical crossing from the Āmbolī to the Kukḍī valley) emphasize the relative paucity. The present road from Poona to Junnar provides reasonably good artifacts in small numbers, at a few places. The one site en route which compares in technique and numbers of artifacts with the best elsewhere is by the village of Cāndolī, near the Bhīmā river, opposite Kheḍ. Just how Junnar developed is still not clear, though its overwhelming position in trade at the beginning of the Christian era is evident from the 135 (or more) caves that surround it.

The tiny group of caves at Beḍsā affords a better illustration for the main ideas of this chapter than does the far more imposing Junnar complex. The relatively small monastery was patronized by merchants and princely donors over a range that included Nāsik and Kuḍā. The water-cisterns seem too numerous for resident monks, hence imply many visitors or pilgrims. The trail that still goes past the monastery over Tiger Pass joined the Paünā valley microlith track to that of the Indrāyaṇī high ground; a good microlith site is found on this path just below the pass, within the limits of Pimpḷolī village. The mother-goddess Beḍsāī of the hamlet below the caves, Yamāī in the *vihāra*, occasional dabs of red pigment on the *stūpa* and the superior prestige enjoyed by the Vetāḷ-like Tiger-god deity of the pass establish the existence of one or more strong prehistoric cults at the junction of primitive tracks which later developed into trade-routes.

A copper-plate charter of the Rāṣṭrakūṭa king Kṛṣṇarāja I (Akālavarṣa) dated March 23, 768 AD donates the village of Koregao-on-the-Muḷā (*Kumārī-grāma*) to a group of brahmins from Karhād (*EI 13.275–292).* The river and all the neighbouring villages have been recognizably named in the grant, when the locality was under permanent agricultural settlement before the 8th century. The only difference is that some of the villages have broken up into segments (Borī. Khāmgāo) while Nāyagāo did not exist, nor Āṣṭe. The low arched doorway of the small

Mahādeva temple at Koregão-Mūḷ is of bricks much larger in size than in the high feudal period, while considerable number of 'hero stones' are built into the inner walls of the shrine. Many of these memorials to the dead show that the particular hero was killed while fighting off cattle-raiders, though two cavaliers and some foot-soldiers were killed in regular battle. The village must have been based upon cattle-breeding when the king (who had the magnificent *Kailāsa* structure carved out of the hill at Ellora) gave it away to priests—who would presumably concentrate upon promoting cultivation of untilled land. The several dozen megalithic tumuli of this locality must by then have been in neglect for centuries. Local tradition of the adjacent village of Āḷandī, as reported orally by Mr. S. B. Tikhe, supplements field archaeology and the record of donation. Āḷandī, now "of the Thief" began as Āḷandī-Sāṇḍas on the edge of the high Karhā basin, just across the steep pass dominated by Malhārgaḍ. The original situation retains marks of human occupation, while large water cisterns carved into the rocks of the pass show that the route was important for trade caravans. The old settlement was divided between two clans, Bāndhāṭe and Gorgal. Of these, the former were the first to come down into the valley, and founded the present village of Rāmośīvāḍī near Āḷandī station on the Southern Railway. The name shows tribal origin and continued predilection for brigandage. The Gorgal descended a bit later to found Āḷandī "of the Brigands", which shows that they too were then wild tribesmen. The settlement was not in its present locus but almost a mile nearer to the Poona-Sholapur road, on the "old white earth" (*junī pāṇḍharī*). Foundations of houses are still visible, as well as microliths that must have been deposited before the village moved down. The foundation stones are small undressed boulders, mostly round; no megaliths occur in this area. This was the village referred to by Kṛṣṇa I as Alandiya; the crude old Śiva temple (accompanied by beautiful hero-stones) which is at the margin of this deserted site goes back to that period. But even this earlier settlement developed only because cattlemen from Jāvaḷī, headed by two chiefs Māyabā and Sāyabā, joined it with their herds. They became the dominating influence which converted the savage tribal Gorgals into a comparatively docile peasantry. To this day, the leading peasant families of Corācī Āḷandī are surnamed Jāvaḷkar. The unknown, date of the immigration was earlier than the 8th century BC. All the villages we have studied must have found it possible to come down to the valleys at about the same period. What made the migration and change to real agriculture possible was, in every case, the cattle and iron. Terraces on steep hillsides sometimes mark the earlier slash-and-burn cultivation, and may be seen high up in the Muḷā valley, at Kalyāṇ (behind Siṃhagaḍ), beyond Koṇḍaṇpūr and elsewhere. Older villagers can generally point out the ancient site of the village in such cases even when the terraces have fallen into disrepair and are marked only by regular lines of shrubs. At Thief's Āḷandī, the rainfall was apparently not sufficient for this type of cultivation; no hillside terraces are to be seen by the pass. With the Jāvaḷī herds came, inevitably, Mhātobā and his wife Jogūbāī; these are still the main patron deities of the village, though the best construction and finest icons are in the temple of Pāṇḍuraṅga built late in the feudal period. It was rebuilt by the Tikhe who rose to high ministerial position under the Scindias at the end of the 18th century, only to commit suicide when his defalcations were about to be exposed. Not all the wild traditions were civilized away. The famous Rāmośī brigand Umājī Nāik (hanged 1831) and the rebel Vāsudev Baḷvant Phaḍke (died 1883) drew their inspiration and some followers from this locality.

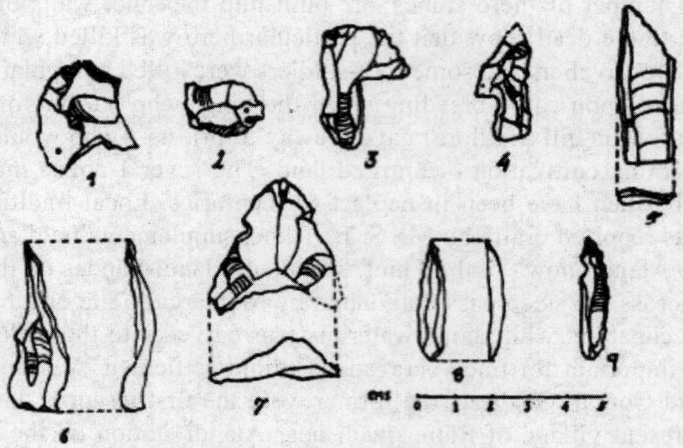

Fig. 4.21. Specialized microlith tools—(1) Pierced amulet or charm, Yeraṇḍavṇe. (2) Fish-shaped drilled amulet from the same site; the pit for the point of the drill has been carefully prepared. (3) Hook from Deulgão. (4) Barbed harpoon (?) point from Varvaṇd; the barb has been drilled, and can also be threaded, like nos. 1 and 2, though the hole is finer. (5) Blade, carefully retouched on slanting edge, Deuḷgão. (6) Fine-pointed piercing tool, Pātas; probably awl for stitching hides. (7) Arrowhead with notched point, from spur near the Mother-Goddess's grove, Phagṇe. (8) Pointed tool from Perṇem, stronger than 6; perhaps a burin for engraving bone. (9) Thin blade with doubly notched tip. Deuḷgão; this may have been a surgical implement, in view of its delicacy and fine retouching.
The material of all these microliths is Chalcedony and except no. 7, which comes from a crossroads site, they all represent important centers of the lowland industry.

NOTES TO CHAPTER 4

General use has been made of the old Bombay Presidency *Gazetteers* (1882 onwards), especially for Poona, Satara, Sholapur, Ahmadnagar, Thana and Colaba districts, to supplement my own field notes. The second and eighth chapters of my book *Introduction to the Study of Indian History* (Bombay 1956) give the methodology and historical background.

1. Cf. in particular J. Przyluski: *JRAS* 1929, 273–279. Footnote 9 of *JAOS* 75, p. 41 should also be of interest.
2. *EI* 8.60–65 (Senart). The list of Gotamiputa's provinces reads: Asika, Asaka, Mulaka, Suraṭha, Kukura, Aparanta. Anupa, Vidabha, Ākarāva(n)ti. The second and third would correspond to the *SN* account of Bāvari's settlement.
3. Published by G. Bühler in the *Arch. Survey of Western India* 5, 60–74. Though now in poor condition, enough survives of the inscription to prove the generous *dakṣīnā* gifts: 12 cattle and a horse; 1700 cattle, 10 elephants; 11,000 cattle, a hundred horses; a very good village; 24,400; *kāhāpaṇas;* 6001 *kāhāpaṇas*, one chariot; 100 cattle; 12 pieces of gold; 14,000 *kāhāpaṇas*, one village, elephants..; village, bullock-cart of grain; 17 cows, one or more mules (?); pieces of gold, silver ornaments; 10,000 *kāhāpaṇa* fee; 20,000 cattle; 10,001 cattle, and so on, for various *yajña* fire-sacrifices, some of which are explicitly named in what survives.
4. The reports of H. D. Sankalia and his colleagues have, unfortunately, sometimes added to the confusion that their most valuable pioneer excavations ought to have reduced. In the *Illustrated London News* for Sept. 5, 1959, pp. 181–3, we are shown Nāvḍā Tolī potters neatly dressed in white cotton at a period not later than 1300 BC, though no evidence is published for the plough, or for local cotton growing. Inasmuch as potters were not so well off in historical times, this reconstruction of a vanished society demands more support than has been produced. Sankalia emphasizes the northern Haihayas, and their etymological connection with the horse, though nothing has been published among his chalcolithic finds to prove the existence of horse or chariot at the site. He presents

a certain number of historical alternatives in the *Journal* of the Bombay Asiatic Society (vols. 31–2; 1956–7; pp. 229–239) but transgresses his own cautious bounds in describing the finds. There is no evidence whatever for connection with Purāṇic 'history', such as it is. (The Purāṇas have suffered continuous priestly revision still a thousand years ago; the *Mahābhārata* epic upon which so many of them are based was also rewritten for religious purposes, just before the Gupta age). The map opposite p. 233 is labelled 'Chalcolithic Culture of the Black Soil People'—though the black soil extends well beyond the Deccan trap area. (The main linguistic division into Aryan and Dravidian, ignored in the paper cited, corresponds not to change of soil, but roughly to that of substratum from basalt to granite). Page 233 states: "And it is possible that such a pressure-flaking was achieved by the use of metal tools"—a remark best passed by in silence. On p. 236, we read again of 'the Aryan or Puranic colonization of the Narmadā valley'. (The Purāṇas affirm that the Ikṣvāku line was extinguished with king Sumitra of Mithilā before the birth of the Buddha. The southern 'Ikṣvakus', like so many other upstarts, had their unknown tribal ancestry improved by some convenient genealogy found or invented for the purpose by the brahmin parasites they attracted. The Purāṇas, rewritten for this purpose, are much less reliable than classical genealogies derived from the Homeric 'catalogue of ships' before Troy). The same page reports an anonymous local tradition of *Rāmāyaṇa* stations on the rivers, one *yojana*—"about 28 miles" apart (the *yojana* is never known to have exceeded nine miles). On p. 234, we find the Assakas equated to Aśvakas who came down from Afghanistan; on p. 238 they became the Aśmakas, translated 'The Blade-using people', a rendering that has no justification whatever. I, personally, find Sankalia's work encouraging. If he can describe (*Deccan College Monograph* No. 10, 1952) the Godavari palaeolithic industry from 64 artifacts found at three sites (foundation trenches for dams) within a range of no more than two miles, my present note, based upon fieldwork over a range of 200 miles and finds of 18000 microliths, should not seem too ambitious.

5. The age given in a report accompanying a letter of Mr. Douglas Barrett of the British Museum (No. 28, 1960) is 2240±150 years. The BM laboratory uses acetylene instead of carbon dioxide, which gives more carbon atoms per molecule, and their electronic circuits are more sophisticated than those first used for radiocarbon dating.
6. D. D. Kosambi: *Dhenukākaṭa; JBBRAS* 30 (ii), 1956, pp. 50–71 and 4 plates.
7. Ṭer was proposed for Tagara by J. F. Fleet in *JRAS* 1901, 537–552. If accepted, it would mean that the *Periplus* and Ptolemy ignored the greatest peninsular trading city of this period, Junnar.
8. Sylvain Lévi in *JA* 5 1915 (pt. i) pp. 19–138: *Le Catalogue géographique des Yakṣsas dans la Mahāmāyūrī;* lines 41 and 44 of the Sanskrit text. The list is composed from several overlapping and somewhat divergent sources.
9. *EI*. 8, 24–36 for the rather poetic account of the Talaguṇḍa pillar. The Bāṇas seem to have had their capital at Tiruvallam (Vanapura) in North Arcot district, and were rooted out by the Coḷa king Parāntaka (907–948 AD) according to L. de la Vallée Poussin: *Dynasties et Histoire de l'Inde* (Paris 1935), p. 269, footnote 2. The connection with Bāṇāī and the Dhangars is frankly doubtful, but what is one conjecture among so many?
10. Bombay Presidency *Gazetteer*, vol. XIX (1885), p. 105, for Birobā, and eastward movement during the rains.
11. *Śrī-nātha Maskobā Devācē Caritra* (in Marāṭhī), originally printed at Poona in 1889. A copy of the second edition (1926) which is also out of print, was kindly supplied by the *pāṭīl* of Vīr. Local tradition, unfortunately, is generally discordant and the information obtained from one Elder may not always tally with that furnished by someone else; this account seems to be generally agreed upon in its essential features.
12. H. Kephart: *Camping And Woodcraft* (New York 1924), vol. II, p. 327. Desmond Clark: *The Prehistory Of Southern Africa* (Pelican Books A458, London 1959), p. 233, fig. 51, *et passim* for the use of mastic. For bored stones as digging-stick weights, *ibid* p. 207, figure 42.
13. G. H. Khare: *Śrī-Viṭṭhala Āṇi Paṇḍharpūr* (in Marāṭhī) 2nd ed. Poona 1953. See also the same author's *Mahārāṣṭrācīṃ Cār Daivateṃ* for a discussion of the medieval origins of the four major cults in the State. That this development was based upon the growth of a common market, which was responsible also for the growth of the Marāṭhī language, should have been mentioned by the able scholar. See also G. A. Deleury: *The Cult of Viṭhobā* (Poona, 1960) for the Paṇḍharpur pilgrimages.
14. In D. H. Gordon's report: *Ancient India* 6, 1950, p. 74. K. R. U. Todd in *Ancient India* 6 (1950) pp. 4–11, describing the stone-age industry of Bombay island, calls a stone ring a 'mace-head', though it could not have served as one with any efficiency and is presumably a digging-stick weight. In the same issue, D. H. Gordon (pp. 64–90) surveys the stone industries of the Holocene in India and Pakistan. Some of the conclusions are

definitely misleading, particularly the association of microliths with copper on p. 83. No tracks are mentioned, only sites. In the region upon which I have concentrated, a good case can be made out for direct transition from the stone to the iron age, without tools of polished stone, or copper in any quantity. Dharwar outcrops often show thick encrustations of iron oxide flakes, which can be removed bodily, reduced by roasting in a charcoal fire, and hammered into usable iron. Vessels, particularly frying pans, locally made in this way by wandering Dhāvaḍ tribal artizans could be purchased at Heḷvāk near Chipḷūṇ, at least till World War II; also at Bhadrāvatī in Mysore State. Copper, on the other hand, is scarce. The knowledge of iron came presumably from traders. The plough is certainly not of local origin.

15. R. V. Joshi: *Pḷeistocene Studies In The Malaprabhā Basin* (Poona-Dharwar 1955). The author shows no microlith site nearer to Poona than Kandivli in his first map, whereas he could have seen a good one from the window of the very laboratory in which his material was organized. The report of his own work is valuable.
16. K. Kenyon: *Digging Up Jericho* (London, 1957); p. 57, absence of larger stone tools: digging-stick weights (not mistaken for 'mace-heads'); p. 74, foot-note C-14 dating well before 6800 BC. Also, *Antiquity* 129.5–9, C-14 dating at 7800 BC, of the burnt-down mesolithic shrine. *Antiquity* 120.185: "There are almost no axes, adzes, hoes or heavy chisels, which is a curious lack among people who made a considerable use of wood". The finds of Pre-pottery Jericho *B* are perhaps the most significant for interpretation of Deccan-track microliths.
17. For megaliths in India, see: *AI* no. 19, 1953, pp. 103–115: K. R. Srinivasan and N. R. Banerjee: "Survey of South Indian Megaliths" For the most careful excavation: R. E. M. Wheeler, *AI* no. 4, pp. 180–310: "Brahmagiri and Chandravalli, 1947: Megalithic and other Cultures in Mysore State". This is the only dated megalithic culture in India, extending from about 200 BC to 50 AD; none of the rest, though all of the iron age, have been so carefully delimited in time. For other work, see *AI* 2, 1–2, 9–16; 3, 11–57; 4, 4–13 (V. G. Childe, megaliths as group-graves); 5, 35–45; 8, 3–16; 12, 21–34; 13, 4–142; 15, 4–42. A general survey also in M. Seshadri: *The stone-using cultures of pre-historic and proto-historic Mysore* (Uni. of Mysore, London 1956). The Bombay *Gazetteer* vol. 18, pt. 3, 1885, p. 118 noted 'ancient remains' at Bhosari, some 8½ miles north of Poona. These were reported upon by H. D. Sankalia: "Megalithic Monuments Near Poona", *Bulletin* of the Deccan College Research Institute, vol. I, 1939–40, pp. 178–184, and plates. The title of the report is singularly unfortunate in the implication that prehistoric remains are described. On p. 182, it is admitted that 'Dolmen-like building is even now constructed', and in fact the memorial was for people that 'died only 2 or 3 years ago'. The Muñjābā shrine, similarly, was built by people still alive but who escaped the investigators' notice. An upright slab, described and illustrated as a Menhir, is set at the corner of a house built in the year 1842 AD; its sole purpose was to protect the house from damage from the wheels of ox-carts that turned the narrow corner—a function that it still performs. The boulders used so extensively by the villagers might derive from prehistoric construction, but no evidence is presented to that effect. On the other hand, the real megaliths that lie half a mile outside the village and bear the engraved circles or ovals that guarantee their antiquity have been left unnoticed. The village was founded by people of the Lāṇḍge ('Wolf') clan, whose traditions and existence have been ignored completely. It need not be added that megaliths in ruined condition but unquestioned antiquity survive much nearer Poona.
18. W. H. Schoff: *The Periplus of the Erythraean Sea*/travel and trade in the Indian Ocean/by a merchant of the first century/translated from the Greek and annotated. The dating seems to me to be reasonable, in spite of numerous criticisms. The alternative is to doubt the general reliability of the *Periplus*, which does not mention the most prominent feature of the west coast and its principal trade commodity, the coconut. This would certainly have been noted by intelligent merchant-travellers later than 120 AD. The sections used here are numbered 51 and 53, and I take a few of R. G. Bhandarkar's identifications of harbours in preference to those in Schoff's notes; both ignore the valuable trade-index furnished by Buddhist caves.

5 The Village Community in the "Old Conquests" of Goa: History versus the Skanda Purāṇa

Goa is a little slice of Portuguese territory on the west coast of India, stradding the 47th degree of east longitude and 15th of north latitude. The area of this little green patch is reported as 1,301 square miles, and the territory proper is wholly contained in a rectangle of about 60 miles by thirty. This region, small as it is, divided into eleven administrative districts (*concelhos*) of which we are concerned with those of Ilhas, Bardez, Salcete (including Mormugão, originally in Salcete but separated after the turn of this century) which constitute the old conquests that came under Portuguese dominion soon after Albuquerque's final victory in 1511, while the remaining districts were annexed after 1763. What interests us here about the village communities of the Old Conquests is that *the best rice producing land is still common property*, but to see the actual bearing of this statement, we have to enter into a fairly complicated historical analysis, and to build up a picture of the locality without which the actual situation can hardly become clear to any reader in Europe or the USA. If, in attempting this I sometimes have to give personal experiences and reminiscences, the reader should not misunderstand my purpose.

5.1. LAND AND PEOPLE

The land itself is one of the most beautiful sights of the world. A heavy rainfall of over 110 inches annual average, compressed mostly into the monsoon months of June to September, covers the earth with dense vegetation whose vivid green contrasts wonderfully well with the red of the laterite soil, and the silvery ribbons of the estuaries. The mountains of the Western Ghats taper off into hills that roll right down to the sea. The inhabitants, however, are much less happy than the idyllic scene would indicate. The comparatively thinly populated[1] New Conquests are less heathy while the Old Conquests are definitely overpopulated for a region devoid of industry. Moreover, this has been so for a long time, as can be seen from the following considerations. The principal food is rice, eaten boiled, supplemented with a little fish from the teeming sea, and a small amount of condiments locally grown. Per working man, 8 khandis of unhusked rice yielding 9/20th of that amount by volume on husking (and other preparation for cooking) are needed annually according to the rate of computation generally used in Goa. In the district of Ilhas the 1844 census showed a population of 47,762 for 10,238 families and that of 1900 54,540 for 11,528 households, while the production of unhusked rice in 1895 came only to 111,440 khandis (*X.* 2.5). For Salcete we find 23,959 households with 95,967 heads in 1844 against a rice yield of 83,980 khandis in 1847; 27,437 hearths with 113,061 people in 1900 against a rice crop of 17,720 khandis (*X.* 2.265). The most densely settled of these, Bardez, showed in 1847, 110,132 khandis of rice for a population in 1844 of 90,077 people in 22,168 households (*X.* 2.413). The 1940 census, apparently unpublished as yet, gives 540,925 people for the whole of Goa while the 1937 estimate[2] for rice was 600,711 khandis of 160 litres each whence, I take it, that the rice given is husked and the number of the old unhusked measures would be about the same. In any case, allowing as little as half a litre of husked rice per person per day, this would look barely sufficient for the needs of the population. As a matter of fact, the modern figures are known to be fictitious, based on the average yield for a few selected fields for each district multiplied by the total area sown though about 65 per cent of the cultivated land is unsurveyed. In the 1920's, the bright idea struck the administration that rice production should be encouraged in Goa, and so tax remission of sorts was allowed for areas under rice. This led, with the strikingly lax, inefficient, and corrupt administration, to all sorts of land being reported as sown with rice merely to secure the remission. When the total yield seemed to reach sufficiency—which is what the official 1937 figures are supposed to prove like other reports before them—a duty was put upon the British rice imports always necessary for feeding Goa. This brought a very heavy retaliatory customs duty upon all food products from Goa to British India, and (along with the 1929–33 depression) ruined the market for one of the principal exports to British India, coconuts. Commercial statistics[3] show that as much 72 per cent of Goa's imports were from British India till 1929 while the retaliatory tariffs had cut this down to below 60 per cent in 1938; the corresponding drop in exports was from about 95 per cent to 70 per cent. The entire economic tragedy of Portuguese India is summed up by our graph[4] in fig. 1, which shows the effect of the customs barrier added to poor land transport in spite of a good harbour at Mormugão (Panjim, or Goa proper, was good for sailing ships which did not fare in the Monsoon season, but is barred after the first heavy rains in June by a deposit of silt at the river mouth Agoada). The annual deficit is almost exactly 12 million rupees, and very steady from year to year; this sum is a fair estimate of the total amount sent home by hard working Goanese all over British India, in British and Portuguese Africa, (and on many boats) by labour in menial and clerical jobs. For, Goa has no capital investments abroad. During the war years, there was a certain amount of capital sent to Goa for safety, and the government made some money by the higher exchange rate of Portuguese currency, but the net effect was in fact disastrous as the fall of Burma and food control in British territory cut off all rice imports. About half the population of Goa managed to live on starvation rations, while the rest emigrated. This constant emigration accounts (along with administrative slackness and inaccuracy of statistics) for the

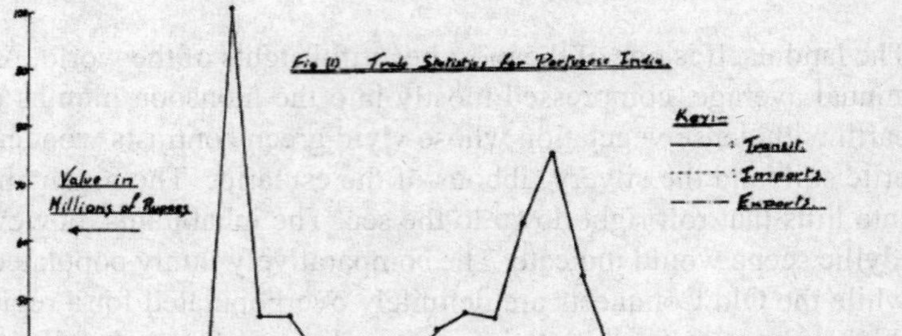

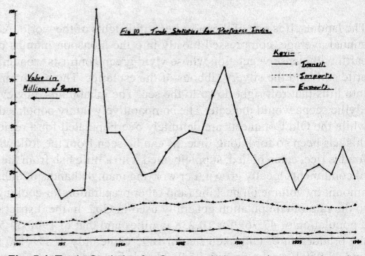

Fig. 5.1 Trade Statistics for Goa; goods imported, exported, and passing through in transit.
The above figure is for representation purpose only.

fluctuation in the population of Goa which has always the same level of about half a million, while in districts like Bardez the number of women rises steadily as the males have emigrated to earn money outside the territory.

There is no real estimate of this emigration though the fact itself is quite clear as may be seen from the following. The 1931 census (the last available in full detail) showed, for example, (my analysis of data, pp. 18–21), that for the period 1921–31 there was a steady annual excess of births over deaths averaging 4412.8 per year for the whole of Portuguese India. Nevertheless, as has been noted, the population does not show a corresponding increase. Furthermore, the same census shows (calculations from Table I page 3 and Table VI page 7) that the excess of females over males for the whole of Portuguese India is 21,179, for Goa alone 21,409; but for the three concelhos of Ilhas, Salcete (without Mormugão) and Bardez the excess is actually 22,670. The excess for Bardez alone is no less than 13,576. It is instructive to note that the ratio of females to males for the

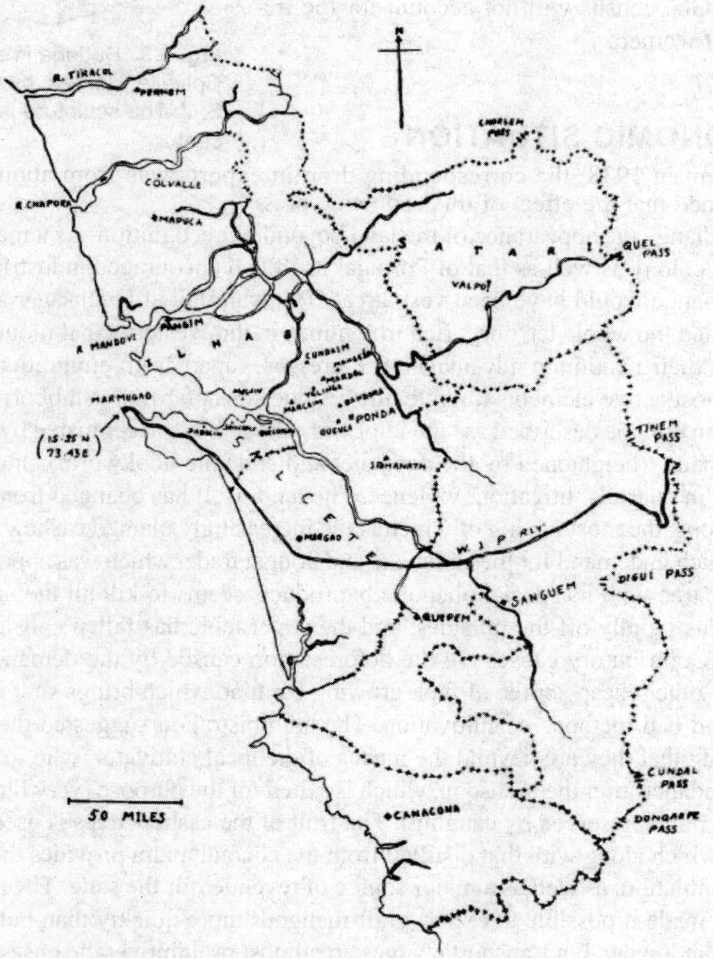

Fig. 5.2. Map of Goa; triangles mark the main temple sites.
The above figure is for representation purpose only.

whole of Portuguese India is 1.0758, for Goa 1.0885, for Bardez 1.2957. To go into further detail the Bardez ratios are: females to male below the age of 14 years 1.00997, but for the adults, *i.e.*, over 14, 1.4693. In happier countries the males are actually in excess at birth and the ratio decreases slowly till in old age the females exceed the males. The only conclusion I can draw from this, no matter how much the unreliability of the statistics may be discounted, is that the abler males always emigrate, particularly from the more densely populated regions of Goa; and this seems to me well borne out by the composition of the emigrant population which one sees in British India, particularly in cities like Bombay. Certainly the number of absentees recorded as counted in the Goa census will not account for the tremendous excess of women.

Fig. 5.3. Buddha image found at Colvalle, Bardez, by the late H. Heras, S. J. The sculpture is of about the 11th century.

5.2. THE ECONOMIC SITUATION

It would be imagined that the effect of this economic pressure should be to change the appearance of the land beyond all recognition. As a matter of fact, if the government of the colony as well as that of Portugal itself had encouraged industrialization, or even permitted it, the change would have been very great. The waterfall at Dudhsagar and other sources could have electrified the whole territory; rich iron mines in the Western Ghat mountains could have been developed to their maximum advantage. The pressure, apart from emigration, has acted indirectly and as the most active elements migrate, the residue sticks far more stubbornly than would be believed to what can only be described as "the idiocy of village life", accentuated by a certain amount of actual idiocy, apathy (heightened by the poor diet and endemic hookworm), and at the other end energy manifested in quarrels, litigation, violence. The land itself has changed from the necessity of growing money crops, the most paying of which is the increasingly planted cashew nut (*Anacardium occidentale*), so much in demand for the chocolate and nougat trade, which was apparently introduced by the Jesuits. The tree with its special phenolic byproducts seems to kill all the underbrush so that the rain-water drains rapidly off the hillsides, and the water table has fallen considerably wherever the tree is grown. Contributory causes are the deforestation caused by the demand for firewood in the absence of any other cheap source of fuel, growing bamboo which brings spot cash but ruins the ground entirely, and bad methods of cultivation. The administration suggested the use of chemical fertilizers, forgetting that they are beyond the means of the local cultivator, who in any case can use fish, caught in abundance after the monsoon, which is salted for the purpose (very little being dried for food purposes and none preserved by canning). The fruit of the cashew trees is used to distil a peculiarly heady wine which along with that distilled from the coconut palm provides the chief relaxation for the working population, as well as a major source of revenue[5] for the state. The railway at the end of the last century made it possible to export graft-mangoes more quickly than before and added to the income of the landowner, but transport charges are almost prohibitive; the buses which started on a proper scale only after 1930 add to the need for ready cash while relieving the lack of transport. The cinema reached Margão, principal city of Salcete and second in the whole of Goa, as late as 1932; and few have money enough to cultivate the fashions imported from Bombay or Lisbon.

5.3. HETEROGENEITY OF THE POPULATION

Under the appearance of uniformity—be it only of squalor and misery—Goa actually offers a tremendous variety to the discerning eye. The Konkani language,[6] or dialect, is itself not uniform so that it was possible for the practised ear (in 1925: motor transport and the war have mixed things up more) to place any individual to within five miles of locality of origin by his speech. There is even a greater diversity in customs and manners. Slightly over a half of the population is still Hindu,[7] about 7,000 Mohammedans, and the rest Catholics. The Hindus are oriented towards British India, being based upon Bombay in matters of trade or profession (but for the few locally employed) and Banaras or some such holy place for religion; the Catholics look naturally to Lisbon and Rome, though in matter of practice Bombay furnishes them with a nearer goal, particularly in modern times. Among the Hindus, at any rate, customs die very hard. All sorts of taboos and superstitions have continued, even spread to or survived among the Christian converts, who have in return given a few superstitions of their own. As most of the leading churches are built upon the sites of former temples, it is not unusual for desperate people, particularly women, to make votive offerings to deities and Madonnas impartially. Tracing the older tradition is, however, not so difficult as it may seem in spite of this mutual influence. Not only does the Koṅkaṇī language differ as said above for locality, but also for profession, class, sex, and education. The same may be said of dress, manners, beliefs, traditions, diet, accommodation, and outlook on life. The oldest Hindu households are not patriarchal but still contain enough of the older style of living to show the careful analyst what the patriarchal household must have been. Anyone brought up in an enormous adobe house where 150 people were fed every day, where servants could not be hired or dismissed, where the women's world was separate from that of the men without the Mohammedan harem seclusion, and where hospitality went to the extreme of feeding even a stray guest at the risk of the host's going hungry needs less stretching of the imagination than one who has to reconstruct the older days from books alone. Being the first male child in the direct line after the death of my grandfather, I automatically inherited his soul, nickname, was given his actual name on the twelfth day, and though my widowed grandmother's favourite grandson, had to be addressed by her in the indirect discourse necessary for every modest woman of the class, so real was the transmigration of the soul. Yet my grandfather was so strict in his observances that even after talking with any of his numerous Christian friends, he would go home and take the ritual bath of purification. When he migrated in his boyhood with his aged parents to the deserted community of Sancoale (which had reverted to jungle (*X*. 2.385–6) after some unknown epidemic, perhaps the plague, of about 1785 cf. X. 2.370) he was seeking his fortune as the pioneer for one Gama who had taken the deserted community on a nine year lease-hold, and for a distant relative Naik, who had agreed to supply the labour. The family had then migrated for the second time in its tradition (third if the ninth or fourth century migration from Bihar be true) after having been driven out of the nearby village of Loutulim in the 16th century to become feudal landlords in what later became the new conquests. But these feudal acquisitions were lost by the incapacity of my great-grandfather. On the second migration, the small family was followed by two slaves who worked in the fields and turned their earnings over to "their" family though there was no organized slave market as in the USA, slavery was not a recognized institution, and nothing except tradition held the slaves to the decayed feudal houshold.

5.4. THE FEUDAL PERIOD

Feudalism in Goa, as apparently in the rest of India, is a survival of the Mohammedan period. In the old conquests, it does not exist; for the Mohammedan period there lasted only from Yusuf Adil Shah in 1482 to the final victory of Albuquerque in 1511. To this fortunate accident, the Old Conquests owe the survival of the community form of settlement which also extended to the New, but with feudal overlapping. The Mohammedans in their final period (there was a transient raid by Malik Kafur in 1310, a slightly more durable conquest by Hassan Gangu Bahmani before 1348, and evidence for penetration in the intervening period, cf. M_3) settled down to exploiting the country whereas the previous desire was for a valuable emporium on the west coast. In fact, both for trade with Arab countries and as a port of embarkation for South Indian Muslim pilgrims to Mecca, Goa proper had become valuable by the middle of the 11th century, when under Jayakeśi I (M_1 pp. 167–216) Mohammedans rose to be governors of the port of Goa and a regular table of port dues was drafted. The intervening period fell under the domination of the Hindu kingdom of Vijayānagara, to which is ascribed by tradition the Kanarese influence (mainly script, occasionally language) still to be seen among the older people. As a matter of fact, Goa culture has always had, in historical times, a marginal character due to its situation beyond a mountain barrier, at the common apex of two distinct linguistic, perhaps ethnic, groups. The population seems never to have been large enough to form an effective cultural mass of its own. To the Vijayānagara regime is supposed to be due the first real land tax in Goa, the *khuśivrat* which still survives in places as the *coxivorado*. The Bijāpūr rulers who took over in 1482 introduced military governors whose armed retinues were supported by another tax, the *goddevorado* or horse-tax. This is the only known period when the communities thought of armed conflict among themselves, though encroachment whenever profitable upon the territory of a weaker community has gone on in almost all times, my own village of Sancoale having acquired its conch-like shape and enormous extent through this type of expansion in the days when it was the most populous community of Salcete. The military governors under the Mohammedans, themselves local men except for the chief of the main garrison, were called the Dessais and hated for their autocratic behaviour which went as far as forcing their former equals to work as menials in the household, and treating the communal land as feudal if not private property. This hatred led to the local population welcoming the Portuguese and therefore to the guarantee given immediately after the conquest that all their ancient local institutions would be preserved, the Dessais being abolished. It may be noted here that wherever the Mohammedan conquest lasted longer, the European conquerors found it much more convenient to recognize those feudal underlings who submitted as rightful lords of their lands, and even to create new ones for simplifying tax collections. The property became, in most cases, the personal property of the holder, the feudal title surviving at most in the inalienability—which has generally been overcome by mortgage. To revert to the Portuguese, the rights of the communities and their founders the *gancares* was recognised explicitly in the *Foral* of 1526 (*X.* 1.206–7 for an abstract), a document issued by the chancellor of the exchequer Affonço Mexias. The community was treated as a corporate unit responsible to the state, and there was to be no disturbance of custom or usage for the taxes, which all survived. This happy state lasted for a very short time, for though the district of Ilhas (= islands) was an ideal base for a maritime power whose colonial empire spread from China to Africa, the progress of Christianity was not rapid enough for the missionaries who accompanied the expeditions. Of these the most hated were the Jesuits, though their early activities introduced the Cashew tree, the pineapple, potatoes (not an important crop for Goa), and best of all graft mangoes developed from local varieties. In 1566 (*X.* 2.262–265) a viceregal decree forbade the construction of new temples as well as the conservation of older ones, and the exodus began which transported the local deities and on occasion the names of their villages to what later became the New Conquests. In 1567 one Diogo Rodrigues called *do Forte* set fire to the chief temple of Loutulim because it had been repaired in disobedience to the decree, and when the captain was sentenced to rebuild this temple at his own expense, an appeal was preferred to the viceroy by the Jesuits and the Archbishop with the result that the captain was authorized to destroy as many temples as he could, which he did to the extent of 280[8]. The temples in Ilhas had been destroyed in 1540 and their lands confiscated for the use of the Church: In 1559 came a decree forbidding the Hindus from holding any public office but the really effective decree was that of December 4, 1567 which forbade marriages, cremation, investiture according to Hindu rites. The effect actually was through the tenure of land to which succession was henceforth impossible unless legitimacy was proved, which meant that the marriage had to be solemnized in the church according to Christian rites. This caused a general emigration of higher caste Hindus, and the tradition is that one brother of an extensive joint family would stay behind to be converted with his wife and children, for the sake of the land, while the rest fled. This led to the breakup of what would have been the final type of patriarchal family. But a subsidiary effect was curious, in that henceforth Goa had "Brahmin Christians" and Christians of lower castes, the caste mechanism having been transferred in its essence to a casteless religion because of the transfer of classes with essentially the same productive relations. The Jesuit order here made the mistake of acquiring too much property, for which they had to pay with virtual extinction when an expansionist policy made it necessary in the eighteenth century to placate Hindu rulers of adjoining territories. What concerns us here is not the religious policy nor the rage which the Portuguese transferred from their Mohammedan enemies to the Hindus who had been their allies and were now their subjects, but the survival of the communal form of ownership for some landed property in the villages.

5.5. INCREASE IN TAXATION

Left to themselves, the religious orders might have worked out some methods for a compromise, which in any case took place later on as is seen from the slight majority that the Hindu population enjoys to-day over the rest. For a while, special orders such as those of the Theatins and the Oratorians were reserved for "Brahmin" Christians who would themselves become missionaries and make new converts. One of these Brahmin Oratorians, José Vaz (*GC*, 49), was long a candidate for canonization; his original house still survives in Sancoale in spite of the long desolation of the community. But the State began to make its own demands upon the communities. New taxes began with the Tombo Geral of 1595. The first charges were religious (*X.* 207–223), and as long as Goa was the trade centre of a prosperous empire, the remaining general taxes were only those of pre-Portuguese days. But special requisitions were always made, usually for the support of a certain number of soldiers, ostensibly for defence but in the imperialistic manner to make the conquered pay for their chains (*X.* 1.238–242). On occasion, the communal lands were leased out by force (*X.* 1.247–251). But there were church tithes, then half-tithes which became permanent taxes too. As the trade of Portugal went down and its own position on the Iberian peninsula became subordinate to that of Spain, taxes went up in Goa, the expenses of the administration devolving more and more upon the local population. There are repeated petitions for relief from taxes levied for purposes which were not fulfilled or which had lapsed (*X*, appended source documents). In 1733 (*X.* 1.267–273) the general assembly (*camara geral*) of Salcete, being made responsible as usual for more taxes, protested against another levy for the support of 1,000 soldiers. In 1740, the *camara geral* of Bardez proved that they had had to pay 50,000 xerafins ransom[9] to the Bhonslas (*X.* 1.279); the district seems never to have been recompensed for this; their net reward was having to pay their share from December 1753 for the maintenance of three companies of soldiers *which were never in existence!* There were payments for the support of the judges imposed upon the districts. In 1776, the three districts had to contribute no less than 390,000 xerafins towards rebuilding the city of old Goa. In 1795, a third of the total yield of the communities was to be paid to the central authority (*X.* 1.130–131). To all these, naturally, had to be added the extortions of any officials and tax farmers that were appointed. A certain amount of relief from taxes and regularization of their collection came only with the 19th century, by which time both the ruling country and the colony had become archaic survivals.

Till the 1880's, the main tax, *i.e.*, the property tithe, was collected in kind and converted into cash for payment to the state by the contractor (tax-farmer) who had bid successfully. But with the conversion into regular cash payments came the rise of another official who completed the supersession of the community in practice, though in theory they still retain ownership of their inalienable lands—subject always to the will of a state in the composition of which they have never had any voice. This official, the civil administrator of the district, is now the virtual ruler in all affairs relating to the community. In this, he was supported by another measure which actually alienated the profit of the community without alienating the land. By 1886, forms of interest in the communal lands had been converted into alienable shares, which are now owned in many cases by people far away from the community in question and who have no interest in the development of the community. The final step, which is only a formality, came within the last decade. Communal lands were for the greater part leased out triennially and the profit was the residue from the rent after communal expenses had been paid. But so acute had internal quarrels among the landholding classes become that the prices were forced up at the auction to quite impossible levels, and the cultivators who actually worked the land could not show a profit under any circumstances. The ever benign government stepped in with a law to the effect that the lands would hereafter be leased out after the fashion of the British permanent settlement on the fixed average rent of the ten years before the law came into force; the lease went directly to the person who actually tilled the land, without the intermediacy of any bidder from among the landholders who usually competed. The function of the communal assembly is therefore almost nothing, as are its profits in the majority of the cases.

5.6. STRUCTURE OF THE COMMUNITY

We have, hitherto, said a great deal about the development since the 15th century without saying much about the structure of the community itself. The village lands comprise a certain amount of forest on the hillside and a frontage upon an estuary or the seashore. The hilltops are generally bare and the softer laterite has been worn down ages ago by the action of the terrific rainfall, leaving only a harder rock exposed. On this is to be traced the oldest track, a foot-track worn deep into the iron-hard surface by centuries of barefoot travel. The reason is that a great part of the goods was always carried by head loads and the hilltops were the only portion clear enough from forest and mud. The only improvement needed was easing an occasional grade, and rests for headloads every mile or so, which are still to be seen even when the track is almost abandoned. On a much lower level, but still on the hillside were (and are) the actual residential houses, clustered together in settlements (*bairros*) for mutual protection, and connected by roads which have developed only in recent years from the cart tracks of a generation or two ago. The house level depended upon that of the water, for the houses had to be high enough to escape all danger of being flooded out in the rains but low enough to yield water (always drawn by hand) without digging a well to an impossible depth. The lowest level would, then, have been swampy or a ravine whose sole function would be to drain off the rain water. But as there are no plains in the region under discussion, this part was the cultivated portion, the only part where rice, the staple food of the people, could be grown. As a result, we have the edge of the lowlands, which is also the edge of the house level, very carefully built up with substantial embankments neatly revetted with mortarless stone. This prevents the whole hillside from being washed down into the rice land. From embankment to embankment, the entire valley has been cultivated for so long a time that the ground has taken on the same level, broken only by a little stream of water that shows the original nature of the valley. This stream serves to keep the water-table constant, and is regulated by small dykes when necessary with larger dykes at its mouth, and wooden floodgates of a simple design that swing shut at high tide to keep the salt water out, opening at the ebb to allow the stream to flow. The smallest floodgates are automatic, but their construction, care, operation, the upkeep of tracks, roads, embankments, are communal charges. The most fertile land is that reclaimed from the sea (*casana*) by large dykes or levees of clay and earth. These may be managed by private enterprise or by the community (older days), but the dykes need constant watching to keep crab-holes from being enlarged into breaches which would flood and wipe out the whole of the *casana*. So, the leasehold and tenancy of these is generally for nine years whereas the other lands as well as the commercial repairs were farmed out for from one to more, generally three, years by aùction (*arrematacão*) amongst the members, generally the *gāncares* of the community. At present, the lowest land and the hilltops generally belong to the community (in spite of encroachments) whereas the middle level is in private hands.

By the community, however, is meant not the whole of the population but a comparatively small section of oligarchic families, the "settlers" or *gāncares*. With very few exceptions like that of the Dumé family which represented the Portuguese at the Peshwa court of Poona, the Bhāṇḍārés at Adossim, the Gaitoṇḍés as Uskai, these *gāncaṛes* had to be Christians from the 16th century till the advent of the Marquis de Pombal who abolished the exclusive rights of Christians about 1761. So, in the new conquests we have feudal landlords along with Hindu *gāncares* for communities not in feudal ownership. The profits of the communal farming derived in older days from the absence of cash taxes, and indeed of heavy taxes of any sort, though the auctioning of lands meant very little competition as internal quarrels had not reached the level of modern times with their unremitting economic pressure. Besides the rice lands at low level, the community leased out on occasion the bare rock at high level; a thin layer of earth and a little levelling enables the holder to grow a crop of rice in the rainy season. A smaller income was derived from the lands leased out for permanent plantation under the limited rent (*foro limitado*) scheme by which any holder was guaranteed leasehold title to some plantation which he would develop at his own cost, generally planting coconuts which were the principal export crop even in the oldest days. To a considerable extent these are in the form of causeways across the rice land in the valley which connect the two opposed hillsides and are planted with two or more rows of coconuts; often these were pure encroachment as was the transfer of a considerable amount of the hillside land to private ownership.

After the charges for communal services, which included those for the communal barber, porter, temples (or churches), etc. had been met, the profit was divided among the *gāncares*, who were the actual shareholders. The conversion of these into modern transferable shares was one of the main reasons for ruin of the community. The older form, however, was represented by tokens held by the *gāncares*, generally in the form of minted pieces (*tāngas*) which represented each share. The division of the profit would then take place in two or three ways. The first charge upon the net profit was that of the *jono*, the individual share which was of two types. The first was as at Adossim or Uskai where the share is a fixed sum per male adult head from the *gancar* families, and the other as at Kholgor where the share is itself subdivisible but fixed by group (*vangor*) of families. The group, incidentally, represented in communal meetings by its head, was the voting unit in communal enterprises, though every *gāncar* entitled to a *jono* could be present and speak his mind; the voting was generally by sense of the assembly, not in the straight counting of votes which characterizes democratic institutions of a capitalist age. The *joneiros*, though entitled to the profit, were not entitled to all of it beyond the *jono*, and on the other hand they were not obliged to bear any of the losses, which now fall upon the holders of the alienable *acções* to which all sorts of originally distinct types of "shares" have been converted indiscriminately (except the inalienable *jono* which survives). As there was usually an extra profit beyond that needed for the *jono* in older days, this was apportioned according to individual needs and enterprise, being assigned to each landholder by the said *tāngas*, which went with the amount of land he cultivated for himself for coconuts or other money crops, and which were transferred with the land. These, however, meant sharing the loss as well in bad years, according to proportionate shares.

This remarkable form of profit sharing, which is not known in so clear-cut and recognizable a form elsewhere in India today, could be and was extended on occasion. With the heavy taxes of the seventeenth century or even earlier, a further class of landholders was admitted to the share of the estate type. These *interessados*, however, had no *jono, and no vote in the assembly*. In most of the New Conquests there are no *interessados*, which is taken to prove that their creation is later. Our tradition, however, is that they were present from the earliest times, when the first settlement took place. The *gāncares* settled the locality, but could not possibly provide all the labour so that worker families had to be interested. To this end, the ultimate profits (after deducting the *jono*, if any) were divided into three portions, of which one-third went to the *gāncares* according to their holdings, and two-thirds was divided among the working families by shares fixed originally in proportion to the workers in each group, and revised from time to time by mutual consent as the numbers changed. The workers, however, had no vote, though in both the systems described above they have to be paid for their labour either in cash or much more generally by share of the final yield. I suggest that both types of *interessados* are historically genuine, and that there were different types in different localities, depending upon the difficulty of settlement.

5.7. THE HISTORICAL BACKGROUND

The community that we can see in the background of all these changes was totally different from the one actually extant today, and the remarkable feature is that the older form of tenure should remain at least in name. It is seen at once that the older type of land-holding could be possible only in a newly opened region where the population was very thin and where a constant fight had to be waged against the jungle to hold it back. Land was therefore assigned by communal agreement, not only to the settlers (*gãncares*) themselves but also to the workers' households for the residential needs of each, and enough besides to provide a vegetable patch at least; what was given besides this depended upon the enterprise of the holder, who might wish to take the risk of a coconut plantation large enough to allow export. This meant a considerable outlay investment, and land, instead of being a capital asset, was at the earliest stage a test of energy. The question that we shall try to settle now on the basis of available evidence is: when did this almost unique form of pioneer enterprise originate?

There is very little reliable evidence that the archaeologists can give us, not only because the archaeology of Goa is in amateur hands but also because the Portuguese conquest was destructive of the crucial buildings, the temples; furthermore, construction in Goa is generally of mud, or soft laterite which can be quarried to any size and shape in blocks, but which is quickly eroded by exposure to a few seasons' rains. Of surviving institutions, the land system described is striking enough to demand explanation from antiquity, and we cannot use it to explain itself. Clothes and other fashions have developed quite obviously in modern times. The most striking feature of the country to be noticed by any casual visitor is the unique sanitation system which serves even the Old Conquests with their population of well over a thousand per square mile though there is no drainage, not even latrines in general; pigs clean up all the excrement and offal, the balance of nature being restored by eating the pigs. This, one believes, is just a later development. The temple records give nothing, for the oldest temples located in the New Conquests by flight at the end of the 16th century, were built in the 17 century or later to their present dimensions—and built in direct if not very well understood copy of the Baroque Christian churches of the city of Old Goa (though the general style of Goa churches is that of Borromini's Jesuit construction). This is understandable, as the Old Goa churches were the most imposing buildings extant, with Hindu workmen trained in that type of construction, when the emigré temples acquired funds enough for their rebuildings; what is surprising is that the incongruity seems not to have been noticed by the local Brahmins. Temple records, if any survived the transfer, have generally been destroyed by sloth, vermin, time, the climate, and on occasion fear of losing property acquired by encroachment without legal title. Much the same is true of family records. The last records of the Lāḍ family, who were given property and status by an 18th century general (Lakhbādādā Lāḍ) of the Peshwas at Poona were destroyed by white ants or used up in covering temporary assembly halls in my boyhood; the family house itself sprawls in a gigantic ruin at Chicalim. The most that can be expected from a search of this sort is an occasional copper plate recording some ancient land grant, and those that have been discovered say nothing of the community organization.

All extant evidence seems to me to point to an ancient migration of Brahmins from the Gangetic plain of India over a thousand miles away, and the settlement in communities with a profit-sharing must have come with them. The U. P. Brahmin to this day cannot put his hand to a plough, no matter what other work he does. To settle a wilderness, the Brahmins would have to interest labour to join them. Traditions of this sort exist, and are contested. The *Sahyādri Khaṇḍa* gives on p. 305 a story of migration from Tirhūt in Western Bengal; on p. 333 we have the Kadamba king Mayūravarmā (4th century) import some Brahmins for supporting his throne. Moraes (M_2 p. 166) speaks of "the myth of northern descent" and propounds, on the strength of works like the *Grāmapaddhati* the theory that local priests just converted themselves into Brahmins, assuming northern origin to cover up this usurpation. This *may* have happened in *some* localities, but can hardly explain why a new land system arose, and is in fact contradicted by a good deal of other evidence. In the first place, local pre-Brāhmaṇic priests of the *gāvḍos* still survive in places like Kholgor; their deities, where unabsorbed by Brāhmaṇic synthesis, have been converted to cacodemons, known generally as *devchār* but still worshipped by the lower castes as well as the *gāvḍos*. With this superbly fashioned *gāvḍos* race or tribe was associated only a meagre agriculture, that of the *nāchnī* (*Eleusine coracana*) which needs nothing but a little clearing in the jungle, easily obtained by fire. Far more important, the structure of the Koṅkaṇī language, in spite of Portuguese influence in modern times and a goodly number of Arabic or Persian words (*GC*, 20–22), still remains quite distinct from that of Kanarese, and even of Marāṭhī of which it is supposed so often to be a dialect. As a matter of fact, the descent from Sanskrit and Prakrit (*GC*, 17–18) occurs in a line parallel to that of Marāṭhī, but it is still true, as I can vouch from personal observation, that the language retains many idiomatic similarities to spoken Bengali, and to the dialects of Bihar as well as Eastern U. P. This could hardly have happened without a significant migration from the Gangetic plain. There are subsidiary factors, such as the strong concentration of blood-group *B* among the Sārasvat Brahmins of Goa which would bear this out, but these have to be confirmed by much better sampling analyses than our anthropologists have hitherto been able to provide.

Whether the migration actually took place in the days of Mayuravarmā (or Mayuraśarmā) in the 4th century or not, a study of the cults locally practised can only support to hypothesis. The god *Maṅgeśa*, one of the five principal deities of southern Sārasvat Brahmins, has been forcibly converted into an image, though originally (and still under the golden mask) a stone phallic symbol of Śiva. What influence this change of cult had upon private land ownership we cannot say, but it did not change either the god's name or the community system. The name has been explained as "god of Monghyr (in Bihar)" by people who take as genuine the reference in *Sahyādri Khaṇḍa* (p. 308). Buddhism certainly had its period in Goa, particularly in the northern portions, as shown by a fine image of Buddha discovered at Colvalle by Fr. Heras of the St. Xavier's College, Bombay; at Pernem, in the New Conquests, relics of a Buddhist shrine of some sort are still worshipped in the open under the name of "Boḍko deva", though the building itself must have been obliterated by the temple that stands near the famous spring of Pernem. The really interesting study comes from the names of local deities of Salcete preserved in a list of 1567 (*X*. 2.262–263). These can still be traced after emigration to the New Conquests before the end of that century, the list serving principally to show that they are not later additions. We have, of course, the major Brāhmaṇic deities: Mahādeva, Durgā, Mahālakṣmī, Narasimha, Nārāyaṇa, Rāmanātha, Dāmodara, Gaṇeśa, and so on, making allowances for the incredibly barbarous orthography of the document. But in addition there are some who do not belong to this group. Firstly, Conssua had only the temple of Gotamesvara, which may or may not indicate Buddha, with the Borquodeo of other villages. A considerable number of localities had cults unquestionably associated with the Nātha sect (cf. G. W. Briggs, *Gorakhnāth and the Kānphātha Yogis*, Calcutta 1938) which represents popular superstition of perhaps the twelfth century: Bhairava, Siddhanāth, Nāganath, Candranāth. Then there are a few that cannot be identified either by name or legend of origin without more fieldwork: Santéry Bassonazasso, etc. Here tradition has to be sifted very carefully, as temple songs (which should have preserved tradition best) have been rewritten long after the emigration; the songs of Śāntādurgā near Pondā contain (for example) whole lines of Hindustāni such as *a'lim dunyā tū mātā hamārī* which cannot be mistaken for an archaic heritage. Such imports are quite common; the temple of Śāntādurgā has a water tank with a balustrade adorned by two Chinese porcelain lions. These are the recent present of a temple dancing-girl who exercised the secondary trade of prostitution in Bombay, received the lions as a gift, and presented them to the temple on one of her periodic visits for the service of the deity at major festivals (without which she would have lost her hereditary right to such service).

But when all these deities have been eliminated from the Salcete list which can be identified with known members of the Hindu pantheon or not identified at all, there remain some which are clear evidence of new settlement. Quetrapalle = Kṣetrapāla is quite common; the meaning is "guardian of the fields", and so far as I know, this is not a Brāhmaṇic deity in modern times though the epithet is used—rarely—for Siva, and far less rarely for Śeṣa; in older days it would be established only for new settlements. Grāmapuruṣa, Ādipuruṣa, seem to me to indicate the cult of the founder of the settlement. Chovīsavīr (twenty-four heros), Bārāzon (the Twelve), Eclovīr (the single hero) are either such founders or perhaps historical personages to whom a cult was devoted, but unquestionably by Brahmins and in comparatively ancient times. Such cults arise even later, but not always, to the status of official worship. A patron goddess of Fatorpá after the 16th century migration is such a historical personage, a lower temple servant (bhāvīṇa) and automatically a prostitute, who was killed leading the revolt of five communities; the communities lost their rights after the revolt was suppressed (X. 2.278) in 1583. Older and still worshipped by the poor but without an official cult was Bhāgā, daughter of a *gāncar* of Loutulim married into the household of the Dessai of Vernã, killed warning her father's people of a night attack planned against them by the neighbouring community. The site of her death (which must have taken place about 1500) was marked by a specially planted tree and is still sacred. But making due allowances for such possibilities, there seems to be no doubt about the existence in 1567 of the cult of the original founder in several of the Salcete communities.

5.8. BEYOND THE COMMUNE

This rather uneven exposition finishes most of what we know about the communities of the Old Conquests. Founded as they seem to be by immigrant Brahmins somewhere between the 4th and the 12th centuries of the present era, the locality still bears traces, besides the *camara geral* of each concelho, of a larger organization than the single community. Tisuary, comprising most of Ilhas, means "the thirty settlements", which still exist. Salcete is the Portuguese corruption of Sāsaṣtī, the sixty-six settlements which can also be traced in modern times. Each was originally associated with certain fixed gentes (*gotras*). Of these, it is known that the communities about Margão had a central administration called the Ten, based upon ten major communities who sent representatives that settled matters of general interest. The organization was entirely Brāhmaṇical. The most fertile and populous communities, those on the estuaries were in the hands of Brahmin *gāncares*, and possess fields that give thirty to sixty fold or more while the relatively poorer sea-side communities were settled by a lower caste, the *Chārḍōs* who were converted without exception to Christianity and of whom the precise caste origin in Hinduism is unknown. They seem to have had no voice directly in the Ten, and had to be content with their sandy soil that yielded as little as sixfold. This interesting caste division of the localities might be interpreted as further evidence of an invitation to northern Brahmins by some ancient king, and the opening up of a new region in a new form. The co-operative idea did spread, for the *casanas* are generally taken up by workers' groups on the same profit-sharing basis and we know of now extinct industrial associations that took the same form (X. 2.410–411); in particular of fishermen and weavers.

The tradition is that justice was locally administered by the *gāncares*, which was made easier by the *patria potestas* of Hindu law and division into *vangor* groups. Capital punishment seems to have been inflicted when necessary by the larger organizations which later developed into the *camara geral* of each district, but there are no known records. What was not accomplished by direct violence of the offended party would mean exile of the offender; as long as he did not live in the system of communities, it did not matter whether he lived or not.

The great weakness of the communities was their small total extent and the complete lack of any military organization for defense. This is an inherent defect of any region dominated by Brahmins of the old type. Its results are to be seen in successive conquests. But in this as in many details of the economic drain Goa does not differ from other peripheral rustic localities in India. The principal difference is in the long-preserved ancient type of land ownership in common and inalienable form, with the existence of a certain amount of recorded data from the sixteenth century onwards.

NOTES TO CHAPTER 5

The conditions described as contemporary in this note should be taken as before 1939 AD. The war has caused many changes in Goa, as in other parts of the Indian sub-continent, which it has not been possible to study, primarily because of political barriers.

My chief published sources for this note are: *X* = Filippe Nery Xavier's *Bosquejo historico das Comunidades das aldeas dos concelhos Ilhas, Salcete e Bardez*, second edition revised and augmented by José Maria de Sa, Bastora, Typographia "Rangel", 3 vols. 1903–1907 (copy obtained from Mr. A. K. Priolkar). The first edition of 1852 is apparently not available; it could well have served, but for its having been published in so obscure a corner of the world, as a valuable supporting document for Marx and Engels in their studies of Asiatic society. The editor, unfortunately, has exercised his privilege with more zeal than judgment and in some cases includes extraneous matter without due reference or checking. Thus, for example, in *X*. 2.385, it is reported that the name Sancoale derives from the abundance of conch shells in this village, though anyone who knows the locality well will vouch for the fact that none have been founded there. This has been taken bodily from the *Sahyādri Khaṇḍa* (*SK*, a section of the Skanda Purāṇa) published by J. Gerson da Cunha, Bombay 1877, p. 562 and derives from the fact that *śankhāvalī* in Sanskrit means both the shape of a conch-shell (which the locality actually bears) or the abode of the shells, which was understood by the author of the *SK*. In this connection, we may add to the critique of the *SK*, often brushed aside as a late and worthless forgery, by noting that the apparent reference to the Sikhs (*SK*, p. 176) should not be adduced in evidence, being hypermetric in the stanza, and probably a mislection for *siddheśam* = *sikhadeśam*. Gerson da Cunha's valuable study on *The Koṅkaṇi Language & Literature* (Bombay 1881) I denote by *GC*. For the ancient history of Goa, most of what is known is contained in three studies by G. M. Moraes: M_1 = *The Kadamba Kula* (Bombay 1931); M_2 = Notes on the Pre-Kadamba history of Goa, in the *Trans. Vth Ind. Hist. Con.* 1941, pp. 164–174; M_3 = A forgotten chapter in the history of the Konkan, in *Bhārata Kaumudī* (Rādhā Kamal Mukherjee Festschrift) Allahabad 1945, pp. 441–475. Besides these I have drawn upon the published statistical data (inaccurate as it generally is) from official sources, made available to me by kindness of Sr. Tristão Bragança Cunha of Cansaulim, Goa; to him is also due the hard work that led to the publication of a nationalist pamphlet *Denationalization of Goans* by the Goa Congress Committee, Bombay

1944—promptly suppressed by the British Government of India in sympathy to objections by the Government of Goa. His reward for daring to claim the right of free speech in Goa was a sentence to eight years of transportation followed by premature death.

Besides the published sources, I draw in large measure, as does *X*, upon generally unpublished tradition. Usually, our reports coincide, but often I find my own version slightly more accurate, for the ancient tradition of Goa is necessarily Hindu and Brāhmanical, and may have been misreported to or misunderstood by the industrious Filippe Nery Xavier. For the reliability of all tradition, I cannot vouch; the defect of verbal lore is that it is either timeless or attaches to the wrong person. My grandfather is certainly reported to have seen the brilliant light cast at night by the jewel that a king cobra had laid aside while feeding, though no such jewel has ever been found in the head of any cobra in spite of the most active search, (for it is traditionally the one effective antidote for snakebite). In my great-grandfather's time, some relative had apparently seen a cattle trough made of half a gigantic egg; there were, of course, other stories reminiscent of Sindbad such as the party that landed on the back of a great turtle, mistaking it for an island—though turtles of large size are not found off the coast of Goa. A commoner story is that of certain fishermen who passed in deep waters between what seemed like two tall coconut trees, and found, that the "trees" came together just after they had sailed through; unlike Jason, they took this to mean that they had escaped from the claw of a monstrous crab. On the other hand, tradition as separated from folk-lore has always a certain element of truth. Under the crumbling triumphal arch of Vasco da Gama in Old Goa, I was told (in spite of its clear if bombastic Latin inscription) that the statue was that of a sailor who came from afar and became king of the country, which represents the facts better than one could have expected.

1. *Censo da População do Estado da India*—1931 (published Nova Goa 1935) gives on chart *C* over 1000 per square mile or the Velhas Conquistas, with a maximum of 1200 per square mile in Bardez. Satari has only 105 per square mile and Sanguem 64 per square mile, concentrated in small hamlets in the dense and malarious forests.
2. *Estatistica da superficie cultivada de arroz, e sua produção, no distrito de Goa, durante o ano de* 1937 (Nova Goa, 1939) p. 13. I do not give detailed figures for this is a useless bit of armchair statistics.
3. *Denationalization of Goanș*, p. 54. Supporting figures in *Estatistica do Comercio e Navegação ano de* 1940 (Nova Goa 1944) pp. 14–15. The same publication, p. 16 shows well over 100,000 double khandis of husked rice *imported* annually into Portuguese India, including Daman and Diu as well as Goa, though the share of the former can be easily written off in the excess over 100,000 khandis.
4. From Table VII, p. 6 in *Estatistica do Comercio e Navegação*, inclusive of Daman and Diu whose share is not above 13 per cent of the total in any single product of importance so that the graph represents substantially the plight of Goa.
5. *Orçamento Geral para o ano economico de* 1945 (Nova Goa, 1945) p. 8, pp. *xviii-xix* shows this to be about 8 per cent of the total budget of 6.7 million rupees.
6. For sources beyond *GC*, Cunha Rivara's *Ensaio Historico da Lingua Concani* (Nova Goa 1857) is quite superficial. A.K. Priolkar in his edition of the poem *A Paixão de Cristo* (J. Uni. Bombay IX, 1940 pp. 182–211) shows that the literary Koṅkaṇi. of the *Khrista Purāṇa* of Fr. Thomas Stephens (1614) may be regarded as a branch of Marāṭhī. This does not necessarily make all of Koṇkaṅī a dialect of Marāṭhī as Mr. Priolkar has so often proposed; on the other hand the studies of S. M. Katre, more imposing from the linguistic standpoint, show little acquaintance with the actual variation in the Koṅkaṇī which that author regards as a separate language. Other studies have appeared in Portugal,, but are not available to me at present.
7. *Censo da População do Estado da India* 1931 (Nova Goa, 1935) p. 4, Table IV.
8. The ruins still exist in some places. I owned till 1936 a farm which was the site of the original service settlement and dancing-girls' houses for the main temple of Sancoale, the Narasiṃha temple on the site of which was built a chapel (elevated in 1840 to the status of a church). My aunt at Quelossim lived in a house built on the site of another temple, whose bell with its chain survives as an object of worship by the wayside. At *old* Mardol, the charred ruins of the principal temple are still to be seen.
9. But the Pondichery records show that the French colony, under its governor Dumas, was strong enough to refuse the same Bhonslas tribute in 1741, though Pondichery was, unlike Bardez, leased from the Marāṭhās.

Index

Numbers refer to pages. The orthography of books and maps in English and Portuguese make it difficult to follow any consistent scheme of Romanization; e.g. Poona would be difficult to recognize as puṇẽ or puṇeṃ. The local variations of rustic pronunciation have not been reproduced; but the omission of the vowel a at the end of a word or syllable in Marāṭhī has been shown, even at the cost of uniformity. The symbols m and M denote localities with microlith deposits and megaliths, respectively.

A

B

H

I

J

L

M

N

O

U

V